Fruit & Veg Grower's Cookbook

First published in 2009 by New Holland Publishers (UK) Ltd
London • Cape Town • Sydney • Auckland

Garfield House
86–88 Edgware Road
London W2 2EA
United Kingdom
www.newhollandpublishers.com

80 McKenzie Street
Cape Town 8001
South Africa

Level 1, Unit 4
14 Aquatic Drive
Frenchs Forest
NSW 2086
Australia

218 Lake Road
Northcote
Auckland
New Zealand

1 3 5 7 9 10 8 6 4 2

ISBN 978 1 84773 408 2

Senior Editor: Corinne Masciocchi
Copy Editor: Clare Hubbard
Art direction and design: Fiona Andreanelli (www.andreanelli.com)
Design assistance: Vanessa Bowerman & Kerry Silver
Photographer: Ian Garlick
Food stylist: Kathryn Hawkins
Editorial Direction: Rosemary Wilkinson
Production: Laurence Poos

Printed and bound in India by Replika Press Pvt. Ltd

Fruit & Veg Grower's Cookbook

Kathryn Hawkins

NEW
HOLLAND

Contents

Introduction

When I sat down to write this book and to plan my fruit and vegetable garden, I did so as an inexperienced gardener. I was very keen and full of enthusiasm to get started, but I soon realized that I had much to learn and prepare before getting stuck in. In fact, a life time's knowledge only goes some way to understanding how Mother Nature works in the garden; I can now truly appreciate the famous line by Thomas Jefferson, 'Though an old man, I am but a young gardener.'

The more I thought about the project ahead, the more I saw planning my garden as being like writing the book itself. You have to do your research and reading around your subject, and you have to make your preparations a few months prior to getting started – for the garden, this would be in the autumn. I enrolled on some general gardening evening classes that taught me the basics about soil types, climatic conditions, improving your soil, as well as general planting and maintenance tips. I became a frequent visitor to my local garden centre and an avid listener of Gardeners' Question Time on BBC Radio 4!

Once you've gathered your information, you need to draw up plans and decide what you want to include (or grow). Then you have to be realistic and edit down your list, and pinpoint what is most relevant to your work – or, in the garden, what you have space for and how those plants suit your conditions. Only after all this research can the real work start. On completion of the digging, sowing and planting (the manuscript), you then have some general maintenance (proofreading) before finally reaping the rewards and being showered with praise for your wonderful produce (or published book!).

I got the gardening bug a few years ago when I was lucky enough to buy a house with an established apple tree and enough garden to experiment with. I started small with a few herbs, strawberry plants and raspberry canes, and then gradually expanded to include tomato plants and other fruit bushes. Now I also have a rhubarb plant, a root vegetable patch, runner beans, Jerusalem artichokes and salad leaves, along with a renovated greenhouse with hothouse vegetables, and other greenery waiting to be planted this summer. I'll admit to not having had 100 per cent success, but on the whole I'm feeling pretty pleased with myself as I write this.

This book is aimed at people like me, who want to have a go at growing their own, but aren't too sure where to start. I've found that there are many sources of information out there, some are very in-depth, and the more you read the more you find conflicting methods, so it can soon become very confusing. As a result, what's included in this book is what has worked for me and my friends and family. I've had some expert help along the way. Genetics have played their part (I come from a family of gardeners); my brother is an experienced gardener and has made a living out of horticulture. He has been my right-hand man throughout this project and I owe him a huge favour for all his advice and help. My mother, too, has been growing her own fruit and vegetables for several years, and she's also been a good source of tips and techniques.

As well as reading around your subject, have a chat with other gardeners and find out what works for them in your local conditions, it's amazing what tips you can pick up. The Internet is an excellent resource and look out for evening classes in your area or join the local horticultural society. My local garden centre runs different courses at certain times of the year to demonstrate seasonal techniques, and I thoroughly recommend taking a course in pruning. I have covered this subject in a general way, but I find a topic like this is better learnt by watching a practical demonstration. When I was faced with pruning my aged apple tree for the first time I didn't know where to start and was terrified I'd end up killing the tree. I was lucky enough to be able to call on a gardener friend to help me, and now I find pruning it quite straightforward.

I've got to get outside now and water my garden, we've been having a dry few days and my newly sown seeds will be getting parched. So, as the chairman says each week on Gardeners' Question Time at the end of the programme, 'Goodbye and good gardening'!

Introduction

So you've decided you want to have a go at 'growing your own'. Before you rush headlong into the garden armed with your spade, it's worth taking a moment or two to think about what you actually want from the garden. Here are some questions you should consider.

1. What space is available? If you have a small plot or you're going to sacrifice a flowerbed for a vegetable patch, you should consider the visual look of the garden and whether you want some areas to be decorative as well as practical. Have a look in a garden design book or in magazines for ideas.
2. What are the conditions like (soil, weather, climate etc.)? You'll see that I've highlighted the ideal growing conditions for each fruit and vegetable entry in the following chapters.
3. How much time will you have to work in the garden? The bigger the plot, the more crops you can grow, but the more time it will take to maintain it. Good maintenance is essential for producing good crops and keeping pests and diseases to a minimum.
4. What fruit and vegetables will you get the most use from and which ones are suitable for your plot?

Once you've had the chance to mull these things over, the fun begins. Draw up a plan of your garden and work out where specific crops can be grown. When you sow or plant, keep a record of where you plant what, along with the date. As the crop develops, make a note of any problems you incur and then record the date of your harvest. A crop plan is important if you become a regular grower (see Rotation on page 10) and it also helps you keep track of when you can expect some produce.

Tools of the trade

Take a trip to any garden centre or DIY store and you'll find a wide array of garden tools, all with their own specific use. Rather than spend a fortune, you might be able to get hold of some second-hand tools, or, as I did, get some cast-offs from your family! Here are a few basic tools that I've found useful when working in my fruit and vegetable garden.

Dibber: an inexpensive piece of kit that enables you to make a perfect hole in the ground or in a pot into which you put a seed or seedling. You can make holes of various depths depending on how far you

push the dibber into the soil. Available in different circumferences, ideally buy a slim dibber for seeds and tiny seedlings, and a wider one for bigger specimens.

Hoe: a draw hoe (small, flat blade with a triangular top) enables you to get in between plants for weeding, and a push, plate or Dutch hoe (hooked with a small diamond-shaped blade) enables you to make a perfect furrow or drill in the ground – ideal for making neat rows. This hoe can have a long or short handle.

Rake: helps keep the soil even and neat ready for sowing and planting.

Spade and fork: 'must-haves' for digging up and turning over the soil prior to planting and after the vegetation has died back.

String, marking-out pegs and labels: marking out each end of a row with pegs and then tying a length of string between them is a fail-safe method of making a straight line. Don't forget to put a label at each end so you know where and what you've planted!

Trowel and hand fork: good for getting in to small areas and in between plants to weed and turn the soil over. Trowels enable you to make larger holes than a dibber, necessary for planting larger seedlings and specimens, and you don't have to disturb the soil as much as you would using a spade or large fork.

Soil

Any garden's biggest asset is its soil, which can be improved to make it suitable for fruit and vegetable growing. Although it may take a bit of time and effort to get your soil to the right consistency, it is well worth it in order to produce good-quality crops. Have a look at the garden the next time it rains and see how the water drains, make a note of where the best plants grow and jot down areas of the garden where certain crops aren't so successful. You can buy soil testing kits from a garden centre to test for all sorts of nutritional defects to help with problem diagnosis; the more you know about your soil the better. Even if you've got good soil, you still have to maintain it.

Soil types

The first thing you need to determine is what sort of soil you have in your garden.

Clay

If you have clay soil, it will be heavy and stick together

in clods or clumps. It certainly makes gardening heavy work but isn't impossible to work with, and quite a lot of gardens are built on this substance. Clay soils drain slowly; they take a while to warm up, but they can be fertile. When our family first moved to Sussex back in the late 1970s, we bought a brand new house with a builder's yard of a garden. During the first summer I can remember my parents spending many back-breaking hours removing rubble and turning over great clods of clay soil until it was suitable for laying down a lawn and planting shrubs and plants. Although their effort was tremendous, we ended up with a fantastic, fertile garden.

Sand
This soil type is the other extreme. It drains very quickly and is free-flowing, so nutrients tend to wash away. It warms up quickly and makes for an easy dig, but it can be difficult to raise healthy crops without some attention.

Loam
The perfect mix of clay and sand, with the best qualities of each. In short, every gardener's dream. However, it still needs looking after.

Stones
While stones improve drainage, too many can be a problem for growing vegetables that form underground – they will be misshapen and difficult to pull. You can remove some stones as you dig and prepare the soil prior to planting, but in most cases, you will end up fighting a losing battle against stony soil – I am writing from personal experience. It is best to avoid varieties of root vegetables that are long and tapering, choose shorter or stumpy varieties instead.

Acid/alkaline
You can buy a pH testing kit quite easily and inexpensively from any garden centre. It is definitely worth testing different parts of the garden to check the soil pH level, because this can affect the produce you grow. The gardener's scale for pH levels ranges from 1 to 14 (very acid to very alkaline, although the extremes are unlikely). Ideally, vegetables grow at their best between pH 5.5 and 7.5, with pH 6.5 (neutral) being the optimum level.

Improving your soil
Listed below are some of the measures you can take to improve your soil and keep it in tip-top condition.

Organic material
The most important thing you can do to your soil is enrich it with organic matter. Substances like manure and compost will help enrich the earth and improve its texture. Make sure you use well-rotted material – it will be odourless – otherwise it will carry on breaking down in your soil, using valuable nitrogen in the process (nitrogen is essential for good cropping). Dig your organic matter deeply (see Digging on page 10) so that it reaches the roots of your plants and gives stability to the plant above. Deeply dug, enriched soil helps retain moisture and nutrients. The best time to apply organic matter is in the autumn when the soil needs replenishing after the previous growing season.

Vegetables and fruit that stay in the ground longer than one season can have an application of organic matter as a 'top dressing'. Sprinkle it around the plants and carefully dig it in to a depth of 5–7 cm (2–3 in) without disturbing the roots. It will then slowly be worked into the ground by earthworms.

A quick boost can be given to soil just prior to planting seeds and seedlings by sprinkling a general-purpose fertilizer (organic or non-organic, it's up to personal preference) and then raking it or lightly digging it into the soil surface. Remember that some crops, especially some root vegetables, don't like fresh organic matter or fertilizers, so take note of my planting instructions for specific soil preparation information.

Changing the soil's pH
Soil can often be too acidic (like mine) for some vegetables, and the simplest way to change this is by adding ordinary garden 'lime' (calcium carbonate) to your soil in accordance with the manufacturer's guidance and safety instructions. Lime is widely available from garden centres and DIY stores and is usually simply forked into prepared soil about a month prior to planting. More rarely, a soil is too alkaline, and this can be more tricky to deal with. Peat used to be recommended for the purpose, but peat products are not environmentally friendly. It is best to seek advice from your garden centre or a specialist to see what treatments are currently available.

Improving drainage
Once you start digging in organic matter you should start to see an improvement in slow-draining, wet soil, as the fibre will help break down the clods. For a more persistent problem, you may want to consider adding horticultural grit to your soil, which will alter the texture and give it a more free-draining consistency. For a serious problem, you may have to consider an underground drainage system to channel water away from your plot. It is worth seeking

specialist advice before spending out lots of money on quick-fix solutions that may not solve this type of problem. Another tip worth remembering is that if the soil is wet, avoid working and trampling all over it, as this will compact it down and consequently lose the texture you've spent ages digging in. If you have to stand on the soil, try to work standing on a plank of wood and limit the area you compact down.

Digging

Take a look in any gardening book and you'll see different methods for proper digging. I'm only going to explain the 'single digging' method that I use in my garden. If your soil is well worked already or quite light and sandy, you can get away with simply turning the ground over with a fork and replacing the soil in the same position; then rake the top to break it down further.

To incorporate organic material, you will have to dig a trench system across the width of your plot. Starting at one end, dig a trench to the depth of your spade blade, and put the soil in a wheelbarrow. Put organic matter in the bottom of the trench. Start digging another trench alongside and use the soil from your digging to fill in the first trench. Continue the digging, filling and composting, working your way through the whole plot until you get to the final trench. Fill this one with the soil from your wheelbarrow. Rake over the soil to neaten it up and even out the surface.

Gardening techniques

In the next eight chapters that deal with growing specific types of fruit and vegetables, I mention various techniques that are required in order to produce a good crop. The necessary techniques are detailed and explained below.

Rotation

Different types of plants take different nutrients from the soil as they grow, so the soil can become depleted after a season's growth and harvesting. Pests and diseases can get a stronghold in the soil and spread to the next crop if planted again on the same patch. Farmers and gardeners have practised crop rotation for hundreds of years in order to obtain consistent results and reduce infection. Depending on the size of your garden or the different types of produce you want to grow, you should allocate certain areas for growing specific varieties. The following year, you should aim to move everything around. I base my plot on a three-year rotation cycle. I grow my permanent vegetables elsewhere in the garden, but if you haven't the capacity to do this, divide your patch into four, put the permanent vegetables together, and rotate the other three types as below:

Patch one: alliums; legumes; courgettes, marrows, squash and pumpkins; sweetcorn; lettuces.
Patch two: potatoes; parsnips; beetroots; carrots; tomatoes.
Patch three: brassicas; radishes.
Permanent patch: rhubarb; Jerusalem artichokes.

This is the theory anyway. In a small garden, it is often very difficult to keep this system going, especially if disease strikes – there is often not enough space to put adequate distance between new crops. If you've planted brassicas, such as swedes, which need to stay in the ground for a long time, you'll automatically be restricted with space for other plants. As a shortcut, avoid planting the same vegetable types in the same patch for 2 years running; legumes need rotating each year. By the way, after you've picked all your beans and peas, the foliage can be dug into the soil to provide nutritious green manure for the following year's new varieties.

Planting from seed

Seedbed: some seeds need to be germinated before they can be planted in the growing plot. An outdoor seedbed is ideal for this. Choose a small area, ideally somewhere that has fine, free-flowing soil (not too many stones). Shorter rows for planting seeds are best so that you don't have to stand on the soil when you are sowing the seeds and maintaining the bed afterwards. Once the seedlings reach the desired size, they can be carefully removed and transplanted into the growing area.

Seedbed alternative: if you don't have the space for an outdoor seedbed, you can plant seeds in specially designed trays with individual compartments or modules. You should fill the seed modules to the top with seed compost, level off the surface by pulling a piece of flat wood over the top and then tapping the trays on the workbench to compact the compost down. You can then make a hole in the centre of each module using a fine dibber or a short length of cane, and drop a few seeds in each – larger seeds can be planted individually. Sprinkle the top lightly with a little more compost and water with a fine droplet nozzle – this will naturally level off the surface. Keep the seed trays in a warm, light position until they germinate.

Drill: a shallow furrow or indent in prepared soil ready for planting seeds or small specimens. The depth will depend on the species planted. Place a length of wood straight across the seedbed or plot and using a short-handled Dutch hoe (you can also use a stick or trowel for narrow drills), pull the soil down the length of the wood to draw out a drill to the desired depth.

Seed planting: when planting seeds it's important not to clump them together. Often the seeds are very small and this can be quite difficult to prevent. Either take a pinch of seeds between your index finger and thumb and lightly scatter them down the drill, or trickle them from the corner of the open seed packet. If you have more time and patience, wet the end of a cocktail stick and dip it in the seed packet to enable you to get one seed at a time. Use the back of a rake to gently cover the seeds with soil and then gently pat down the soil with the head of the rake. Water the seeds and don't forget to label them before you forget what you've planted!

Thinning out: when vegetable seeds are so tiny, it is difficult to sow them individually. While care should be taken to sow as thinly as possible (see above), when the seedlings appear and become large enough to handle, you can simply pluck out the excess until you have the required density left in the ground. The 'thinnings' or leftover seedlings are fragile and are usually discarded.

Earthing-up

Earthing-up or 'hilling' is a technique that helps the underground tubers of root vegetables develop properly. It keeps them out of the light and gives stability to lanky plants. First break up the soil

between the rows and remove any weeds. Using a hoe, draw up the soil and pile it against the plant stems to gradually produce a mound with a flattish top, about 18 cm (7 in) high. You'll probably need to repeat this process as the foliage develops. You can stop when the foliage meets across each row.

Firming

Some plants, like rhubarb, need to be supported by the soil after planting. Depending on the size of the plant and the area you have to work in, you can either push the soil down with your foot, hand or the end of a trowel.

Staking

Fruit and vegetable plants that grow tall often don't have strong enough stems to support themselves and their produce, so they need a bit of help. Depending on what you're growing, you can use simple bamboo canes or more elaborate, purpose-built frames. Secure the plant to the support using garden string, special plant ties or clips. It is best to put the supports in place before the plants get established so that the root system isn't damaged at a later stage, and to encourage the plants to grow up the support as they develop.

Watering

Most vegetables and fruit need a good, steady supply of moisture in order to develop and grow properly. In dry conditions, plants tend to run to seed quickly (this is called 'bolting') and their taste and texture will be inferior; root vegetables may split underground. Overwatering root vegetables will encourage the leaves to grow more than the root. Keep the supply of water consistent – feast or famine where water is concerned will result in irregular growth patterns. If you have the time and only a small garden, use a watering can to get to the base of a plant where water is most needed. If you are not under a control ban, use a hose with a sprinkler attachment in the same way. Sprinklers are very useful for large gardens, but of course, with water a rare commodity these days, they must be used sensibly. A drip hose (a hosepipe with holes in) will give a good, steady supply of water without the danger of flooding your soil.

However you water, make sure the ground is soaked but not flooded. A light sprinkling will be of little use, and flooding an area causes puddling and erosion of the soil as the water runs away. The best time to water is in the morning so that the water has chance to soak in before the sun gets too hot and causes evaporation. If you can't fit morning watering into your daily routine, choose a time when the sun is not too hot to avoid foliage scorching. There is more chance of spreading pests around if you water late in the day as a moist atmosphere will be more ideally suited to them.

Mulch

Water is lost from the soil by the sun's rays and the wind. You can keep moisture in the ground by digging in well-rotted organic matter, and by applying a 'mulch' of loose-textured organic matter such as grass cuttings, some less well-rotted compost or coarse bark chippings. Water before mulching and apply to a depth of not more than 7 cm (3 in) around the base of the plant. Non-organic mulches like polythene prevent even less evaporation, but of course they will not let moisture in and they don't look very nice either. Mulch can also be used as a protection against a light frost.

Protection from the weather and garden wildlife

Tender young plants can be susceptible to damage from the cold, wind and an unexpected frost; they also make tempting treats for pigeons, other birds, mice, slugs and snails. There are a number of measures you can take and you'll find several solutions at a garden centre or DIY store. A cloche is the most traditional method. This is a glass or plastic dome that can be put directly over an individual plant *in situ*. For a row of new seedlings you can use a glass or plastic tunnel for protecting against the elements (you will have to remove it to water) or for simple pest protection you can buy netting tunnels or plain netting to put over your own frames. Garden fleece is available for putting over newly sown seeds – this helps keep the soil warm for germination and allows rain and light to penetrate. With regards to slugs and snails, it's a matter of personal preference how you deal with them. Humane traps are available or you can scatter a handful of slug pellets around the seedlings at the time of planting.

Pest and disease control

There are all sorts of chemical treatments available, but there are some organic compounds you can try. Derris dust, sulphur dust and soft soap spray can be used without causing harm, but they need to be applied regularly and act only on contact with the actual pest or disease. You can also set organic 'traps'. Earwigs are attracted to inverted flowerpots filled with dried grass, set on a short garden cane – remove the pot and burn the grass every other day. Wireworms can be drawn towards old potatoes or carrots, skewered on a stick and buried. Plant garlic and strong-smelling herbs like mint nearby to keep

pests like carrot fly at bay, and parsley will help deter onion fly. Some plants can be used to deflect pests from your vegetable patch, for example, nasturtiums (*Tropaeolum*) attract aphids and French marigolds (*Tagetes patula*) attract hoverflies, which in turn feed on aphids. Finally, good garden maintenance is one of the most important ways to keep pests and diseases away. Keep a regular check on your plants and immediately get rid of anything that has become diseased. Any debris from infected plants should be burned to reduce the risk of reinfestation.

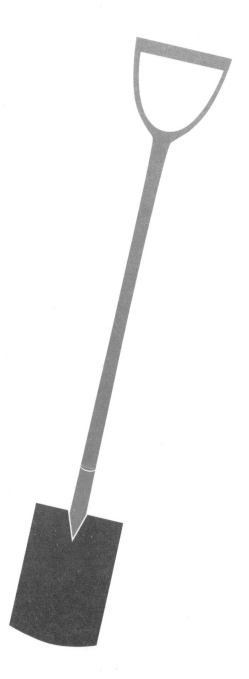

Chapter 2
Alliums

The vegetables covered in this chapter are members of the same genus, and have been around for centuries. Onions, shallots, leeks, garlic and spring onions are all *Alliums* used in the kitchen. They are highly prized for their flavouring abilities and it is hard to imagine life without them – many recipes would be very dull indeed without their unique savouriness.

The good news from the gardening point of view is that they are relatively easy to grow and require little skill or specific technique. Some *Alliums*, like leeks, do take up quite a bit of ground space and require a long growing season, so that's something to think about when planning your crop. A little advance preparation is required: during the late autumn/early winter before you start planting, you'll need to dig over your vegetable patch and enrich the soil with compost and well-rotted manure. Also, *Alliums* don't like acid soil so liming may be necessary to bring the pH to 7 or more (see page 9). You'll see that I've concentrated on the easiest and quickest way to raise some of these vegetables, which is from the already developed seed called a 'set'. If you have time, space and the right facilities, you may prefer to grow from seed yourself. Of the *Allium* genus, leeks and spring onions are usually grown from seed and you'll find all the instructions for seed planting on pages 10 and 11.

Even with all the best plans put into place, some things will go wrong and you may well incur some problems with pests or growing inconsistencies. Here are some of the most common invaders and diseases that may attack the *Allium* genus.

☠ Pests and diseases

Eelworm: affects onions, garlic and shallots, usually in midsummer. Symptoms include bloated and swollen stems, leaves and bulbs. Dig up infected plants and burn them or destroy completely. Do not plant other *Alliums* in the same site for 2 years.

Onion fly: these flies lay their eggs on onions, leeks and shallots. As the maggots hatch, they turn bulbs and stems to mush as they feed on them. The danger period is usually between May and August, and the risk of infestation is increased if the leaves get bruised and the oniony odour is released. It is best to avoid thinning out where possible. Dig up infected plants and burn them or destroy completely.

Onion neck rot: occurs in stored onions and also during the growing period. It is a grey velvety mould that forms on the neck and quickly rots it. Choose treated sets and seeds. Store only onions in tip-top condition and check them regularly. Dig up infected plants and burn them or destroy completely.

Onion white rot: a fungal disease of spring onions and also onions, leeks, shallots and garlic. A white fungus forms on *Alliums* as they grow and quickly causes rot. Dig up infected plants and burn them or destroy completely. Do not plant other *Alliums* in the same site for eight years.

Tip

Parsley is regarded as a natural deterrent to onion flies, so plant it around your *Allium* rows.

Garlic
Allium sativum

👁 At-a-glance

Plant: late February–March or early spring. If you live a very mild area, you can plant in the autumn.

Ideal growing conditions: sunny position; light, non-acid soil.

Believed to have originated in Asia, garlic has been used as a unique flavouring for centuries, and has been grown in the UK since the 16th century. To describe the flavour of garlic is very difficult, but its intensely pungent savouriness makes it a powerful flavouring. It also has antiseptic, antibiotic and antifungal properties. You'll find white, pink and purple varieties, small to gigantic bulbs, and flavours from sweet and mild to very strong. Garlic can be eaten fresh or 'green', or it can be dried and stored for several weeks.

It is best to get your garlic from a nursery or garden centre and not the greengrocers. This will ensure that it is disease-free and suited to the UK climate.

✍ Crop planner
Garlic grows best in the sunshine. It prefers light, sandy soil that drains well and is non-acid. A longer growing season will yield the biggest bulbs, so if possible plant in the autumn. If your soil is heavy and you live in a cold area, delay planting until early spring. Garlic can also be grown successfully in plant pots. Due to the distinct aroma of garlic, it is said that the bulbs act as a deterrent to many pests.

Remember that a little garlic goes a long way. Between 12 and 20 plants, depending on your requirements, should be ample. Approximate time from sowing to lifting is 16–36 weeks, depending on when the garlic has been planted.

✿ Varieties
'Cristo': large garlic bulbs with very white skin and a thick growing stem. Each bulb has up to 15 large chunky cloves that have a strong flavour.
'Elephant': the name speaks for itself in terms of its size, yet although the cloves are huge, they taste mild and sweet. Great for roasting.
'Marco': distinct white, compact bulbs with a strong, biting flavour. This garlic is ideal for storing.
'Sultop': pretty pink-skinned cloves, with a mild, slightly sweet flavour.

✿ Tips and techniques
Either in autumn or early spring, depending on climate, choose bulbs with plump cloves. Strip the papery skin from the bulb and split up into cloves – discard small ones. Using a dibber or trowel, make a shallow hole about 2.5 cm (1 in) deep in the ground for each clove. Space the holes about 10 cm (4 in) apart, using a line of string to keep the line straight. Plant the cloves upright, flat end down, and just cover with soil to the tip of the clove. Keep the plot well weeded and water during dry spells.

✿ Possible problems
Garlic is usually trouble-free, but it can attract general *Allium* fungal or viral diseases (see page 13). If the attack is severe, the bulbs should be removed and burnt or destroyed.

✿ Harvesting and storing
Lift garlic when the foliage turns yellow and starts to die down in late summer – leaving the the bulbs too long will result in them drying out. Ease the bulbs from the ground by carefully digging round with a fork. If drying, dry the bulbs thoroughly in the sun, preferably covered – a greenhouse is ideal, then remove any earth and long roots. Either plait the dried leaves together in bunches, or if you prefer to remove the leaves, put them in net bags or in trays. Store in a cool, dry place. Put aside a few good-quality bulbs for replanting the next year.

✿ Preparation and cooking
Green garlic has a delicate, fresh flavour and aroma, and can be used as a replacement for dry garlic, onions or leeks. To prepare it, simply chop up the bulbs – there is no need to peel or separate the cloves. The stem can be prepared in the same way to give colour and a slightly more delicate flavour.

Dry garlic needs to be peeled of its papery skin for most dishes. The more you chop up garlic the more flavour that is released. Using a garlic crusher means that you get an intense flavour in a dish, but a little chopping yields a lesser garlicky hit.

Garlic can be roasted whole in its skin and the long, slow cooking develops a sweet/savoury flavour and pastelike texture that's delicious smeared over toasted bread to serve with a hearty soup or roast.

✳ Freezing: the flavour of garlic deteriorates with prolonged freezing, so it is best used fresh. If you do freeze a garlicky dish, make sure it is well wrapped to avoid flavour transfer between food items.

Leek
Allium porrum

👁 At-a-glance

Plant: early–mid spring.

Ideal growing conditions: fertile, well-drained, non-acid soil in an open site.

Harvest: early autumn–late spring (depending on variety).

Like other members of the *Allium* genus, leeks have been a popular vegetable for hundreds of years, and a valued flavouring at times of the year when other vegetables were scarce. They are an easy-to-grow, robust crop with hardy varieties for winter and early types for late summer, the latter being tall and slim, while hardy leek varieties are usually more stocky in size or have bluer-green foliage; there are also mid-season varieties available. Leeks do require a long growing season in order to enable them to mature sufficiently, although younger, smaller leeks can be enjoyed as a delicious late spring vegetable in their own right.

✍ Crop planner
Leeks will grow in any reasonable soil unless it is compacted or waterlogged. Choose an open, sunny site for planting. Leeks like some nutrition to yield a good crop, so adding compost or well-rotted manure the previous late autumn/winter is a good idea to help them on their way. For best results the soil should be non-acid. Incorporate a general fertilizer into the surface about a week before planting. Although they are relatively easy to grow, they do require some care and attention and they do occupy the ground for several months. However, they are still a viable crop and look attractive as they develop.

A 3 m (10 ft) row will yield about 5 kg (11 lb) leeks. Therefore, two rows should be sufficient for most families. Approximate time from sowing to lifting is 30–45 weeks, depending on variety.

✿ Varieties
Earlies
'King Richard': this is a good all-round leek that can be grown as a mid-season variety as well (making excellent baby or 'mini' leeks). It is high yielding, with a long white body and paler green leaves. The taste is mild and sweet.
Mid-season
'Argenta': ready for harvesting in early winter, this variety withstands frosts to give a thickish white

stem, with crisp flesh and a mild flavour.
'Musselburgh': a Scottish variety and much-loved favourite. This leek is hardy and reliable. It has thick, shortish stems that have a fine flavour.
Late
'Giant Winter Catalina': long, thick stems with a mild flavour. This looks impressive growing and can be left in the ground for some time.
'Yates Empire': long, thick stems that are pure white. It will stay in the ground until mid-April.

🜚 Tips and techniques
Leeks need a long growing season, so start them as early in the season as possible. Make a drill about 1 cm (½ in) deep in an outdoor seedbed in late March, when the soil is workable and warm enough to permit germination, and sow the seeds thinly. In late June or July, when the plants are 20 cm (8 in) tall and about as thick as a pencil, they are ready for transplantation. Water the seedbed the day before so that the soil softens if it is dry. Carefully remove from the bed and trim the tops down.

Using a dibber, make holes 15 cm (6 in) deep, and 23 cm (9 in) apart. Drop the young leeks into the holes. Do not replace any soil, simply fill with water, allowing the soil to naturally settle around the roots. Subsequent rows should be planted about 38 cm (15 in) apart.

For the rest of the summer, hoe the soil to keep it free from weeds and make sure the leeks are kept watered during dry weather – the planting holes will fill naturally over time. As the plants develop, gradually draw soil up (earth-up) the lower stems in order to keep them white ('blanching').

🌢 Possible problems
Generally trouble-free; however, could be susceptible to any of the problems on page 13.

⌐ Harvesting and storing
Leeks are best harvested before they get too large, when they are about 2 cm (¾ in) thick is ideal. If you begin picking them when they are still quite small, this will help to extend the season. Carefully ease them out of the soil by loosening the earth around them to avoid breaking them as you pull them out. Leeks can be kept outside in the soil and then lifted throughout winter as they are needed. To do this, dig a shallow v-shaped trench, lift the leeks and lay them against one side of the trench. Cover the roots and white stems with soil and pack down gently. Lift and use when required.

Chapter 2: Alliums

ⅼ Preparation and cooking

To clean leeks for cooking, slice off the root, cut off the tops of the leaves and remove any tough or damaged outer leaves. For cooking whole or in large pieces, slice halfway through down the length of the stem and prise open. Rinse under cold running water to flush out any trapped earth. Shake well to remove excess water before cooking.

Boil leeks in a small amount of lightly salted water for 8–10 minutes for large or whole pieces; about 3–5 minutes for small chunks. Drain well and then return to the pan and cook very gently to steam away any remaining water. Leek flavour is sweet and mild, and is popular mixed with cheese. Slice, shred or chop and stir-fry as you would an onion. Younger, smaller leeks are delicious steamed whole or eaten raw, shredded and tossed into salads.

✱ Freezing: the leeks should be prepared as above and cut into 2.5 cm (1 in) lengths. Blanch for 2 minutes, cool and dry well. Leeks are quite soft and watery once they have been frozen, so it is a good idea to use the thawing liquid in your recipe for extra flavour.

⏱ Short recipe: serves 4
Hearty cheesy leek soup

Prepare 450 g (1 lb) leeks as above and shred finely. Melt 50 g (2 oz) butter in a saucepan and gently fry the leeks for about 5 minutes until tender. Stir in 25 g (1 oz) medium oatmeal and 1.2 L (2 pt) chicken or vegetable stock. Bring to the boil, cover and simmer for 20 minutes. Just before serving, stir in 100 g (3½ oz) grated mature Cheddar cheese, season to taste and ladle into bowls. Serve immediately sprinkled with finely chopped parsley.

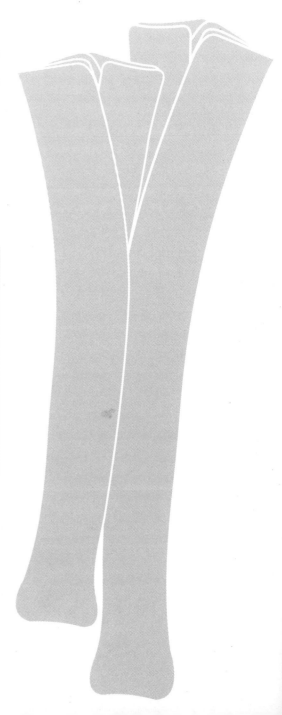

Onion
Allium cepa

👁 At-a-glance (from sets)

Plant: early–late spring (depending on variety).

Ideal growing conditions: light, non-acid soil, manured the previous autumn; open site.

Harvest: mid- or late summer (depending on variety).

The onion is probably the most widely used of all vegetables because of its flavouring and versatility. For most cooks/gardeners, growing a sufficient supply to keep up with demand can be quite a challenge! The choice of onion is seemingly endless: brown-, yellow-, white- and red/purple-skinned varieties, differing in shape from the familiar bulbous to the long and ovular, and a wealth of sizes and flavours. Different onion varieties can be grown for harvesting at different times of the year, and some store better than others.

The easiest way to grow this kitchen staple is from an immature bulb grown from the seed of the previous season, called a 'set'. There are several advantages to growing onions in this way (as opposed to seed), especially if you live in a colder part of the country. Onion sets are easy to plant and require less demanding growing conditions. They mature relatively quickly, are more reliable and the sets are less likely to be attacked by pests. Onion sets are widely available to buy from seed merchants and garden centres from the late winter months. Look out for heat-treated sets that reduce the possibilities of bolting (see page 11).

✍ Crop planner
Onion sets require an open site. The soil doesn't have to be too light or highly organic, but it is a good idea to incorporate manure or compost in late winter before planting in spring. Onions prefer a non-acid soil.

A 3 m (10 ft) row of onion sets will yield about 30 onions. Approximate time from planting to lifting is 20 weeks.

✿ Varieties
'Centurion F1': smooth, brown-skinned onion that crops well and matures early. This onion also stores well.
'Hercules F1': a strong flavoured onion, elongated in shape. It is resistant to bolting and stores well.

'Red Baron': deep pink/purple onion with attractive purple-ringed white flesh. Sweeter than white varieties. It is quite an early onion, and stores well.
'Sturon': large onion, globe-shaped with golden skin. It has a good rich flavour, and stores very successfully for a long time.

⊕ Tips and techniques
Plant sets in early to mid-March, and heat-treated sets from late March to mid-April. Using a dibber, make a hole about 2.5 cm (1 in) deep in the ground for each set, about 10 cm (4 in) between onions, in rows about 30 cm (12 in) apart. Plant the bulb root-end down, and cover so that only the shooting tip is showing. Keep well weeded and watered until established, and then only water if the conditions are exceptionally dry or they begin to wilt. If you have a garden that attracts birds you may need to cover the bed with netting or put in bird scarers in order to prevent the sets being lifted out.

♠ Possible problems
The main pest is onion fly. Onion eelworm and other *Allium* fungal diseases can also be a potential problem (see page 13).

⌁ Harvesting and storing
Onions can be lifted at any point for immediate use, but you must let them mature fully if you want to store them. In late summer, when the leaves begin to yellow, bend over the tops to encourage ripening and leave for about 2 weeks. Loosen the soil around the onions with a fork and carefully loosen the bulbs. Depending on the weather, after a further 2 weeks, the onions can be lifted and spread out in a dry, warm place to continue ripening – too much wet weather at this stage will determine how long the bulbs can be left before they split and start to spoil. Ripening can take days to weeks depending on variety and storage conditions. Take care not to bruise the onions and keep the withering leaves intact if you want to tie the onions together for bunching and hanging on rope. Otherwise, onions can be put in net bags and hung similarly in a cool, dry place. Keep checking the onions during storage in case any start to rot.

▯ Preparation and cooking
For cooking, cut off the stalk and root end and peel away the dry, papery outer layers of skin, and any tougher inner layers. Either halve, slice, chop or cut into thick wedges depending on the recipe. Onion is usually fried or mixed directly into a recipe. Large sweet varieties can be stuffed and roasted whole, while smaller ones are peeled and left whole and either boiled or pickled.

✱ **Freezing:** usually onion is only frozen for convenience sake because if you have a sufficient supply of fresh this is preferable. Peel and slice or chop, then wrap well and seal to prevent transmitting odour. Small onions can be peeled and left whole, and require about 3 minutes blanching, then allow to cool and dry, before packing as above and freezing. Use all onion within 6 months of freezing.

Small onions can be added to soups and casseroles directly from frozen, while prepared onion is best semi-thawed and used as fresh. Like leeks, onions go quite soft and watery once they have been frozen, so it is a good idea to use the thawing liquid in your recipe for extra flavour.

🕐 **Short recipe: serves 4**
Baked onions

Preheat the oven to 180ºC/350ºF/gas 4. Slice the tops off 4 medium onions and reserve. Do not peel. Carefully top each onion with 1 tsp of light brown sugar and seasoning. Cut 25 g (1 oz) butter into 4 pieces and place a piece of butter on top of each onion. Press the tops back on the onions and wrap each completely in foil. Stand in a small roasting tin and bake in the oven for about 1½–2 hours until tender. To serve, remove the onions from the foil; take off the lid and top with a dollop of garlic and herb flavoured soft cheese, sprinkle with freshly chopped chives and black pepper, and quickly replace the lid. Serve immediately with grilled pork, gammon or sausages, scooping out the flesh from the skins to eat.

Shallot
Allium cepa Aggregatum Group

👁 At-a-glance

Plant: February–March.

Ideal growing conditions: open site; light, non-acid soil, manured the previous autumn.

Harvest: midsummer.

Many cooks prefer the flavour of shallots to onions; it is often finer and sweeter, and the flesh is tinged pink. Shallots are a good choice as an alternative to larger onions if you find a whole onion too much to use in one recipe. The leaves can be used as a substitute for chives and small shallots make a good alternative to pickling onions for preserving in vinegar. Shallots store well.

Shallots are planted like bulb onions but grow in a cluster of about five small bulbs. They are planted earlier and are hardier than onion sets; they grow more quickly and are ready before the main crop of onions appears. They can also be grown from seed. Compared to onions, most seed merchants are unlikely to sell as many varieties of shallots.

✍ Crop planner
Traditionally, shallots were planted on Boxing Day, but this time of year is usually inconvenient and cold, so put back planting until February or March. Choose a sunny site that has been manured during the previous autumn. Light soil is best for easier planting and shallots prefer a non-acid soil.

A 3 m (10 ft) row of shallot sets will yield about 15 clusters of shallots. Approximate time from planting to lifting is 18 weeks.

✿ Varieties
'Golden Gourmet': yellow-skinned and pear-shaped; stores well.
'Hative de Niort': largish, perfect pear-shaped bulbs with deep brown skin.

۹ Tips and techniques
On light soil, push the bulbs into the soil so that they are three-quarters buried. If the soil is firm, use a dibber to make a shallow hole first. In both cases leave only the tip of the bulb above soil level. Leave 15 cm (6 in) between shallots in rows spaced 30 cm (12 in) apart. Replant any bulbs that have become dislodged. Keep weeded and water in early summer if necessary.

۶ Possible problems
On the whole, shallots are quite easy to grow, but they can succumb to the general infections of other onions (see page 13).

⊶ Harvesting and storing
Shallots are usually ready to harvest in July and August. When the foliage dies back lift the bulb clusters and dry for a few days as for onions. Loosen the soil around the shallots with a fork and carefully loosen the bulbs. Depending on the weather, after a further 2 weeks, the shallots can be lifted and spread out in a dry, warm place to continue ripening – too much wet weather at this stage will determine how long the bulbs can be left before they split and start to spoil. Ripening can take days to weeks, depending on variety and storage conditions. Take care not to bruise the shallots and keep the withering leaves intact if you want to tie them together for bunching and hanging on rope. Once the foliage has completely died back, split the clusters into individual bulbs and leave to ripen for a few more days. The shallots can then be stored in a net or basket in a cool, dry place throughout the winter months.

⫶ Preparation and cooking
Shallots are used as a flavouring rather than as a vegetable in their own right. Their milder onion flavour enhances any dish. Prepare by peeling away the outer papery skin, slice off the top and bottom, and then chop the bulb or slice into thin rings.

✳ Freezing: shallots are best used fresh, although if you do want to freeze them, follow the instructions for chopped onion (see page 18).

🕐 Short recipe: serves 4
Sweet and sour shallot sauce
Peel and thinly slice 225 g (8 oz) shallots. Place in a glass bowl and mix in 2 Tbsp of raspberry vinegar. Stand for 5 minutes. Melt 25 g (1 oz) unsalted butter in a frying pan and fry the shallots with the soaking vinegar for 5 minutes until tender but not browned. Stir in 2 tsp of caster sugar, pour over 75 ml (3 fl oz) dry white wine and 75 ml (3 fl oz) chicken or vegetable stock, bring to the boil and simmer for 5 minutes. Mix 1 tsp of cornflour with 1 Tbsp of water and stir into the shallot mixture. Cook for a further minute until slightly thickened, then season and stir in 2 Tbsp of freshly chopped parsley. Serve with oily fish or grilled chicken or pork.

Spring (Salad) onion
Allium cepa

👁 At-a-glance

Plant: mid-spring (late March) onwards.

Ideal growing conditions: open site; light non-acid soil, manured the previous autumn.

Harvest: end of May onwards.

These are the most refined members of the onion family, although some varieties can be planted out to withstand winter. They get their name because they are ready before main crop onions, and can be ready for harvesting as little as 8 weeks after sowing. The spring onion is best used as fresh as possible and is usually eaten raw as a salad vegetable and has a strong pungent flavour. The leaves can be used like chives. Both bulb and leaves can be shredded and used in stir-fries.

✍ Crop planner

Choose a sunny site that has been manured during the previous autumn. The soil should be non-acid.

A 3 m (10 ft) row of spring onions will yield sufficient spring onions for most people's requirements. They are ready about 8 weeks from sowing.

✿ Varieties

'Ishikura': a slender, long-stemmed onion that doesn't form a bulb at the end; for summer use.
'North Holland Blood Red': a lovely red-skinned variety that's white on the inside; this is a summer salad onion.
'White Lisbon': widely grown variety that is quick growing and mildly flavoured. Good choice for growing in successive crops. Suitable for summer and winter use.
'Winter White Bunching': strong, vigorous spring onion that will withstand winter planting.

❡ Tips and techniques

Make a drill about 1 cm (½ in) deep and sow the seeds thinly in March, then at 3–4 week intervals in order to give a successive crop until July. If you sow them thinly, there should be no need to thin them out. Leave about 15 cm (6 in) between rows.

Spring onions are best grown quickly in order to prevent the leaves toughening, so water them frequently to encourage growth.

🔥 Possible problems

Onion fly is the main concern when growing spring onions but other fungal diseases of the onion family may also be a problem (see page 13).

⚓ Harvesting and storing

Early crop spring onions will be ready in the spring, and later crops from June to October. Spring onions do not keep well and are best used as soon after harvesting as possible. Pull the onions as required, in bunches, when they reach about 15 cm (6 in) in height. If you do want to keep spring onions, rinse well and store in the fridge for 2–3 days.

🍴 Preparation and cooking

For eating raw or cooking, rinse well and pat dry, slice off the root end and remove any damaged outer leaves. Leave whole for serving as crudités or chop finely and add to salads or mix with sandwich fillings for extra oniony 'bite'. Slice or chop and add to sauces and stir-fries – spring onions require only a short amount of cooking.

❋ Freezing: spring onions are not suitable for freezing.

🕐 Short recipe: serves 4
Low-fat spring onion mash

Peel and cut 900 g (2 lb) main crop potatoes into small pieces. Put the potatoes in a saucepan with a pinch of salt. Cover with water, bring to the boil and cook for 12–15 minutes until tender. Drain well and return to the saucepan. Mash and keep warm. Prepare 8 spring onions as described above and chop the white and green parts finely. Stir into the mashed potato along with a small carton of chive-flavoured cottage cheese and plenty of salt and pepper. Serve immediately to accompany grilled fish, chicken or vegetables.

Chapter 3
Root vegetables

Where would we be without this hearty, wholesome group of vegetables? Potatoes, carrots, parsnips and turnips are staples of our everyday recipes and traditional culinary history. Beetroots, radishes, Jerusalem artichokes, radishes and swedes are also included in this chapter. To get the best roots you can, you'll need deep and sandy or fine soil that drains well, but almost any reasonable land will produce good crops if it is adequately prepared. The late autumn/early winter before you start planting, you'll generally need to dig over your vegetable patch and enrich the soil with compost and well-rotted manure – check the individual entries for each vegetable for specific information. About 1–2 weeks before planting, it is advisable to rake in some general-purpose fertilizer.

There's nothing too complicated about growing roots. Some grow from seed sown in the ground, while others need to be started off indoors and reach seedling stage before they can be planted out into the vegetable patch. You should be able to grow successive crops of the smaller, quicker-growing roots for a longer harvesting period, while some roots, like swedes, do occupy the ground for some time, so you might want to consider growing half-rows to make the most of your space.

☠ Pests and diseases

Blackleg: stems blacken at and below ground level. The leaves yellow and wilt. It is an early-season disease and it occurs especially if the soil is heavy and there is lots of rain. Plants should be pulled up and destroyed.

Canker: roots succumbing to this will turn black and rot. Plants should be pulled up and destroyed. Choosing a canker-resistant variety means you shouldn't have to concern yourself with this problem.

Carrot fly: eggs are laid on the carrots and as the maggots hatch, they burrow into the flesh to feed, and the roots begin to rot. Attacks are worse in dry conditions. The affected carrots should be pulled up and destroyed.

Cyst eelworm: plants appear weak and stunted and only marble-sized tuber appear. Affected plants should be pulled up and destroyed.

Potato blight: the foliage will yellow and brown, and begin to curl. This causes the potatoes to rot and turn to slime. Avoid planting potatoes on the same site for a year. Look out for blight-resistant varieties. There are also fungicides available if you decide to use such measures.

Potato scab: can be caused if the soil is dry and too light. It makes the skin of the tubers malformed and ragged. It doesn't affect the eating qualities. Dig in compost but do not lime before planting. Look out for resistant varieties.

Violet root rot: you may see a slight yellowing of the foliage, but often the symptoms only show when the carrot or parsnip is pulled. The root shows a mass of purple feltlike threads. Burn or destroy affected roots and do not plant carrots in this ground for 2 years.

Wireworm: a serious potato pest in new gardens, especially in wet summers. Tubers are riddled with narrow tunnels. Affected plants should be pulled up and destroyed.

Tip
Planting garlic or mint nearby is a natural carrot fly deterrent.

Beetroot
Beta vulgaris

👁 At-a-glance

Plant: mid-March–April onwards (depending on variety).

Ideal growing conditions: open sunny site; light, non-acid soil; manure the previous autumn.

Harvest: mid-May onwards.

A sweet-tasting, earthy-flavoured root that has been popular in our kitchens since Tudor times, but it dates back to the Roman Empire. There are two main types: the familiar round shape called 'globe', and a longer, chunky, rooted variety. They are usually grown from seeds, although from mid-spring you can buy seedlings from nurseries and garden centres. Globe beetroots are mostly used for summer/autumn eating and used fresh in salads, while the long-rooted varieties can be stored for winter use. You'll find different coloured beetroots available to plant, ranging from the traditional deep red/purple to paler golden or white varieties.

Cooked beetroot makes a delicious hot or cold vegetable and it preserves very well for enjoying later on in the year. Small beetroot leaves make a colourful and lively addition to the salad bowl, and older leaves will cook up like spinach, although most of the stunning red veining will be lost during cooking.

✍ Crop planner

Choose a sunny site which has been manured during the previous autumn. Do not grow on freshly manured ground otherwise the roots will divide. The soil needs to have good drainage properties and be limed if it is acid. Beetroot is usually grown from seed, straight in the ground, but the seed usually comes in clusters and resembles a small piece of cork. This is really the dried fruit that contains several true seeds. To save time thinning out, look out for beetroot seed classified as 'monogerm' or 'single seed'; this means that you'll only get one seedling from each seed.

A 3 m (10 ft) row of beetroot will provide approximately 4.5 kg (10 lb) globe, or 8.1 kg (18 lb) long-rooted beetroot. Approximate time from sowing to harvesting is 8–14 weeks, depending on variety.

✿ Varieties

'Albina Vereduna' or 'Snowhite': the most popular white variety; not as widely available as other globe types, but does have an excellent flavour.

'Boltardy': widely grown variety that is bolt-resistant and suits early sowing. It is round, smooth and deep red.

'Burpees Golden': a round, orange-skinned, golden-fleshed beetroot with an excellent flavour. The flesh doesn't bleed when cut.

'Cheltenham Green Top': a classic beetroot that is one of the most popular and recommended long-rooted varieties grown. It has deep pink flesh.

'Monopoly': a dark red-fleshed globe beetroot that grows from monogerm seed.

'Perfect 3': smooth, globe-shaped beetroot with deep red flesh. Good for early lifting or for mature beetroot.

✪ Tips and techniques

If you are using monogerm seed, presoak the seed for about 30 minutes before planting to soften the coating. All beetroot seed can be planted outside when a minimum germination temperature of the soil, about 7°C (45°F), is reached. In warmer areas this may be from mid-March, but in more northern gardens, this will be well into April. Choose a sunny spot and make a drill about 2 cm (¾ in) deep and sow the seeds about 2.5 cm (1 in) apart. Leave about 20 cm (8 in) between rows. Subsequent sowings can be made every 2–3 weeks for successive crops. In June, change to a main crop variety.

When the seedlings are about 2.5 cm (1 in) high, thin them out to leave a single plant in each station. Discard the thinnings. You may need to protect seedlings from birds by erecting netting or putting in bird scarers. Keep the beetroots weed-free, but take care when hoeing to avoid damaging the roots. Water steadily (see page 11).

💣 Possible problems

Beetroots are usually trouble-free. The leaves may become damaged by aphids; if this happens just pick off the affected leaves and discard.

⚏ Harvesting and storing

Pull globe beetroots by hand as they are needed. Younger beetroots, about the size of a golf ball, are tastier and have a better texture; the flesh of older roots can become a little 'woolly'. As a general guideline, globe beetroots are best pulled by the time they reach tennis-ball size. Once out of the ground, hold the base of the leaves in one hand and twist off the leaves with the other. If you cut into the root stem it will 'bleed' and the juice stains.

Long-rooted beetroots are ready to dig in November. Put a fork alongside the row and loosen the soil around the beetroots that you want so that they can be more easily pulled out of the ground. Once the leaves have been removed, the roots can be stored in boxes of sand in a frost-free shed or outbuilding.

⫶ Preparation and cooking

Beetroot can be eaten raw, grated in fine shreds for salads, but it bleeds on to other ingredients and dries out quickly, so it is best prepared and added at the last minute. When preparing beetroot it is advisable to wear thin latex gloves to avoid staining your hands; wash the roots well, peel thinly and grate coarsely.

For cooking, carefully rinse the beetroots, taking care not to cut into the skin or bruise it. Place in a saucepan, unpeeled. Cover with water and bring to the boil. Cook for 1–2 hours, depending on size (gently press a skewer or round bladed knife into the beetroot to test for 'doneness'). Refresh in cold water and then carefully rub off the skin. Small beetroots are a classic pickled vegetable to serve with cold meats and salads, and are also delicious made into a soup (see page 128) or even added to a cake mixture to keep it moist (see page 163).

✱ **Freezing:** choose small golf ball-sized beetroots and cook in their skins as above. Drain and cool, rub off the skins and pack into freezer bags. If using larger roots, these are better sliced before freezing. Keep in the freezer for up to 6 months. Defrost for 4–6 hours in the fridge before using.

⏱ Short recipe: serves 4
Baked beetroot

Preheat the oven to 200ºC/400ºF/gas 6. Rinse and wrap 4 medium-sized whole unpeeled beetroots individually in foil parcels – add a sprig of thyme and a sprinkling of caraway seeds before sealing up. Bake for 1–1½ hours until they feel tender when squeezed. Remove from the foil, split the top, season and add a dollop of sour cream and sprinkle with fresh chives. Baked beetroots make a tasty accompaniment to serve with duck, game and other rich meats.

Carrot
Daucus carota

👁 At-a-glance

Plant: early spring–early summer.

Ideal growing conditions: open sunny site; sandy or light soil.

Harvest: late spring onwards.

A home-grown carrot eaten fresh out of the ground is so markedly different in taste from any carrot I've ever bought. The taste is far superior, sweet and spicy, and makes it well worth the effort to grow them. This striking root has been around since the days of the ancient Egyptians. It has evolved from an unpleasant-tasting white root, through to yellow and purple, but it wasn't until the 16th century that the orange carrot was cultivated and eaten in Britain. Different varieties of shape and colour mean that we can enjoy this colourful vegetable all year round, and it can be eaten both raw and cooked.

✍ Crop planner

Choose a sunny site. Do not manure the previous autumn or grow on freshly manured ground otherwise the roots will deform. The soil needs to have good drainage properties and should be treated about 2 weeks before planting with a general-purpose fertilizer. A heavy clay soil or lots of stones in your soil will make long roots difficult to achieve, so you are better choosing shorter-rooted varieties. Carrots are grown from fine, dustlike seed sown straight in the ground. Some varieties are more prone to carrot fly than others.

A 3 m (10 ft) row of carrots will provide approximately 4.5 kg (10 lb) early carrots, or up to 6.75 kg (15 lb) main crop carrots in ideal conditions. Approximate time from sowing to harvesting is 12–16 weeks, depending on variety.

✿ Varieties

'**Amsterdam Forcing**': traditional, much-grown early orange carrot. It is cylindrical, but has a blunt end and there is a little central core. It is ideal for freezing.
'**Autumn King**': a large, long, cylindrical orange root with a stumpy end. It is hardy and can grow for a long time and still retain flavour. It stores well.
'**Chantenay Red Cored 2**': high-yielding main crop carrot, with stocky, wedge-shaped roots and a small core. It has a good crunchy texture.
'**Early Nantes**': a traditional carrot for successional planting. Similar to 'Amsterdam Forcing' but with

longer, more tapered roots. It is early, tender and suitable for freezing.
'**Nantes 2**': this is the variety to plant as an early main crop.
'**Flyaway**': a stumpy carrot with sweet orange flesh. Carrot fly resistant.
'**Rondo**': a short, round, orange carrot, best harvested when still quite small.

☿ Tips and techniques

Carrot seed can be planted outside when a minimum germination temperature of the soil, about 7°C (45°F), is reached. In warmer areas this may be from mid-March, but in more northern gardens this will be well into April. Choose a sunny spot and make a drill about 1 cm (½ in) deep and sow the fine seeds as thinly as possible. Sift a very thin covering of soil over the top. Leave about 30 cm (12 in) between rows. Subsequent sowings can be made every 2–3 weeks for successive crops until early winter. For storing, sow in May or June ready for an autumn harvest.

When the seedlings are large enough to handle, thin them out to about 5–8 cm (2–3 in) apart. Discard the thinnings. Take care with this process, as you can attract carrot fly with the smell of bruised foliage. You can protect your seedlings with a low barrier of netting if necessary, but this is quite difficult to erect. Keep the carrots weed-free, but it will be difficult to use a large hoe once the foliage develops. Water, with care, if the conditions are dry.

☂ Possible problems

The main pest is the carrot fly and look out for violet root rot (see page 21).

☞ Harvesting and storing

Early, short-rooted carrots will be ready for pulling in June and July – loosen the ground around the carrots with a garden fork if the soil is compacted. Main crop carrots will be ready for harvesting in early October. To store carrots, remove as much soil as possible and trim off the leaves close to the top of the carrot. Lay the carrots in boxes, between layers of sand, and store in an airy, dry, frost-proof shed or outbuilding.

✂ Preparation and cooking

Trim off the leaves and wispy root end. Scrape small, young carrots under cold running water, and peel older carrots thinly using a vegetable peeler. Either grate, cut finely or chop into small pieces to serve raw in salads, or serve in chunkier sticks as crudités. Small carrots can be left whole or halved lengthways for cooking, while larger ones should be sliced, diced or cut into batons. Cook in lightly salted boiling water for 8–15 minutes depending on size, age and method of preparation. Drain well.

✱ **Freezing:** small, whole, scraped carrots freeze well, otherwise prepare older carrots as above. Blanch for 2–3 minutes depending on thickness, drain and cool. Either open-freeze on trays for later packing, or pack straightaway into freezer bags or rigid containers. Keep for up to 12 months. Cook from frozen for 5 minutes in boiling water, or add directly to soups and stews.

🕐 Short recipe: serves 4
Spiced carrot dip

Peel 450 g (1 lb) carrots and dice. Put in a saucepan and cover with water. Add a pinch of salt, bring to the boil and cook for 8–10 minutes or until tender. Drain and return to the saucepan. Mash well until smooth using a fork or potato masher. Cover and set aside. Heat 2 Tbsp of olive oil in a small frying pan and gently cook a chopped garlic clove and a deseeded and chopped green chilli for 3–4 minutes until softened but not browned. Stir the cooked garlic and chilli mixture into the still-warm carrots, along with 1 tsp of granulated sugar, 1 tsp of ground cumin and 2 tsp of ground coriander. Set aside to cool. Add more salt if necessary, then cover and chill until required. Best served at room temperature sprinkled with freshly chopped coriander.

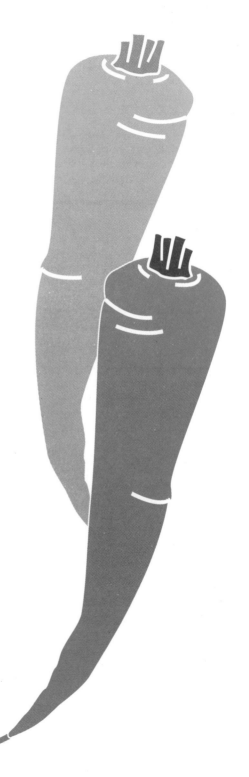

Jerusalem artichoke
Helianthus tuberosus

A relation of the sunflower family, the name is thought to derive from the Italian name for sunflower, *girasole*. An autumn/winter vegetable that's rich in phosphorus and potassium, the potato-like tubers can be knobbly or smooth depending on the variety and have a distinct sweet, almost smoky flavour. It is an easy vegetable to grow as it isn't that fussy about the conditions it grows in. It is grown from tubers and while it is advisable to obtain them from a nursery so you know the variety you are growing, you can plant from the ones the greengrocer sells. Note that the leafy foliage grows rapidly and can become quite tall (sometimes up to 3 m/10 ft!), however, this can act as a good windbreak, so keep them to the edge of the plot.

✍ Crop planner

Planting time is not too critical for Jerusalem artichokes, so any time in spring will be fine. Unless conditions are extreme, Jerusalem artichokes can be grown in any soil, either in sun or shade.

A 3 m (10 ft) row of six Jerusalem artichoke plants will provide approximately 10.8 kg (24 lb) of root vegetable. Approximate time from sowing to harvesting is 12–16 weeks, depending on variety.

✿ Varieties

Note: Often available simply as 'Jerusalem Artichoke'.
'Dwarf Sunray': a smooth, white-skinned variety that doesn't need peeling. It is quite compact when growing.
'Fuseau': a traditional variety that has long, white tubers with a smooth surface. It is more compact when growing than other varieties.

⚓ Tips and techniques

Dig holes about 10–13 cm (4–5 in) deep, spaced about 38 cm (15 in) apart – rows should be spaced with 90 cm (3 ft) between them. Replace the earth carefully over the tubers and make a low ridge of soil above using a rake. Use a hoe to earth-up the base of the stems when the plants reach about 30 cm (12 in) high. Once the plants become established, push a cane into the ground at the end of each row and run a plastic-coated wire on either side of the plants in order to protect them from the wind.

Water the plants in dry weather. During summer months, pick off flower buds to improve the crop.

💣 Possible problems

Jerusalem artichokes rarely attract pests. The main problem is that they can grow quite rampantly. They are also quite difficult to get rid of if you decide not to grow them again; a single piece left in the ground will resprout to produce a new plant. However, the regrowth usually appears in the same place and they do not spread beyond the plot.

⚓ Harvesting and storing

The tubers will be ready for lifting in October, once the leaves start to wither. Cut off the stems and then carefully dig right under the roots. Sift through the soil to make sure no pieces have been left behind. They are frost-hardy so are best stored in the ground until required. Once dug, they don't store for long. However, if the ground looks set to freeze, they can be dug, cleaned and stored in trays of dampish sand for a few weeks – after this they will begin to shrivel.

⚕ Preparation and cooking

Scrub under cold running water before peeling thinly with a vegetable knife or potato peeler. However, some varieties don't need any peeling, just a light scrub. You will find some varieties are smooth skinned and easy to peel, while others are quite knobbly and the skin is more difficult to remove. Jerusalem artichokes can be prepared and cooked like potatoes, but the creamy white flesh discolours quickly so add lemon juice to the rinsing and cooking water.

Cook in boiling, salted, lemony water for 15–20 minutes depending on size. Drain and serve with melted butter. Parboiled Jerusalem artichokes can be sautéed in butter, deep-fried in hot oil or roasted around a joint like potatoes. Prepared artichokes also steam well – whole ones will take 35–40 minutes, while halves or quarters will take 25–30 minutes.

✱ Freezing: Jerusalem artichokes are unsuitable for freezing whole. You can, however, freeze them in 'chip' (see page 29) or 'mash' form. For mash, cool, mash and pack into a rigid freezer container. Freeze for up to 6 months. Allow to defrost in the fridge overnight, then place in a covered saucepan over a low heat with a little milk or butter, and cook gently, stirring occasionally, for 10 minutes until hot.

Parsnip
Pastinaca sativa

👁 At-a-glance

Plant: mid-March–April.

Ideal growing conditions: sunny site; light, non-acid soil, good drainage.

Harvest: from September

No roast dinner is complete without this favourite on the roasting tray! Traditionally they were grown to full maturity as a coarse, thick vegetable as they are one of the most slow growing of crops. They would occupy the ground for almost the whole year, and are reputed to need the first frost to sweeten their flavour. New developments mean that it is possible to have parsnips at other times of the year, and you'll find short and long varieties, some fat and stocky, others thin and tapering. Parsnips need little attention once they have been thinned out, they are hardy and can be harvested fresh when other vegetables are scarce. They have a sweet, nutty flavour that is great served with roast beef and Yorkshire puddings, and they are ideal for seasoning with Indian spices.

✍ Crop planner
Choose a sunny site. Like carrot planting, do not manure the previous autumn or grow on freshly manured ground otherwise the roots will deform. The soil needs to have good drainage properties; it should be non-acid and treated about 2 weeks before planting with a general-purpose fertilizer. A heavy clay soil or lots of stones in the soil will make long roots difficult to achieve, so choose shorter-rooted varieties. Parsnips are grown from seed sown straight in the ground. The seeds are very light and germination is slowed down by cold weather.

A 3 m (10 ft) row of parsnips will provide approximately 3.6 kg (8 lb) vegetable. Approximate time from sowing to harvesting is 30 weeks.

✿ Varieties
'Gladiator': has smooth, pale skin and long roots. It is vigorous growing with good yield. Canker resistant.
'Patriot F1': smooth, neat, wedge-shaped parsnip that gives high yields. It has good tolerance to disease.
'Tender and True': an old variety with long, tapering roots for good-quality soil. It is canker resistant and has a great sweet flavour.
'White Gem': this variety adapts to any soil. It has quite long roots, white skin and is sweet tasting. Resistant to canker.

⚘ Tips and techniques
Parsnip seeds can be planted outside when a minimum germination temperature of the soil, about 7°C (45°F), is reached. In warmer areas this may be from mid-March, but in more northern gardens this will be well into April. Choose a sunny spot and make a drill about 2.5 cm (1 in) deep and sow in groups of three seeds, about 13cm (5 in) apart. Sift a very thin covering of compost over the top. Leave about 38 cm (15 in) between rows. Parsnip seeds can take up to a month to germinate.

When the seedlings are large enough to handle, thin them out to one per station. Discard the thinnings. Keep weed–free, but it will be difficult to hoe once the foliage develops. Water if the conditions are dry but too much moisture may cause the roots to split. If the weather turns very cold, cover the developing parsnips with straw to protect them.

✦ Possible problems
Parsnips can be attacked by carrot fly and canker (see page 21).

⚬ Harvesting and storing
Once the leaves die back in autumn parsnips can be pulled, but it is claimed that the flavour will be better after the first frost. Dig carefully around the roots with a fork to loosen, taking care not to damage them, before you lift them. Parsnips can be left in the ground until needed, but by February the remaining roots should be lifted before new shoots begin. Parsnips can be stored in trays, covered lightly with soil, in a cool, dry shed.

🍴 Preparation and cooking
To prepare for cooking, wash thoroughly, then cut off the top and tapering root. Peel thinly and cut into thick slices. Small parsnip can be left whole or sliced lengthways. If parsnips are very large, cut into pieces and cut out the central 'woody' core. Boil in lightly salted water for 10–20 minutes depending on size. Drain and serve with a knob of butter and chopped parsley. For roasting, boil for 5 minutes and cook as you would for potatoes. They can also be chipped, deep-fried and steamed in the same way as potatoes.

❋ Freezing: prepare as above and cut into 2.5 cm (1 in) thick pieces. Blanch for 2 minutes, drain, cool and dry. Pack into rigid containers and freeze for up to 12 months. Cook from frozen for 10 minutes in boiling water, or add directly to soups and stews.

Potato
Solanum tuberosum

Plant: first earlies – early spring; second earlies – mid-spring; main crop – mid–late spring.

Ideal growing conditions: open, sunny site; fertile soil but not recently manured.

Harvest: first earlies – early summer; second earlies – midsummer onwards; main crop – autumn

What would the culinary landscape look like if we didn't have this vegetable? The versatile tattie is one of the most important food crops throughout the world, and it's certainly one of our main staples. It's also nutritious, and the best news is it's easy to grow yourself!

The most challenging thing about potato growing is deciding which variety to grow. It can be pretty daunting when you're faced with all the different potatoes on offer at your local nursery or seed merchant. Potatoes are divided into two categories, earlies and main crop, and these categories determine when they can be planted and harvested. Earlies are divided further into 'first' and 'second' earlies. Different varieties are more suited to specific uses, so have a think about your own requirements to help you decide which one is right for you. Other considerations are flavour, texture and colour – all of which are down to personal preference.

Because of the choice on offer you might be tempted to grow several different varieties, but you should know that potato plants take up quite a bit of space in the garden. Have a look out for 'taster' bags that offer the grower a chance to try out different varieties without having to buy lots of bags of seed potatoes. You can grow two or three varieties in the same row (remember to label which is which!) and then you'll learn which ones you like best and concentrate on those varieties next time. If you're still unable to make up your mind, most people choose an early crop because these usually have the best flavour. Another way round the space problem, of course, is to grow potato plants in containers, and there are now several containers specifically available for this purpose.

✍ Crop planner

Choose a sunny site, which has been manured the previous autumn – the soil should not be freshly fertilized. The soil needs to have good drainage properties. Potatoes are grown from a 'seed' potato from a nursery (not a greengrocer), which needs to be 'chitted'. This involves standing the potatoes in a tray (egg boxes are good for this), the most rounded end uppermost, so that any sprouts or 'eyes' can grow upwards. Put the trays in a cool, frost-free place that is light but not directly in the sun. In a few weeks, short shoots appear. When the shoots are 2.5–5 cm (1–2 in) long, you're potatoes are ready to plant.

A 3 m (10 ft) row of potatoes will provide approximately 5.4 kg (12 lb) earlies or 9 kg (20 lb) main crop potatoes. Approximate time from sowing to harvesting is 12 weeks for earlies and 22 weeks for main crop.

✿ Varieties
Earlies

'Arran Pilot': an old favourite that crops well. It has a long shape, white skin and white flesh, with a slightly waxy texture.
'Epicure': a hardier, traditional variety with a good flavour. It has a rounded shape and white skin and flesh.
'Foremost': introduced in the 1950s, it has white skin, waxy yellow flesh and good flavour.
'Winston': a large, even potato, suitable for baking. It has excellent flavour and flaky flesh.

Second earlies

'Catriona': an attractive potato with deep pink patching, long tubers with yellowy skin and creamy flesh. Gives a good crop but doesn't store.
'Estima': oval potato with waxy yellow flesh; ideal for boiling.
'Kondor': red skin and waxy yellow flesh. It has good flavour and boils and bakes well.
'Nadine': round, smooth tubers and creamy white flesh with good flavour. A good cropper.

Main crop

'Cara': one of the late varieties, it has a round shape, pink skin and white, floury flesh. Stores well.
'King Edward': oval in shape, with creamy flesh and deep pinkish-red patches. It has excellent flavoured floury flesh, making it one of the best all-round potatoes.
'Pink Fir': long, thin, smallish knobbly potato with yellow waxy flesh; perfect for salads. Not so high yielding but worth growing for the flavour alone.
'Romano': oval shape with red skin and white, waxy flesh. Needs watering if conditions are dry. Stores well.

✆ Tips and techniques

First earlies need to be planted in early spring, and because there is still a chance of frost, a sheltered, sunny spot is preferable. Second earlies require planting 2 weeks later and main crop about the same time or later still; they both need a sunny site.

For the first earlies, dig a shallow trench about 10 cm (4 in) deep and sow shoots uppermost, spaced about 30 cm (12 in) apart. Alternatively, dig individual holes with a trowel. Leave about 45 cm (18 in) between rows. Cover with soil and draw up more soil to form a low ridge on top. If there is a danger of frosts as the first shoots begin to show, draw over a little more soil to protect them. When the shoots are about 23 cm (9 in) high, you need to earth-up (see page 11) by drawing the soil up the stems of the foliage. Continue doing this as the foliage grows and develops fully.

Follow the same procedures for second earlies and main crop, but plant them about 38 cm (15 in) apart. The rows for seconds need to be about 60 cm (24 in) apart, and for mains, about 75 cm (30 in) apart.

Water if the conditions are dry, especially for the earlies; this is important once the tubers develop.

🌢 Possible problems

Blight and scab are the biggest problems, especially if there has been lots of rain. Other pests include cyst eelworms, wireworms, blackleg and slugs (see page 21). Rotation is very important for potato growing – don't plant in the same place the next year (see page 10). Always make sure you dig up all the potatoes from the patch, especially if you have had problems with disease.

⚬ Harvesting and storing

Potatoes are not hardy and should be lifted before the first frosts.

Harvest early potatoes just as their flowers begin to open – about 12 weeks after planting. These varieties don't store very well, so it is better to use them up while they are fresh and in season. Having said this, you might like to try a trick of my grandfather's. He used to put a selection of his newly dug early potatoes in an old biscuit tin, still in their soil, and bury them in the garden. The tin lay undisturbed until Christmas, when my mum and the rest of the family would enjoy the flavour of freshly dug new potatoes with their Christmas dinner! For earlies, dig a fork in well below the tubers and lever them out, pulling on the foliage at the same time.

Main crop potatoes are ready for harvesting in the autumn. Remove the foliage about 2 weeks before

digging in order to help the skins firm up. Choose a dry, warmish day for harvesting and leave the potatoes to air-dry for a couple of hours. Discard any that are damaged or diseased, then pack in thick brown paper potato sacks or hessian bags and tie the top closed. Keep in a cool (frost-free) dark, dry place for up to 3 months. These bags allow air to circulate but prevent light getting in – exposure to light will cause the potatoes to turn green. Check frequently for rot or mould.

🍴 Preparation and cooking

In general, wash and scrub using a small brush and remove any 'eyes' or blemishes. Cook small potatoes in their skins. Otherwise, thinly peel using a vegetable peeler or a small, sharp knife, and cut according to cooking method. Remember that the greatest amount of nutrients lie just under the skin, so cut away as little as possible. Most potatoes discolour if peeled and exposed to the air, so try and prepare them just before cooking. If you do want to prepare them in advance, cover them with cold water to keep the air out, but they will lose some vitamin C.

✱ **Freezing:** cook the potatoes in the form of boiled, whole new potatoes, mash, roast or baked in their jackets. Cool, pack and freeze for up to 6 months. Thaw before reheating. Raw potato can be frozen in the form of chips: blanch uncooked chips in boiling water for 1 minute, drain and cool quickly. Open-freeze until solid and then pack into freezer bags. Seal, label and store for up to 6 months. To use, defrost, pat dry and cook in hot oil.

> ### 🕐 Short recipe: serves 4
> #### My favourite mash
>
> Thinly peel 900 g (2 lb) main crop potatoes such as King Edward. Cut into medium-sized pieces and put in a saucepan. Cover with water, add a good pinch of salt and bring to the boil. Cook for 12–18 minutes until tender. Drain well through a colander and air-dry for 10 minutes before returning to the saucepan and mashing well.
> Meanwhile, heat 4 Tbsp of olive oil in a small frying pan and gently fry 3–4 finely chopped garlic cloves for 2–3 minutes until softened but not browned. Set aside. Stir the oil and garlic into the mash along with 6 Tbsp of freshly chopped parsley. Add salt and pepper to taste and serve with roasted or grilled salmon.

Radish
Raphanus sativus

👁 At-a-glance

Plant: early spring onwards for summer radishes/midsummer for winter radishes.

Ideal growing conditions: open sunny site for summer radish, some shade for winter; plenty of water.

Harvest: late spring onwards for summer radishes/autumn for winter radishes.

One of the prettiest, daintiest roots you can grow, and they're very tasty too! Radishes were grown by the ancient Egyptians and were probably introduced to the UK by the Romans. Radishes remind me of a typical British vegetable patch, just like the one frequented by Peter Rabbit! Varieties can be deep pink/red, white, even black skinned. They can be small and round, elongated, or the size and shape of a huge parsnip. What they all have in common is crisp, white flesh with a mild to strong mustardy flavour. Summer radishes are among the quickest growing of vegetables. Winter radishes, which include the Oriental *mooli*, or Japanese radish, have leaves that can be eaten like cabbage.

✍ Crop planner

Choose a sunny site for your summer radishes and some shelter for winter varieties – you can always sow these radishes between other vegetables to provide some shade. The soil should be treated about 2 weeks before planting with a general-purpose fertilizer. Radishes like plenty of water.

A 3 m (10 ft) row of radishes will provide approximately 1.8 kg (4 lb) summer radishes and 4.5 kg (10 lb) winter radishes. Approximate time from sowing to harvesting is 4–6 weeks for summer varieties and 10–12 weeks for winter radishes.

✿ Varieties
Summer

'Cherry Belle': a popular globe-shaped radish with a cherry-red-coloured skin. It can stay in the ground a while before the flesh texture deteriorates.

'French Breakfast': elongated, cylindrical red/white radish. It has a mild flavour if harvested quickly; the longer it is left in the soil the more hot and woody it becomes.

'Minowase Summer': this is a *mooli*/Japanese radish type that yields a root about 30 cm (12 in) long. Good for stir-fries as well as salads.

Winter

'China Rose': deep pink-red skin, with elongated, chunky roots and crisp flesh.

'Black Spanish Round/Black Spanish Long': globe or tapered varieties with black skin and white flesh.

❂ Tips and techniques

Make a drill about 1 cm (½ in) deep and sow the fine seeds as thinly as possible so that little thinning is required. Sift a very thin covering of compost over the top and water well. Leave about 15 cm (6 in) between rows. Summer radishes do not like staying in the soil once they are mature – their texture declines rapidly – so it is probably better to sow successively in 2-week intervals rather than planting several rows at the same time. When the radishes' shoots are big enough to handle, thin to about 2.5–10 cm (1–4 in) apart, depending on the expected size. Discard the thinnings. Winter radishes should be sown as above, in rows about 25 cm (10 in) apart. Thin to about 18 cm (7 in) apart.

Keep weed-free. Water radish crops throughout the summer to prevent them drying out. You may need to protect a radish crop with netting or bird scarers.

✦ Possible problems

Although classified as a root vegetable, radishes are related to cabbage and succumb to the same pests (see page 39).

⚬ Harvesting and storing

From 4–6 weeks after sowing, summer radishes will be ready for pulling. Pull as many as are needed when they are young and tender. In the autumn, winter radish roots are ready. They can be left in the ground until required, but if heavy frost and cold weather threaten, they are best lifted, cleaned and stored in boxes of sand in a cool, airy place over the winter.

🍴 Preparation and cooking

For globe radish, trim away the root end and top for salads, leaving a 2.5 cm (1 in) shoot of stalk if serving to be dipped or as a cheese board accompaniment. Wash and pat dry before serving. For cooking larger radish, scrub or even peel if the skin is blemished or particularly tough. Cook whole, or dice if very large, and cook in lightly salted boiling water for 7–10 minutes until tender. Drain well, season with black pepper and serve with butter. Black radishes can be quite pungent and are often salted before being used like celery in a salad. Large radishes can be cut into thin strips or coarsely grated and added to stir-fries.

✱ **Freezing:** not suitable.

Swede (or Yellow turnip)
Brassica napus (Napobrassica Group)

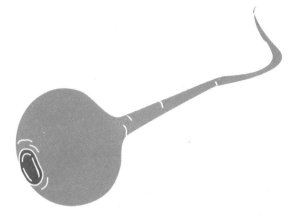

👁 At-a-glance

Plant: late spring/early summer.

Ideal growing conditions: open site; light non-acid soil with good drainage; soil manured the previous autumn.

Harvest: autumn onwards.

Swedes (or (yellow) turnips as they are known in Scotland) are a field crop and benefit from space and light. They are extremely hardy and provide a good vegetable source in the winter months. The light yellowy-golden flesh is sweetly earthy in flavour and firm in texture. Often considered to be a bit on the hearty side, swede flesh is actually quite light and it should certainly be considered for more than mashing or adding to a stew. Although it is generally the root part that is eaten, the botanical origin of the plant is the same as the cabbage. Look for varieties that are resistant to common *Brassica* diseases (see page 39).

✍ Crop planner

Choose an open site, with light soil that has been manured the previous autumn. Having said this, they will grow quite well on a heavier soil as long as it is well drained. The soil should be treated about a week before sowing with a general-purpose fertilizer, and should have a pH of about 6.5 (see page 9). Swedes are raised from seed and require quite a long growing period. They are also quite a big vegetable, so you might want to think about growing half-rows if you have limited space.

A 3 m (10 ft) row of swede will provide approximately 13.5 kg (30 lb) vegetable in ideal conditions. Approximate time from sowing to harvesting is about 22 weeks, depending on conditions.

✿ Varieties

'Best of All': has purple skin with yellow flesh, and is very hardy and dependable.
'Marian': a good all-rounder, giving good yield, flavour and texture. Also resistant to club root and mildew. More elongated in shape.
'Ruby': good resistance to mildew and has a sweet flavour.
'Western Perfection': quick-growing variety that will be ready for harvesting in September. Has purple-topped roots with yellow flesh of good flavour.

⚘ Tips and techniques

Make a drill about 1 cm (½ in) deep and sow the fine seeds as thinly as possible. Sift a very thin covering of compost over the top. Leave about 38 cm (15 in) between rows.

When the seedlings are large enough to handle, thin them out to about 23 cm (9 in) apart. Discard the thinnings. Keep weed-free by careful hoeing, and water to keep the soil moist during summer to prevent the roots becoming woody.

✶ Possible problems

Swedes can be prone to diseases of the cabbage family, such as flea beetles, mildew and club root (see page 39).

⚬ Harvesting and storing

Swede roots are completely hardy and can be lifted from autumn to winter as required, and some can be left in the ground for greens. For storing beyond this time, lift the roots and cut back the leaves to the top of the root. Keep in a cool, airy outbuilding.

▌ Preparation and cooking

Cut a thick slice off the top and bottom to reveal the yellowy flesh. Slice off the thick skin. Wash in cold water and cut into cubes or slices. Boil in lightly salted water for 15–20 minutes depending on size, until soft. Drain well and serve as is or mash with cream and butter. Can be served on its own or mixed into mashed potato.

Cut into thick fingers, swede can be added to the roasting tin and cooked alongside parsnips to accompany a roast. The sweet flavour is enhanced by adding a pinch of nutmeg or ginger.

❋ **Freezing:** swedes are not recommended for freezing as they go very watery and lose texture.

Turnip
Brassica rapa Rapifera Group

👁 At-a-glance

Plant: earlies – early spring; main crop – mid- to late summer.

Ideal growing conditions: sunny site; non-acid, rich fertile soil, manured the previous autumn.

Harvest: earlies – summer; main crop – autumn onwards

Turnips grow quickly and can be picked young. They may be grown between slower-to-mature roots and will be ready for picking long before crops such as parsnips or swedes. You should be able to plan crops for spring, summer and autumn, and you'll find white, yellow and pink varieties available, some flattish in shape, others long or globe-shaped, some for planting as 'earlies', and others as hardier 'main crop' turnips. Turnips have a mild peppery flavour; care should be taken not to overcook them, as the flesh can easily become soft and lose flavour.

✍ Crop planner
Choose an open site, with light soil that has been manured the previous autumn. Turnips will also grow well on a heavier soil as long as it is well drained and fertile. The soil should be treated about a week before sowing with a general-purpose fertilizer. Lime the soil if necessary (see page 9). Turnips are raised from seed.

A 3 m (10 ft) row of early varieties will provide approximately 3.15 kg (7 lb) vegetable, and 5.4 kg (12 lb) main crop turnips, in ideal conditions. Approximate time from sowing to harvesting is about 6–12 weeks, depending on variety. Main crop turnips can become woody if left in the ground too long, so it is worth considering planting half-rows at different times, so that you achieve a good-textured flesh.

✿ Varieties
Earlies
'Purple-top Milan': a pretty pinkish-purple-topped turnip that is flat and squat. A quick and easy to grow early variety.
'Snowball': a traditional globe-shaped turnip that grows quickly and is dependable. It has creamy white skin and pure white flesh.
Maincrop
'Manchester Market': a round, white-fleshed turnip with a green top. It has a mild flavour and keeps well.
'Market Express': a late variety that's very hardy. Best eaten young when the flesh is tender and sweet.

⊕ Tips and techniques
For earlies, make a drill about 1 cm (½ in) deep and sow the fine seeds as thinly as possible. Sift a very thin covering of compost over the top. Leave about 23 cm (9 in) between rows. Continue to sow at 2-week intervals throughout the summer for a continuous supply of small turnips. When the seedlings are large enough to handle, thin them out to about 13 cm (5 in) apart. Discard the thinnings. For later varieties, sow as above, but make the rows 30 cm (12 in) apart and thin seedlings to 20 cm (8 in) apart. Discard the thinnings.

Hoe to keep weed-free and keep the soil moist during summer to encourage the turnips to grow quickly and prevent the roots drying out.

💣 Possible problems
Turnips can be prone to diseases of the cabbage family such as flea beetles, violet root rot and club root (see page 39).

⚬ Harvesting and storing
Pick early turnips about 6 weeks after planting and do it frequently so that they are not allowed to get too big – they should be the size of a golf ball, and no larger than a tennis ball – otherwise the flavour will be impaired and the texture stringy. Simply pull from the ground when required. They are best used as soon as possible although summer turnips can be frozen (see below). Young turnip leaves can be picked and used as 'greens'. Winter turnip varieties can be pulled when needed, but if the ground looks like it will freeze, turnips should be dug up and stored in the same way as swedes (see page 31).

🍴 Preparing and cooking
Cut off the leafy top and root end. Peel young turnips thinly and main crop more thickly. Wash well. Young turnips can be left whole, while others are best cut up. Cook young turnips in lightly salted water for about 10–15 minutes, and turnip pieces for about the same time, depending on size. Drain well. Young turnips are lovely glazed with sugar and butter, or served with parsley sauce. Other turnips can be mashed and seasoned with lemon juice and a little nutmeg or mace.

✱ Freezing: choose small roots, and trim and prepare as above. Blanch for 2 minutes, drain, cool and pack into rigid containers or freezer bags. Store for up to 12 months and cook from frozen for 8–10 minutes. Large turnips can be cut into dice ready for adding to stews or for mashing. Blanch as for baby turnips, then freeze and cook in the same way.

Chapter 4
Bulb and stem vegetables

This is a short chapter that includes a few of the easier to grow vegetables within this category. I have omitted ones that require more green-fingered confidence and time-consuming gardening techniques, so if you can't find your favourite, these are the reasons why. However, the ones I have chosen are some of the most delicious, flavoursome and versatile veggies you can use in the kitchen. The plants are attractive to grow as well and some have fragrant, herblike foliage. So, not only will you end up with some tasty produce come harvest time, but you can admire it growing in your garden while you wait.

☠ Pests and diseases

Cabbage root fly: see page 39.

Carrot fly: see page 21.

Celery fly: causes blistering on celeriac leaves from May onwards. Pinch out and destroy affected leaves, and spray with suitable insecticide if you want to use one.

Club root: see page 39.

Crown rot: the bud and flesh around the rhubarb crown rots and any resulting stalks will be thin and malformed. Dig up the affected plant and destroy. Do not replant in the same area. Choose a reliable nursery for your stock.

Flea beetle: see page 39.

Honey fungus: the rhubarb crown decays to leave brown and white matter. Orange toadstools appear around the crown. Dig up the affected plant and destroy. Do not replant in the same area. Choose a reliable nursery for your stock.

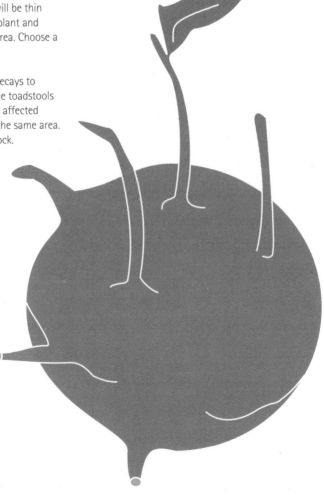

Celeriac
Apium graveolens var. rapaceum

Plant: sow in late winter to mid-spring; plant out in late spring to early summer.

Ideal growing conditions: open sunny site; rich organic, moist soil.

Harvest: autumn onwards.

Celeriac is a close relation to celery, but whereas with celery you eat the shoots, with celeriac you eat the huge, swollen stem base. Celeriac is hardier and less temperamental than celery, although it needs a long growing season; it is usually regarded as a tender winter root vegetable. It can be eaten raw or cooked and the flesh is very savoury like celery. It makes a delicious choice over the winter months when celery and other salad vegetables are scarce.

✍ Crop planner

Choose a sunny site and manure the previous autumn to planting. The soil should be moist and treated about a week before planting with a general-purpose fertilizer. Celeriac is grown from seed and then planted into the ground once the seedlings are robust enough.

A 3 m (10 ft) row will provide approximately 3.15 kg (7 lb) celeriac in ideal conditions. Approximate time from sowing to harvesting is 30–35 weeks, depending on variety.

✿ Varieties

'Balder': an easy-to-grow variety that yields medium-sized roots with a good celery flavour.
'Marble Ball': a well-known variety with a rich celery flavour; medium-sized roots.
'Monarch': smooth-skinned variety, easy to grow, with a good flavour.
'Snow White': large-rooted, with very white flesh, and a more 'nutty' flavour than other varieties.

☯ Tips and techniques

Celeriac seeds need to be germinated indoors. Almost fill a seed tray with moist seed compost and sow the seeds thinly over the surface. Lightly cover with more moist compost. Put in a warm place at about 15–20°C (60–70°F), keep moist and in the light, but not in direct sunlight. When the seedlings reach 5–7 cm (2–3 in) high, transplant them into trays of potting compost about 5 cm (2 in) apart. Gradually

accustom the plants to outside conditions for 2–3 weeks before planting outside in May or June.

Choose a sunny spot. Using a dibber, make holes sufficiently deep so that the base of the stem is level with the surface of the soil, about 25 cm (10 in) apart, and 45 cm (18 in) between rows. Keep weeded and well watered – celeriac does best in moist conditions.

Cut off any side shoots that appear, and from late summer remove the lower leaves to expose the top or 'crown' of the root. Pile earth around the crown to keep it white. If the weather turns very cold, cover with straw to protect from frost.

🜚 Possible problems

Usually untroubled by anything other than slugs, but carrot fly might be a nuisance (see page 21). Celery fly may also be attracted to celeriac leaves (see page 33).

☛ Harvesting and storing

Leave the roots as long as possible so that they reach their maximum size – unlike a lot of other vegetables, there is no advantage to lifting them early. Use the roots as required during late October and November. Once the weather becomes very cold and wintry, any remaining roots can be stored in damp sand in a cool shed or outbuilding. Cleaned celeriac root will keep in the fridge for about 2 weeks before it starts to dehydrate.

🍴 Preparation and cooking

Trim off the leaves – these can be used to flavour stocks and soups. Slice off the root end then scrub under cold running water. The knobbly skin requires quite thick peeling, and as the flesh is exposed, put it in a bowl of water with lemon juice to prevent discolouring and use as soon as possible. Cut into thin strips or grate coarsely for salads. To cook, cut into pieces and cook in boiling salted water for 10–15 minutes, depending on size, until tender. Drain and serve.

✱ **Freezing:** celeriac is suitable for freezing but it is then only suitable for eating cooked. Prepare the celeriac as above; it requires no blanching, so simply pack in rigid containers between layers of freezer sheets, for up to 12 months. Cook from frozen for 8–10 minutes or add pieces directly to stews or soups.

Florence fennel
Foeniculum vulgare var. dulce

Florence fennel is also known as sweet fennel or *finocchio*, and as its name suggests, it originates from Italy. It has a delicate, sweet aniseed flavour and is delicious eaten raw as a salad vegetable or lightly cooked to serve with fish, chicken and other delicate flavours. It has a reputation as being quite difficult to grow, so you do need to make some ground preparations and ensure that you water consistently, also choosing a bolt-resistant variety will help your chances of success. It does take up quite a bit of space because it has masses of fine, feathery, frondlike leaves that can be used as a herb. The bases of the leaves overlap just above ground and form a white, flattish, upright bulb that is the vegetable we all recognize. Fennel is usually planted from seed straight into the ground, but you may find seedlings available from a nursery or garden centre.

✍ Crop planner

Ideally, fennel thrives in a warm, even temperature, however, mature plants can withstand a little frost. Choose an open, sunny site, which is sheltered from the wind. Fennel needs a light soil with good drainage and lots of nutrients, so manure the plot well. It should not be allowed to dry out, and inconsistencies with watering may encourage the plant to bolt if it is a non-resistant variety (see page 11).

A 3 m (10 ft) row will yield approximately 10–12 fennel bulbs in ideal conditions. Approximate time from sowing to harvesting is 10–15 weeks, depending on conditions.

✿ Varieties

'Carmo F1': well flavoured and quick to grow.
'Zefo Fino': this pretty-looking plant has fleshy, medium-sized bulbs and is bolt resistant.

ℚ Tips and techniques

Wait until the weather warms up before you sow fennel seeds. Early to midsummer is the best time. Make a drill about 1 cm (½ in) deep and sow the seeds as thinly as possible. Sift a very thin covering of compost over the top. Leave about 45 cm (18 in) between rows. When the seedlings are large enough to handle, thin them out to about 30 cm (12 in) apart. Discard the thinnings. Keep well watered, especially during dry weather. Hoe to keep the weeds down.

As the bulbs swell, draw soil up around them to at least half their height. Keep drawing up the soil like this as the bulbs grow in order to keep them white and make them sweet tasting.

◗ Possible problems

Fennel is not prone to pests or diseases. Its biggest battle is with the weather!

⚬ Harvesting and storing

Fennel is ready when the size of the bulb is about the same as a tennis ball. If you cut the stumpy base at the root rather than pulling the whole vegetable out of the ground, it will sprout again and provide you with more feathery foliage. Trim away the leaves for use as a garnish or they can be chopped up and added to salads – the leaves will keep for 2–3 days in a jug of water in the fridge. A fennel bulb is best used as fresh from the garden as possible for maximum crispness and flavour, but it will keep in the fridge for 4–5 days.

ⱷ Preparation and cooking

Trim the root base and wash well in cold water. For eating raw, cut in half lengthways and then cut into thin slices. For cooking, cut in half or quarters and cook in a small amount of lightly salted water for 15–20 minutes, depending on size, until tender. Drain well.

✱ **Freezing:** prepare the fennel as for cooking and cut into 2.5 cm (1 in) thick pieces. Blanch for 3 minutes, drain, reserving the liquid, and cool. Pack into rigid containers and cover with the blanching liquid, leaving a 1 cm (½ in) gap at the top of the container. Keep for up to 6 months. Thaw before cooking and either add pieces to stews or soups or cook in boiling water for about 10 minutes.

Kohl rabi

Brassica oleracea Gongylodes Group

Often regarded as a root vegetable, kohl rabi is in fact the swollen stem of a cabbage. Kohl rabi sits just on the ground, and has a taproot that goes beneath the soil. You'll find purple-red-skinned varieties and pale, bright green ones. Kohl rabi is more popular in Germany and Austria than it is in France and Britain, yet its fresh, mild turnip-like taste and firm texture offers another flavour when grated in a salad, or it can be cooked and used as a vegetable. Unlike swede and turnip leaves, kohl rabi leaves are not eaten. It is usually sown from seed and is quite easy to grow and generally problem-free.

✍ Crop planner

Choose a sunny site with good drainage, which has been manured the previous autumn. The soil should be treated about 2 weeks before planting with a general-purpose fertilizer. Kohl rabies prefer a non-acid soil.

A 3 m (10 ft) row of kohl rabies will provide about 4.5 kg (10 lb) vegetable, sufficient for an average family if other root vegetables are grown. Approximate time from sowing to harvesting is 8–12 weeks, depending on variety.

✿ Varieties

'Purple Danube': a stunning deep purple-pink variety with sweet-tasting flesh.
'Purple Vienna': purple-skinned globes with white flesh. Good choice for late sowing and a winter harvest.
'White Danube': pale green skin with juicy white flesh.
'White Vienna': a traditional pale green-skinned variety.

⚘ Tips and techniques

Kohl rabi seed can be planted outside when a minimum germination temperature of the soil reaches about 10ºC (50ºF). Choose a sunny spot and make a drill about 1 cm (½ in) deep and sow the fine seeds as thinly as possible. Sift a very thin covering of compost over the top. Leave about 30 cm (12 in) between rows. Subsequent sowings can be made every 2–3 weeks for successive crops until autumn.

Thin the seedlings when the first true leaves appear, to about 18 cm (7 in) apart. Discard the thinnings. Keep weed-free but take extra care not to damage the globes if using a hoe. Water if the conditions are dry as they may split if the soil dries out too much.

🪶 Possible problems

The main pests are the same as for cabbages. You may want to consider using protective discs if cabbage root fly is a known problem (see page 39).

⚬ Harvesting and storing

The stems are best harvested when they are about the size of a tennis ball. If they get too large they will become woody in texture. Late crops will survive in the ground until early winter. Pull the plants from the soil by the bulbous stem as required. Eat shortly after harvesting, but if left whole they will keep in the fridge for about 10 days. In colder climes, the last kohl rabies can be pulled, cleaned and stored in trays of dampish sand for a few weeks – after this they will begin to shrivel.

🍴 Preparation and cooking

To prepare, cut off the leafy tops and trim away the taproot. Scrub thoroughly in running water. For eating raw, peel and grate coarsely for adding to salads, or peel and cut into fingers or small chunks ready for cooking. Cook in a small amount of lightly salted water for about 10 minutes. Drain well and serve as an accompanying vegetable with butter and black pepper, or mash and mix with sour cream and a pinch of nutmeg.

✱ Freezing: kohl rabi can be prepared and cut into dice ready for adding to stews or for mashing. Blanch for 2 minutes, drain, cool and pack into rigid containers or freezer bags. Store for up to 12 months and cook from frozen for 5–10 minutes.

Rhubarb
Rheum x cultorum

👁 At-a-glance

Plant: Spring.

Ideal growing conditions: sunny, non-shady position; free-draining, rich, soil, well manured the previous autumn.

Harvest: summer of the second year onwards.

This vegetable has come to be regarded as a fruit because we serve it mostly for pudding. It grows best in an open site but will grow anywhere, although it likes a good mulching, and remember that the roots of an established plant run deep. It is easy to cultivate and a single plant will provide a good yield for a small family. The rhubarb stalks are the only edible part of the plant – the leaves are full of oxalic acid and are very poisonous if eaten. Once a rhubarb plant is established – after three years – it can be forced for early cropping. This rhubarb will have thinner, softer and pinker stalks than those stalks left to mature unforced, and is ready for picking from spring to early summer. Rhubarb can be grown from seed but this is a lengthy process. More usually, you buy a 'crown' or small plant from a nursery or garden centre ready for planting in spring.

✍ Crop planner

Rhubarb is a sun-loving plant and doesn't like shade. It needs lots of rich, fertile soil to grow, and manure should be dug down deep into the soil below your chosen plot, because rhubarb is long rooted. Do this the previous autumn and then just before planting, sprinkle in some fertilizer for extra nutrition.

A rhubarb plant will be productive for between 5 and 10 years, and will yield about 2.25 kg (5 lb) rhubarb each year. Approximate time between planting and pulling is about 15 months.

✿ Varieties

'Champagne Early': also called 'Red Champagne', this traditional reliable rhubarb has deep red stems and is ready early in the season.
'Timperley Early': this thin-stemmed variety is ideal for forcing; ready in early spring.
'Victoria': a popular variety that is ready for pulling in late spring.

۹ Tips and techniques

Rhubarb plants can be planted outside in spring or early summer if they are kept well watered. Dig a hole the size of the root ball and plant so that the bud of the crown is just below the surface. Firm the soil around the plant after filling the hole. Rhubarb plants should be spaced about 90 cm (3 ft) away from each other. Water well in dry weather and remove any flowering shoots that appear. Apply a mulch of well-rotted manure around the plant in autumn and again in spring.

Allow new plants to become established for 12–18 months after planting before pulling.

If you want to 'force' rhubarb for early, fine stems, cover the crown with a large upturned bucket or special terracotta rhubarb forcer in midwinter. The stalks will be ready in about 6 weeks. Do not force the same plant for at least 2 years, otherwise the plant will weaken.

☛ Possible problems

Rhubarb is a relatively trouble-free vegetable. Crown rot and honey fungus are possible threats, but are not very common (see page 33).

↤ Harvesting and storing

Don't pick any stalks in the first year. In the second year, pull a few, leaving about half on the plant, and stop around midsummer to allow the plant to recover. In the following years, pull fully grown stalks as needed. To pull, place your thumb inside the stalk as far down as you can, and twist to pull it away from the crown. Do not cut the stalks. Cut off and discard the leaves. Rhubarb is best used straight from the garden, although you should be able to keep the stalks for 1–2 days in the fridge before they being to wilt.

🍴 Preparation and cooking

Rhubarb is very acidic and requires a lot of sweetening to make it palatable. But its clean taste makes it an excellent choice for dessert to follow a rich, creamy main course. Prepare young rhubarb stalks by trimming off the leafy tops and the pale root end. Wash and dry thoroughly. Older rhubarb can develop a coarse stringy skin that should be peeled away if very tough. Trim and wash as before. Cut rhubarb into chosen length for cooking and either poach in a sugar-based syrup for 7–8 minutes until tender or bake small pieces of raw or stewed rhubarb in a pie, crumble or tart. Rhubarb combines well with redcurrants and raspberries, and makes good jams and preserves.

* **Freezing:** choose tender young stalks and prepare as described on page 37. Cut into 2.5 cm (1 in) lengths and pack in rigid containers or freezer bags; blanching is unnecessary. Keep for up to 6 months. Use for stewed fruit and pies. Alternatively pack as above but sprinkle with sugar in between each layer for using as a ready-sweetened, ready-to-cook compôte once thawed. You will need to put the contents in a saucepan and cook gently for 7–8 minutes until very soft and tender. Rhubarb can also be stewed and/or puréed and then frozen.

🕐 Short recipe: serves 4
Sweet and sour rhubarb sauce

Prepare 4 thin stalks of young rhubarb as described above and cut into 2.5 cm (1 in) lengths. Put the rhubarb in a saucepan with 50 g (2 oz) caster sugar and 2 Tbsp of freshly squeezed orange juice. Heat gently until steaming, then cover and cook for 7–8 minutes until tender and soft. Stir in 1–2 Tbsp of raspberry vinegar and salt to taste; add a pinch of finely grated orange zest and set aside to cool, then cover and chill until ready to serve. Ideal served with oily fish or duck

Chapter 5
Leaf vegetables

I love greens! In fact, I feel very disappointed if I get given a meal with no green vegetables on my plate. It's not because I'm ultra-healthy either, I simply love the look, colour, taste and texture of green leafy vegetables. When it comes to growing greens, some varieties are much easier than others. In general, you do need to make sure your soil is fertile and non-acid, and once planted, leaves do need to be watered regularly.

There are several different leaves to consider for your plot, some take up more space than others and sit in the ground for a long time, so you'll have to do some careful planning. Another point to consider is that most leaf vegetables are started from seed, some sown straight in the ground, others are transplanted from a seed bed or seed container. In spring you will start seeing seedlings of some leaf vegetables in nurseries and garden centres, so this is a good alternative if you don't have the time, space or inclination to raise your own plants from seed.

Just about anyone can grow Swiss chard and tasty salad leaves like rocket and corn salad; they're not fussy about soil, they don't take up too much space or occupy the ground for too long a period if you don't want them to. They are good plants to start with, and from there you can decide which other leaves you might like to try growing.

☠ Pests and diseases
Bird damage: birds are attracted to the seedlings and soft leaves, particularly when other food sources are scarce. Pigeons are especially troublesome. Erect netting over the seedlings or try using bird scarers.
Cabbage root fly: this disease causes the leaves to wilt and develop a blue tinge. Most vulnerable are newly planted seedlings. Insecticides are available if you want to use them, otherwise preventative discs can be applied to the base of the stems of seedlings before transplanting. Fine netting can be erected over young plants to stop the flies laying their eggs.
Caterpillars: holes in leaves appear from April to October, particularly if it's hot. Sprays are available if you want to use them. Inspect the top and underside of the leaves for eggs and remove and crush any eggs that have been laid.

Club root: this is the most serious disease that can affect leafy vegetables. It causes the roots to swell. Any affected plants should be burned or destroyed and cabbages should not be planted in the same spot for several years. Improve the drainage of your soil and lime the soil if necessary to help minimize the risk of this disease. Choose to grow resistant varieties.
Downy mildew: this causes a yellowing of the upper surface of the leaf and the growth of a white fuzzy fungus underneath. Fungicides are available if you want to use them. Avoid planting seedlings in affected areas and sow seeds in sterilized compost.
Flea beetle: the most common problem – you will see holes on the leaves. Insecticides are available if you want to use them.
Greenfly: attacks are worse in a dry spring; they carry viruses and can often make plants unusable because they cover it in thick, sticky dew. While they can't be prevented, you can spray with an appropriate insecticide at the first sign of an attack or use a more natural method (see page 12).
Root aphid: attacks the roots and covers them with white, powdery damage, particularly in dry weather. Destroy damaged and decaying plants. Keep plants watered to minimize the risk, and look out for resistant varieties.
Slugs and snails: attack any fleshy leaf and root in wet, damp weather, usually at night time. Look for the telltale slimy trails. Slug pellets can be scattered around seedlings or other slug traps are available.
Spinach blight: young leaves are often attacked; the leaves narrow and pucker and turn yellow. There is no cure, so destroy affected plants. The virus is carried by greenfly so spray with insecticide or take other precautions as necessary.

Broccoli and Calabrese
Brassica oleracea Cymosa Group and B. oleracea Italica Group

👁 At-a-glance

Plant: mid-spring–early summer (depending on variety).

Ideal growing conditions: sunny site; firm, fertile non-acid soil, manured the previous autumn.

Harvest: late winter–mid-spring (broccoli); late autumn–early winter (calabrese).

The origins of this well-known, flavoursome vegetable date back to 17th-century Italy, where it was developed from a wild cabbage. Its name comes from the Italian *broccolo*, which means 'cabbage sprout'. The name 'broccoli' is also applied to sprouting broccoli and purple sprouting broccoli. Sprouting broccoli grows through the winter months and can be harvested in late winter to early spring. It consists of clusters of small spears that are cut with a length of stem attached. As the spears are cut, more develop over a period of 4 to 6 weeks. Perennial broccoli comes up each year for harvesting in the spring. It grows to be a much larger plant than other varieties and needs supporting; it has white heads similar to cauliflowers. Calabrese is a less hardy plant that has one big, compact head of white, green or purple firm curds; it is a summer crop.

✍ Crop planner

Choose an open site, preferably with some shelter from strong winds, with soil that has been manured the previous autumn. The soil should be treated about 2 weeks before sowing with a general-purpose fertilizer, and should have a pH of about 6.5 (see page 9). Broccoli and calabrese are usually raised from seed but you may prefer to buy seedlings from a nursery or garden centre.

A 3 m (10 ft) row will provide approximately 3.4 kg (7½ lb) vegetable, in ideal conditions. Approximate time from sowing to harvesting is about 12 weeks for calabrese and up to 44 weeks for other varieties.

✿ Varieties

'Claret': a purple sprouting variety that grows tall. It yields well and is ready for harvesting from March.
'Corvet': this summer variety of calabrese produces a large green head first, then subsequent smaller spears.
'Early Purple Sprouting': a traditional hardy variety that is ready for harvesting from the end of February.
'Late Purple Sprouting': this is a sturdy variety that grows throughout winter and is ready for picking in April. It grows to about 90 cm (3 ft) tall.
'Nine Star Perennial': a perennial variety that grows tall and produces small, pale green heads that look like tiny cauliflowers.
'Romanesco': an attractive variety of calabrese with lime green pointed spears, ready in November. It has a delicious flavour and a soft texture, so it is best steamed.

ℚ Tips and techniques

For broccoli varieties, rather than forking and loosening the soil before planting, tread it down gently and rake lightly. Make a drill about 1 cm (½ in) deep in an outdoor seedbed in late March, when the soil is workable and warm enough to permit germination, and sow the seeds thinly. As they grow you may need to thin out the seedlings to keep them about 5 cm (2 in) apart. Discard the thinnings. When the plants are 13 cm (5 in) tall, they are ready for transplantation. Water the bed the day before so that the soil softens if it is dry. Carefully remove the seedlings from the bed. Using a dibber, make sufficiently deep holes for each seedling, 60 cm (24 in) apart. Put the seedlings into the holes, fill them with soil as necessary, then firm them carefully with your heel and water them in. Leave 1 m (3½ ft) between rows.

Calabrese seeds are best sown *in situ* as they are less successfully transplanted. Make a drill about 1 cm (½ in) deep and sow three seeds every 30 cm (12 in). Sift a very thin covering of compost over the top. Leave about 90 cm (3 ft) between rows. When the seedlings are large enough to handle, thin to leave one in each station. Discard the thinnings.

Keep broccoli and calabrese weed-free with careful hoeing, and if birds are a problem, erect some netting or put in bird scarers. Water in dry weather and apply a mulch if preferred. As winter approaches, earth-up the soil to protect the stems, and keep the soil firm if the plants become loosened by the wind.

✿ Possible Problems

Both vegetables can be quite prone to problems, and are susceptible to any of the pests and diseases listed on page 39.

⊶ Harvesting and storing

Cut the heads of calabrese with about 2.5 cm (1 in) of stalk in late summer/autumn when the flower buds are green and tightly closed. Once the main head is cut, side shoots may grow and more heads will form on some varieties. 'Romanesco', however, is a single-headed variety, so once this is cut the remaining plant should be discarded.

Sprouting broccoli should be cut with 10–15 cm (4–6 in) of stem, and cooked as whole stems. The remaining plant should be cut back to just above a pair of side shoots in order to encourage fresh spears to grow. Freshly picked spears can be kept in a jug of water in the fridge for 2–3 days.

⫲ Preparing and cooking

Wash the spears carefully in cold water, strip off any leaves and trim away or peel any coarseness on the stems. Cook in boiling salted water for 8–10 minutes, depending on thickness, or steam for 15–20 minutes.

✳ Freezing: prepare as above then blanch for 1–2 minutes, depending on thickness. Drain and cool, then open-freeze on trays before packing into freezer bags or rigid containers. Keep for up to 12 months. Cook from frozen in boiling water for 5–8 minutes.

🕐 Short recipe: serves 4
Broccoli alla romana

Peel and finely chop 2 cloves of garlic. Heat 4 Tbsp of fruity olive oil in a deep frying pan and gently fry the garlic for 1–2 minutes until softened but not browned. Add 450 g (1 lb) prepared broccoli or calabrese spears and stir for 2–3 minutes until well coated in the hot oil. Pour over 150 ml (¼ pt) Italian dry white wine and season well. Bring to the boil, cover and gently simmer for about 15–20 minutes until tender and just cooked through. Drain, if preferred (use the stock to make a simple white sauce), or serve in the cooking juices to accompany fish or chicken, or toss into freshly cooked pasta.

Brussels sprouts
Brassica oleracea Gemmifera Group

👁 At-a-glance

Plant: early–mid-spring.

Ideal growing conditions: open, sheltered site; non-acid soil manured the previous autumn.

Harvest: mid-autumn–spring.

Brussels sprouts are believed to be a descendant of the wild cabbage and first grown in Belgium. Its distinctive flavour (and cooking smell) will no doubt bring back horrible memories for some of you, of overcooked, khaki-coloured sprouts that used to be piled on to your plate at school. Love them or loathe them, Brussels sprouts are one of the most commonly grown of all green vegetables, and are one of our Christmas Day dinner 'must-have' vegetables. I once heard a mother saying that she managed to get her children to eat sprouts by telling them they were fairies' cabbages – a lovely notion! Brussels sprouts plants are very hardy and will crop during autumn and winter if both early and late varieties are planted.

✍ Crop planner
Choose an open, sheltered spot with soil that has been manured the previous autumn. The soil should be treated about 2 weeks before sowing with a general-purpose fertilizer, and should have a pH of 6.5–7 (see page 9). Brussels sprouts are usually raised from seed but you may prefer to buy seedlings from a nursery or garden centre.

A 3 m (10 ft) row will provide approximately 3.6 kg (8 lb) vegetable, in ideal conditions. Approximate time from sowing to harvesting is about 28 weeks for early varieties and about 36 weeks for later varieties.

✿ Varieties
Early to mid-season
'Oliver': an early that is ready for picking as early as September. This high-yielding plant is quite short and produces big sprouts with plenty of flavour.
'Peer Gynt': a favourite, reliable early variety that produces button sprouts from September to December.
'Roger': tallish plants that produce sprouts in early to midwinter. The sprouts are smooth skinned and pale with a good flavour.
Late
'Fortress': a hardy variety that yields dark green, well-flavoured button sprouts from January to March.
'Noisette': as the name suggests, a French variety with a nutty flavour. Sprouts are ready for picking from October to February.
'Sheriff': this plant yields a large amount of sweet-tasting sprouts from January to March; it has good resistance to powdery mildew.

⬤ Tips and techniques
For early varieties, rather than forking and loosening the soil before planting, tread it down gently and rake lightly. Make a drill about 1 cm (½ in) deep in an outdoor seedbed in mid-March, when the soil is workable and warm enough to permit germination. Sow the Brussels sprouts seeds thinly. As they grow, you may need to thin out the seedlings to keep them about 7 cm (3 in) apart. Discard the thinnings. When the plants are 15 cm (5 in) tall, they are ready for transplantation. Water the bed the day before so that the soil softens if it is dry. Carefully remove the seedlings from the bed. Using a dibber, make sufficiently deep holes for each seedling, so that their lowest leaves are just above the soil. Plant at a distance of 75 cm (30 in) apart. Put the seedlings into the holes, fill them with soil as necessary, then firm them carefully with your heel and water them in. Leave 75 cm (30 in) between rows. For later varieties, follow the instructions above, but sow the seeds a few weeks later.

Keep weed-free with careful hoeing, and if birds are a problem, erect some netting or put in bird scarers. Water young plants in dry weather – mature plants will only need watering in exceptionally dry conditions. As winter approaches earth-up the soil to protect the stems, and keep the soil firm if they become loosened by the wind – you may need to stake the plants if it is very windy. Remove the bottom leaves as they turn yellow.

♠ Possible problems

Brussels sprouts are prone to any disease that affects the cabbage family, particularly club root (see page 39).

⚬ Harvesting and storing

Pick sprouts when they are small and no bigger than the size of a walnut. The leaves should be tight and firm. The sprouts will then be crisp and sweet. Older, 'cabbagey' sprouts will have little flavour. It is widely believed that the first frost heralds the best time to pick Brussels sprouts as it's said to improve their flavour. Pick sprouts as required from lower down the stem first by simply twisting them from the stem. Once all the sprouts have been picked, the top leaves can be cooked as 'greens'. Harvested sprouts are best used as fresh as possible but they can be stored unwrapped in the fridge for 2–3 days.

⫼ Preparation and cooking

Ideally pick the sprouts just before cooking, trim away any loose outer leaves and slice the base of the stalk away from each sprout. Cut an 'X' in the base of each sprout and rinse them in cold water. Cook in a small amount of lightly salted boiling water for 8–10 minutes until just cooked – they should be slightly chewy or 'al dente'. Drain well and serve.

✱ **Freezing:** trim as above, but there is no need to cut an 'X' in the bottom. Blanch for 1–3 minutes depending on size. Drain well and cool. Open-freeze on trays before packing into freezer bags or rigid containers. Keep for up to 12 months. Cook from frozen for 5–8 minutes.

🕐 Short recipe: serves 4
My favourite stir-fried sprouts

Prepare 450 g (1 lb) sprouts, then shred finely. Trim and shred a medium-sized leek and mix with the sprouts. In a large frying pan or wok, stir-fry 6 chopped rashers smoked streaky bacon for 3–4 minutes until the juices run. Add 2 Tbsp of sunflower oil, and when hot, add the sprouts and leeks. Stir-fry for 4–5 minutes until starting to cook down, then add 2 Tbsp of Worcestershire sauce. Stir-fry for a further 2 minutes or until cooked to your liking. Delicious served with a roast.

Cabbage
Brassica oleracea Capitata Group

Plant: early–mid-spring–late summer (depending on variety).

Ideal growing conditions: an open, sunny site; non-acid soil manured the previous autumn.

Harvest: all year round (depending on variety).

The humble cabbage has long been underrated, but with so many varieties, colours and textures, it really deserves more praise than it gets. Its reputation for being 'tasteless' or 'slimy' comes from the fact that it's easily overcooked and spoilt. However, they make magnificent features in the garden, are very hardy and easy to grow, and if cooked correctly, cabbage is delicious too. If you do like cabbage then it's worth planting a few varieties so you can have a succession of different types of cabbage all year long, in a range of sizes, textures and colours from white, to pale yellow-green to dark green to purplish red.

✍ Crop planner

Choose an open, sunny spot with soil that has been manured the previous autumn. The soil should be treated about 2 weeks before sowing with a general-purpose fertilizer, and should have a pH of 6.5–7 (see page 9). You can choose to sow your own cabbage seed or buy seedlings from the nursery or garden centre.

A 3 m (10 ft) row will provide approximately 6–10 cabbages, in ideal conditions, depending on the variety. Approximate time from sowing to harvesting is 4–10 weeks for Chinese, about 35 weeks for spring varieties and 20–35 weeks for summer, winter, savoy and red varieties.

✿ Varieties
Spring

'Durham Early': conical-shaped green heart with loose dark green outer leaves.
'Offenham 1 Myatt's Offenham Compacta': a large cabbage with dark green leaves and a big heart. Sow in August ready for a May harvest the following year.
'Pixie': a small compact cabbage that's ideal if you're short on space because you can grow them closer together.

Summer

'Derby Day': so named because it's ready for cutting on Derby Day in June. It's a round cabbage with bright green leaves.

'Greyhound': a popular compact cabbage with a conical heart; can be sown early and matures quickly.
'Hispi': similar to 'Greyhound' but it is ready earlier, and has dark green, smooth leaves.

Winter and savoy

'Alaska': a dark green, dimpled, small savoy cabbage; ready mid- to late season.
'Best of All': a large savoy with a big heart that is ready in September.
'Celtic': large and leafy traditional favourite with blue-green veiny leaves (it is a hybrid of a winter and savoy); it is very hardy.
'Christmas Drumhead': in spite of its name, this small blue-green cabbage is ready in October.

Red

'Red Drumhead': a compact, much-loved cabbage with dark red leaves. A good choice for small plots.
'Ruby Ball': has a firm centre with a uniform head and few outer leaves. It should be ready in late summer.

Chinese

'Jade Pagoda': longer-headed, cylindrical, looser-leaved cabbage with yellowy-green frilly leaves.
Pak choi or bok choi: small, compact bunches of leaves with a thick yet soft, white stalk. Excellent for braising and stir-fries. Quick growing and ready to harvest in about 3–4 weeks. Try 'Green Revolution F1', which can be used young as a salad leaf or mature into a firmer head.

✿ Tips and techniques

The method for growing most types of cabbage is very similar (see below for spring and Chinese varieties), but the timing varies according to variety. Rather than forking and loosening the soil before planting, tread it down gently and rake lightly. Make a drill about 1 cm (½ in) deep in an outdoor seedbed at the required time, and sow the cabbage seeds thinly. As they grow, you may need to thin out the seedlings to keep them about 7 cm (3 in) apart. Discard the thinnings. When the plants are 15 cm (6 in) tall, they are ready for transplantation. Water the bed so that the soil softens. Carefully remove the seedlings from the bed. Using a dibber, make sufficiently deep holes for each seedling. Plant each at a distance of 30 cm (12 in) for compact and 75 cm (30 in) apart for larger varieties. Put the seedlings into the holes, fill them with soil as necessary, then firm them carefully with your heel and water them in. Leave the same distances between rows.

For spring and Chinese cabbage varieties, sow them *in situ* and thin out to 10 cm (4 in) apart. In spring, thin the seedlings out again to about 30 cm (12 in) apart – you can use the established seedlings as spring greens. Keep them watered well and tie up the leaves with raffia or light string in summer if they start to loosen.

Keep the cabbage patch weed-free with careful hoeing, and if birds are a problem, erect some netting or put in bird scarers. Water young plants in dry weather and keep watering until the plants are established. As winter approaches, earth-up the soil to protect the stems of overwintering varieties, and keep the soil firm if they become loosened by the wind – you may need to stake the plants if it is very breezy. Remove the bottom leaves as they turn yellow.

⚫ Possible problems
Club root is the most serious cabbage disease but also cabbage root fly, caterpillars, flea beetles, slugs and snails all love cabbages. See page 39 for more information.

⚬ Harvesting and storing
Cut cabbages when the hearts are firm. Use a knife to cut through the stem, just below the head and inside the loose leaves. In most cases, cabbages are cut for immediate use. Red and white winter cabbages and those with solid heads can be stored for winter use as they may not be as hardy as other types. Cut off the root and stem, remove any outer leaves and then place in a straw-lined box. If stored in a cool, dry place they should keep for several weeks. Chinese cabbages do not keep and should be picked as required.

⚭ Preparation and cooking
In general, remove the coarse outer leaves from a cabbage, then cut into quarters and slice out the hard central core and base stump. Wash thoroughly and drain, shaking to remove excess water. Cut into wedges or shred. Cook in the minimum amount of salted boiling water – use just enough to stop the cabbage sticking to the pan. Cook for 5–6 minutes if in shreds, or for about 10–15 minutes if in wedges. Drain very well.

Red cabbage makes a great coleslaw if shredded finely, but if cooking it is best cooked slowly as it requires longer than green varieties (see recipe below).

Chinese cabbages have more delicate leaves. They can be shredded and eaten raw, lightly steamed (they make excellent wrappings for fish and other vegetables) or can be shredded and added to a stir-fry to bulk it out – add towards the end of cooking to retain its texture.

✳ **Freezing:** freeze only young, crisp cabbage for best results. Trim and shred, then blanch for 1 minute. Drain well and cool. Pack in freezer bags and use within 6 months. Cook from frozen in boiling water for 6–7 minutes.

🕐 Short recipe: serves 4
Slow-cooked red cabbage
Melt 25 g (1 oz) butter in a large saucepan and gently fry a medium chopped onion with a bay leaf, 6 cloves and 1 small cinnamon stick for 5 minutes until softened but not browned. Add 50 g (2 oz) sultanas and 500 g (1 lb 2 oz) prepared, shredded red cabbage and stir in until thoroughly coated in the onion mixture. Add 4 Tbsp of raspberry or other fruit vinegar, 50 g (2 oz) light brown sugar and season well. Bring to the boil, cover and simmer gently for about 40–50 minutes until tender. Discard the cloves, cinnamon and bay leaf before serving. Great with sausages and mash!

Cauliflower
Brassica oleracea Botrytis Group

👁 At-a-glance

Plant: mid- to late spring and winter (depending on variety).

Ideal growing conditions: an open, sunny, sheltered site; rich, moist, non-acid soil manured the previous autumn.

Harvest: early, mid- and late summer; autumn and winter (depending on variety).

Growing this familiar vegetable can be a real challenge in comparison to other members of the *Brassica* family, but the rewards are great. While new hybrids have been developed to produce less temperamental varieties, good soil preparation and constant watering is essential for a good crop. Cauliflowers can be classified by the season in which they ripen; while the flavour is pretty much the same, the colour of the curd can be bright white, cream, purple, green or even orange.

✍ Crop planner
Choose an open, sunny spot with some shelter. Do not plant winter varieties in any areas where frost is likely. Make sure the soil has been manured the previous autumn. The soil should be treated about 2 weeks before sowing with a general-purpose fertilizer, and should have a pH of 6.5–7 (see page 9). You can sow your own cauliflower seed or buy seedlings from the nursery or garden centre.

A 3 m (10 ft) row will provide approximately 4–5 cauliflowers, in ideal conditions, depending on the variety. Approximate time from sowing to harvesting is about 16–20 weeks for summer and autumn varieties, and about 40 weeks for winter varieties.

✿ Varieties
Summer
'All Year Round': an old favourite with a large, creamy-white curd, ready for cutting in August.
'Plana': midsummer cropper, with a uniform, pale cream curd, that grows quickly.
Autumn
'Marmalade': this is an unusual variety with an orange curd.
'Violet Queen': ready in early autumn, this cauliflower has a deep purple-red curd.
Winter
'Jerome': this cauliflower will be ready in early winter; it is tasty, quite large and a good shape.

'Walcheren Winter': a hardy variety with a good-quality head. There are several strains depending on when they are ready for cutting – 'Armado May', as its name suggests, is ready for cutting in May, for example.

⚡ Tips and techniques
The method for growing different varieties of cauliflower is the same, but the timing varies according to variety. Rather than forking and loosening the soil before planting, tread it down gently and rake lightly. Make a drill about 1 cm (½ in) deep in an outdoor seedbed, at the required time, and sow the cauliflower seeds thinly. As they grow, you need to thin out the seedlings to keep them about 7 cm (3 in) apart. Discard the thinnings.

About 6 weeks or so later, when the plants have five or six leaves, they are ready for transplantation. Water the bed so that the soil softens. Carefully remove the seedlings from the bed. Using a dibber, make sufficiently deep holes for each seedling. Plant each at a distance of 60 cm (24 in) for summer and autumn varieties and 75 cm (30 in) apart for winter varieties. Put the seedlings into the holes, fill them with soil as necessary, then firm them carefully with your heel and water them well. Leave the same distances between rows.

Keep the cauliflowers weed-free with careful hoeing, and if birds are a problem, erect some netting or put in bird scarers. Keep them well watered, especially during dry weather. Once the curds form, break the stems of some of the large outer leaves and fold them over the curds to protect them from the sun and prevent them from discolouring.

💣 Possible problems
Cauliflowers are prone to all of the cabbage diseases (see page 39).

⚘ Harvesting and storing
Cut the heads when they are compact, firm and dome-shaped. If left too long, the curds start to separate as the plant begins to flower. Cut through the stem with a sharp knife, but don't cut off all the leaves as they will help protect the curd. If you do have several ready at the same time, the heads can be tied and hung upside down in a cool, frost-free shed or outbuilding. Spray with water from time to time and stored like this they will keep for 2–3 weeks. Cut cauliflower florets do not keep well in the fridge, so they are best prepared and cooked as quickly as possible.

⌶ Preparation and cooking

To cook, cut off the outer coarse leaves and the stalk stump. The fine inner green leaves can be cooked with the rest of the cauliflower as 'greens'. If you want to cook the cauliflower whole, rinse well and then cut a cross in the bottom. It will take about 15–20 minutes to cook in boiling salted water. Take care not to overcook as it quickly becomes soggy and waterlogged. Alternatively, break into florets and cook for 8–10 minutes. Adding a little lemon juice to the cooking water helps preserve the whiteness of the curd.

✱ **Freezing:** prepare florets as above. Blanch in lemony water for 3 minutes. Drain and cool. Either open-freeze on trays for later packing, or pack straightaway into freezer bags or rigid containers. Keep for up to 6 months. Cook from frozen for about 8 minutes in boiling water.

🕐 Short recipe: serves 4
Spicy golden cauliflower

Peel and chop an onion and 2 cloves of garlic. Heat 2 Tbsp of sunflower oil in a deep frying pan and gently fry the onion and garlic with 1 tsp of crushed mustard seeds, 1 tsp of crushed coriander seeds and 3 cardamom pods for 6–7 minutes until softened but not browned. Add 1 tsp of ground turmeric and 450 g (1 lb) cauliflower florets. Pour over 150 ml (¼ pt) water, add a pinch of salt, bring to the boil, then reduce the heat. Cover and simmer for about 15 minutes, stirring occasionally, until tender. Drain if necessary. Pile on to a serving dish and sprinkle with freshly chopped coriander. Ideal served as part of an Indian meal or with a hearty stew.

Chicory
Cichorium intybus

👁 At-a-glance

Plant: Spring–summer (depending on variety).

Ideal growing conditions: an open, sunny site; soil manured the previous autumn.

Harvest: Autumn–winter (depending on variety).

Related to endive, this Roman leaf, with its crisp, bitter leaves, is popular in the Italian kitchen, and makes an interesting alternative to other vegetables in the autumn as the summer produce starts to run out. Chicory is a perennial leaf that can be cooked as a vegetable or eaten raw. There are several different varieties of chicory ranging in size and colour. The most well known is witloof or Belgian chicory, which has slim, white, tightly packed leaves, fringed with a yellow frilly edge. This is a 'forced' variety and needs quite a bit of attention in order to obtain the white leaves (a method called 'blanching'). For the purposes of this book, I am concentrating on two varieties that don't require forcing: the rounded radicchio or red-leaved chicory, which has tightly packed, small, purplish-pink leaves with bright-white veining; and the sugar loaf variety that has large, green, coslike leaves and a pale heart that is pleasantly mild. Chicory can be grown from seed or you should be able to buy seedlings from a nursery or garden centre.

✍ Crop planner

Chicory isn't that fussy about soil, but ideally you should choose an open, sunny site with soil that has been manured the previous autumn. In a very hot summer you may have to provide some shelter from full sun. It can be sown directly into the vegetable plot, but a few days before sowing, rake a general-purpose fertilizer into the surface.

A 3 m (10 ft) row will provide about 10–12 radicchio or sugar loaf heads. Approximate time from sowing to harvesting is between 18 and 30 weeks, depending on variety.

✿ Varieties

'Palla Rosa': radicchio with dark pinkish-red, longer leaves with bright white veins.
'Rosso di Treviso': deep reddish-brown-leaved radicchio with bright green veins, and a pale central heart; non-hardy.
'Sugar Loaf': a fairly hardy, tall-growing sugar loaf with loose, bright green outer leaves with a pale, tightly packed heart; mild flavour.

'Winter Fare': another sugar loaf variety that is hardier than the others.

ɋ Tips and techniques

For radicchio and sugar loaf chicory, make a drill about 1 cm (½ in) deep in your vegetable plot and sow the seeds thinly. Set the rows about 30 cm (12 in) apart. As they grow, thin out the seedlings to stations about 30 cm (12 in) apart. Discard the thinnings. Keep the chicory well watered and do not let the soil dry out. As winter approaches, protect sugar loaf varieties with cloches.

☛ Possible problems

Slugs and snails are the most likely pests (see page 39).

☛ Harvesting and storing

Cut the heads at the base of the stem and use as soon as possible, although heads can be stored in a cool, dry, frost-free place for up to a month. Cut heads will also keep in the fridge, loosely wrapped to protect them, for about a week.

🍴 Preparation and cooking

Remove the root end and the outer leaves. Halve and discard any core that has formed. Break up the leaves, rinse and shake well to remove excess water. Shred and toss into salads for extra flavour; use the curled leaves as crudités dippers or serving 'cups' for other salads or pâtés. In Italy, radicchio and other red chicories are often cooked (see recipe below).

✱ **Freezing:** not suitable.

🕐 Short recipe: serves 4
Tagliatelle con radicchio

Melt 25 g (1 oz) butter in a large frying pan with 1 Tbsp of olive oil and gently fry a chopped red onion, 2 chopped garlic cloves, ½ tsp of dried chilli flakes and 1 Tbsp of freshly chopped thyme for 7–8 minutes until softened but not browned. Finely shred 1 or 2 prepared heads (depending on size) of radicchio or other red chicory. Add 4 Tbsp of dry white wine to the onion mixture, heat until bubbling, then add the shredded radicchio and stir well for about 5 minutes until wilted. Stir into 450 g (1 lb) freshly cooked and drained tagliatelle, along with 100 g (3½ oz) freshly grated Parmesan cheese, and season to taste. Serve immediately.

Endive
Cichorium endivia

👁 At-a-glance

Plant: Spring–late summer (depending on variety).

Ideal growing conditions: an open, sunny site; moist, fertile soil, manured the previous autumn.

Harvest: Summer, autumn and winter (depending on variety).

Endive is a bitter-tasting, large, lettuce-like salad vegetable related to chicory. In France, however, what we recognize as endive is called chicory, while *chicorée frisée* is the frilly leaf I am writing about here. For the garden, there are two types: curly endive, which grows flat and wide and has lots of fine frilly leaves; and Batavian endive or escarole, with broader, attractive, curled leaves. The latter is hardy and is suitable for winter growing. Endive has been around for centuries – it grows wild in the Middle East and was known to the ancient Egyptians – it is an easy crop to grow and provides a tasty salad leaf when other salad vegetables are thin on the ground. You can buy self-blanching varieties of curly endive, which have finer, paler, sweeter central leaves, or you can do this yourself with non-blanching varieties.

✍ Crop planner
Choose an open sunny site with soil that is fertile and manured the previous autumn. In a very hot summer, you may have to provide some shelter from full sun. Endives can be sown directly into the vegetable plot, but a few days before sowing, dig in a general-purpose fertilizer.

A 3 m (10 ft) row will provide about 10–15 heads. Approximate time from sowing to harvesting is between 15 and 20 weeks, depending on variety.

✿ Varieties
'Batavian': most popular and well known Batavian endive, with soft green, lightly curled leaves.
'Coronet de Bordeaux': a hardy, traditional French variety of Batavian endive, with broad, green, slightly curled leaves.
'Green Curled': a traditional variety of curly endive suitable for blanching, with frilly green leaves.
'Grosse Pancalieri': a curly endive that is self-blanching and has pinkish stalks.

❑ Tips and techniques
For both types of endive, make a drill about 1 cm (½ in) deep in your vegetable plot and sow the seeds thinly. Set the rows about 38 cm (15 in) apart. As they grow, you need to thin out the seedlings to stations about 25 cm (10 in) apart for curly endive, and 38 cm (15 in) for broad-leaved varieties. Discard the thinnings. Keep endives well watered and do not let the soil dry out. As winter approaches, protect Batavian endives with cloches.

For non-blanching endives, place a terracotta plant pot saucer over the centre of the plant for about a week in summer (or up to 3 weeks if the weather is cool) to keep out the light. You can also 'blanch' broader-leaved varieties, but these can simply be tied up with raffia or garden string in order to cover up the central core and keep out the light.

☄ Possible problems
Slugs and snails are the most likely pests (see page 39).

⌀ Harvesting and storing
Cut the heads at the base of the stem and use as soon as possible. Alternatively, pick a few leaves as required – the thin stalks will reshoot. Endive does not store well, especially if it is blanched.

❙ Preparation and cooking
Remove the root end and the outer leaves. Break up the leaves, rinse and shake well to remove excess water. Tear the leaves and toss into salads for extra flavour.

✳ Freezing: not suitable.

🕐 Short recipe: serves 2
Bitter leaf salad
Combine a large handful of prepared endive leaves with a few smaller, sweeter, milder leaves of your choice, and add in segments from 1 pink grapefruit and a few strips of pared, raw cooking apple (tossed in lemon juice to prevent discolouring). Mix 1 tsp of wholegrain mustard with 1 tsp of honey and 2 Tbsp of apple juice. Toss into the leaves and serve with smoked fish or smoked chicken.

Kale

Brassica oleracea Acephala Group

At-a-glance

Plant: late spring.

Ideal growing conditions: an open site; fertile, non-acid soil, manured the previous autumn.

Harvest: Autumn–mid-spring (depending on variety).

This is the hardiest of all the *Brassicas*, and is probably the closest to the original wild cabbage. It is often dismissed as animal fodder and disliked because it is strong tasting and easy to overcook and make bitter. Yet recently it has become a trendier addition to the winter serving plate, with the emergence of varieties like 'Nero di Toscana', with its tall, slim, dark grey/green leaves, and you'll often find it on the menu of many sophisticated Italian bistros. Personally, kale is one of my favourite greens, and it's great served with a rich, dark stew and some creamy mashed potato. Kale is usually sown from seed but you may find pre-grown seedlings in your nursery or garden centre.

Crop planner

Choose an open site with soil that is fertile and manured the previous autumn; lime if necessary. However, kale can be grown quite successfully in poorer soils. It needs to be sown into a seedbed and the seedlings aren't transplanted until June/July.

A 3 m (10 ft) row will provide about 4.5 kg (10 lb) kale. Approximate time from sowing to harvesting is approximately 30–35 weeks.

Varieties

'Fibror': a dwarf variety with dark green, very curly leaves. Good choice if space is at a premium.
'Nero di Toscana': narrow, tall, slightly fleshy leaves, 'black' in colour.
'Pentland Brig': tall growing, less curled green leaves, for picking in November. In spring you can harvest the side shoots and later still the spears, which cook like broccoli.
'Redbor': a tall variety with pinkish-purple/green, very curled leaves

Tips and techniques

Rather than forking and loosening the soil before planting, tread it down gently and rake lightly. Make a drill about 1 cm (½ in) deep in an outdoor seedbed and sow the kale seeds thinly. As they grow, thin out the seedlings to keep them about 7 cm (3 in) apart. Discard the thinnings.

Once the seedlings are about 13 cm (5 in) tall, they are ready for transplanting. Water the rows the day before and plant the seedlings about 45 cm (18 in) apart for smaller varieties, but leave 60 cm (24 in) for larger leaves. Keep 60 cm (24 in) between rows.

Keep kale well watered to encourage growth, and do not let the soil dry out as the plants will be slow to recover should their growing be halted. Weed regularly and remove any yellow leaves.

Possible problems

Kale is generally pest-free, but caterpillars can be a problem in autumn (see page 39).

Harvesting and storing

With early varieties, leaves should be ready in autumn and continue through winter to early spring. Pick or cut a few young leaves from the centre of the plant – taking care not to strip it as it will need time to recover. Leaves towards the outside of the plant will be tougher and more bitter in flavour.

Leaves can be left on the plant until required – it is very hardy. Once picked, the leaves should be used as soon as possible because they will wilt quickly.

Preparation and cooking

If caterpillars are a problem, soak the leaves in salted water to draw them off the plants before you prepare the leaves.

Slice out the long central mid-ribs or stems from larger leaves of kale, and shred the frilly green leaf flesh. Wash well in cold running water. Young tender kale leaves can be tossed raw into winter salads and are excellent dressed with a peppery lemon vinaigrette. To cook, shake off the excess water and either pack into a steamer and cook covered for 15–20 minutes until softened, or pack wet leaves into a saucepan and cook with the lid on and no extra water, turning occasionally, for about 10 minutes, depending on the tenderness of the leaves used. Drain thoroughly and chop finely. Toss in a little butter and season with black pepper and ground nutmeg or ground cloves. Serve with slow-roasted pork or boiled bacon. Chopped kale can be added to a hearty soup for extra flavour.

✱ **Freezing:** not suitable.

Lettuce
Lactuca sativa

There are so many varieties, shapes, sizes, textures and colours of lettuce. The good news is that they are all fairly easy to grow provided that you get the soil right. There are four main varieties: crisphead, butterhead, cos (or romaine) and loose-leaf, the latter being the easiest to grow. Lettuces don't need a special bed, you can put them between slow-to-mature vegetables like parsnips; the lettuces will be picked long before the other crop needs more space. Lettuces can be grown from seed or you can buy seedlings from a nursery or garden centre.

✍ Crop planner

Choose an open sunny site with soil that is fertile and manured the previous autumn. Lime the soil if necessary. In a very hot summer, you may have to provide some shelter from full sun. Lettuces can be sown directly into the vegetable plot, but a few days before sowing, rake in a general-purpose fertilizer.

A 3 m (10 ft) row will provide about 10–20 heads. Approximate time from sowing to harvesting is between 6 and 14 weeks, depending on the variety. A row of lettuces are likely to be ready all at the same time, and because they don't store, you may want to consider growing shorter rows.

✿ Varieties
Crisphead

These lettuces have a firm, large heart of curled, crisp leaves. More resistant to bolting.

'Iceberg': a popular, firmly packed, pale green ball of a lettuce; very crisp.

'Lakeland': similar to 'Iceberg', but crops later and is resistant to root aphids. Dense leaves, full of heart.

Butterhead

The most popular choice for gardeners, these summer salad lettuces have softer, smooth-edged leaves.

'Avondifiance': sow this dark green, large lettuce in June and August. It is mildew, bolt and root aphid resistant.

'Webb's Wonderful': a well known and much loved lettuce with soft, bright green leaves.

Cos (Romaine)

Long-leaved and crisp right to the centre.

'Little Gem': small, firmly packed and delicious, with pale green, sweet leaves in the centre.

'Lobjoit's Green Cos': a well-known, classic cos lettuce with long, dark green, crisp leaves.

Loose-leaf

These lettuces have little or no solid hearts.

'Lollo Biondo' and 'Lollo Rosso': a bright green and a red variety of frilly, soft-leaved lettuce.

'Oak Leaf' or 'Feuille de Chêne': shaped like those of the tree, the leaves are soft and green and reddish-tinted with a slightly bitter flavour.

❡ Tips and techniques

For all varieties, make a drill about 1 cm (½ in) deep and sow the seeds thinly. Set the rows about 30 cm (12 in) apart. As they grow, thin out the seedlings when the first true leaves appear. Water the day before and thin to stations about 15–30 cm (6–12 in) apart, depending on the variety. Discard the thinnings.

Keep lettuces well watered and do not let the soil dry out. Erect some netting or put in bird scarers. As winter approaches, protect overwintering varieties with cloches – these do not have to be so well watered. Carefully hoe to keep the weeds down.

✆ Possible problems

Slugs, snails and greenfly (aphids) are the most likely pests (see page 39).

➻ Harvesting and storing

Lettuces are harvested in the morning when they have a dew on the leaves because they are firmer. Firm head varieties are usually ready when they feel full and solid. If they are left in the ground too long they will run to seed. Pull or cut crispheads, butterheads and cos at the base of the stem. For loose-leaf lettuces, either cut whole or pick a few leaves as required – the thin stalks will reshoot. Whole lettuces can be kept in the fridge for 2–5 days (firmer heads keep longer), but are best used as soon as possible after harvesting.

⫿ Preparation and cooking

Cut away the root end and discard damaged outer leaves. Rinse in cold water and shake to remove excess water. Avoid washing the tender inner hearts as these easily become waterlogged. Usually served raw as a salad vegetable, but firmer varieties can be shredded and stir-fried or blanched in stock for about a minute and served as a light, delicate vegetable.

✱ Freezing: not suitable.

Other salad leaves

Chapter 5: Leaf vegetables

👁 At-a-glance

Plant: Spring, later summer–early autumn (depending on variety).

Ideal growing conditions: cool climate, not too hot; moist, non-acid, fertile soil, manured the previous autumn.

Harvest: late summer, autumn, winter (depending on variety).

If you want to liven up your salad bowl with different flavours and textures, you can grow varieties of individual salad leaves. You'll find several types to choose from and they can all be grown in a similar way. Below are some of the most familiar varieties to choose from.

✿ Varieties

Corn Salad (aka Lamb's Lettuce or Mâche) (*Valerianella locusta, V. eriocarpa*): a gourmet salad leaf with tender, soft green leaves and a delicate, fresh lettucey flavour. It grows easily and self-seeds if permitted. If covered it will survive throughout the winter months so is excellent value. French varieties such as 'Cavallo', 'Jade' or 'Verte de Cambrai' look like tiny compact lettuces and can be lifted whole and used as a garnish or added to a salad. Other varieties are more vigorous and spreading, for example 'Vit'. Approximate time from seed to harvest is 6–12 weeks.

Land Cress (aka American Cress or Winter Cress) (*Barbarea verna*): I'd never seen this before until I found it growing in small clumps in my herb garden. It looks and tastes like watercress and as such is excellent for adding a bit of pepperiness to a winter salad bowl and can be cooked into a sauce or soup. It thrives in a damp, shaded part of the garden. Ready for picking about 8 weeks after sowing.

Mizuna (*Brassica rapa* var. *nipposinica*): a Japanese salad *Brassica* with fine, feathery, dark green leaves, which make a great garnish as well as an attractive addition to the salad bowl. They have a mild, mustardy flavour. Usually sold as 'Mizuna' or 'Mizuna Greens', it is ready for harvesting 4–8 weeks after sowing. The older the leaves get, the less succulent they become – these are better steamed or stir-fried. The flowering stalks can be eaten – simply steam and serve like broccoli.

Mustard Greens (*Brassica juncea*): usually grown as a large cabbage, but if this Chinese *Brassica* is grown as a leafy seedling it makes a lovely mustardy addition to a salad bowl. Choose the red-leaved variety 'Red Giant', which has a pungent flavour and colourful reddish-brown and green veiny leaves.

Rocket (aka Arugula and Rucola) (*Eruca sativa, E. versicaria*): a trendy salad *Brassica*, often classed as a herb but frequently used in the salad bowl. The small, dark green, slightly feathery leaves have a spicy, peppery flavour. Easy to grow, although the leaves seed quickly and need frequent watering. You may not find specific varieties as it usually sold under one of its common names – 'Wild Grazia' is a strongly flavoured variety with lightly forked leaves. Leaves will be ready to harvest 4–12 weeks after sowing.

✍ Crop planner

Ideal for growing in a cool climate, these salad leaves are grown mainly for autumn and winter use, but if you live in a cooler climate, you may find that you can sow in spring for a summer crop. Choose an open site with soil that is fertile and manured the previous autumn. Lime the soil if necessary. Salad leaves can be sown directly into the vegetable plot, but a few days before sowing, rake in a general-purpose fertilizer.

✹ Tips and techniques

For all varieties, make a drill about 1 cm (½ in) deep in your vegetable plot and sow the seeds thinly. As they grow, thin out the seedlings when they are large enough to handle. Water the day before and thin to stations about 10–15 cm (4–6 in) apart, depending on the variety. Discard the thinnings. Set the rows about 30 cm (12 in) apart.

Keep the leaves well watered and do not let the soil dry out. Shelter from the sun if necessary. Birds may be a problem, so erect some netting or put in bird scarers. As winter approaches, protect overwintering varieties with cloches – these do not have to be so well watered. Carefully hoe to keep the weeds down.

☠ Pests and diseases

Usually trouble-free, but rocket can attract flea beetles (see page 39).

⚘ Harvesting and storing

All salad leaves are best picked and used as required. None of them keep well, although you can submerge them in a bowl of cold water and keep in the fridge for up to 24 hours if necessary. Either pick off individual leaves – this way the plants will shoot up again – or remove the whole lot. For land cress, pick the outer leaves first, leaving the centre to produce more. As salad leaves get older they toughen, so you would be better to use only the centre leaves in this instance.

⅋ Preparation and cooking

Any leaves that grow close to the ground will get quite earthy and need careful rinsing and drying before use. Either place in a bowl of cold water to allow the earth to settle, or gently rinse under trickling cold water. Shake off excess water and either put in a salad spinner or pat dry using kitchen paper. Use fresh in salads or as garnishes.

✱ **Freezing:** not suitable.

Pour 1.2 L (2 pt) vegetable stock into a saucepan and bring to the boil. Reduce the heat to a gentle simmer. Meanwhile, melt 50 g (2 oz) butter in a large saucepan and gently fry a chopped onion and garlic clove for 2–3 minutes until softened but not browned. Stir in 400 g (14 oz) Arborio rice and cook, stirring, for 2 minutes, until well coated. Add a pinch of dried chilli flakes and a ladle of stock. Cook gently, stirring, until absorbed. Continue adding the stock, ladle by ladle, until all the stock has been used and the rice is creamy and thick, but not sticky. This will take about 25 minutes. Just before serving, roughly chop a generous handful of washed and dried rocket leaves and carefully fold into the rice along with 100 g (3½ oz) grated Parmesan cheese. Season and serve each portion with a handful of fresh rocket leaves piled high on top.

Chapter 5: Leaf vegetables

Spinach
Spinacia oleracea

👁 At-a-glance

Plant: early–late spring, and later summer–early autumn (depending on variety).

Ideal growing conditions: cool climate, not too hot; moist, non-acid, fertile soil, manured the previous autumn.

Harvest: early–late summer and winter–spring (depending on variety).

A favourite with Popeye, spinach has made a comeback in recent years, mostly as a salad leaf. It's also delicious as a cooked vegetable and mixed with cheese and eggs it makes a great filling for a pastry case. Spinach is related to beetroot and chard; it is a plant for cool climates and doesn't like hot, dry weather. It is important to keep the crop watered, and you'll need to sow several plants to get a good yield. It can be sown for early cutting as a salad leaf, or allowed to mature for cooking. Spinach is usually grown from seed, and sown successively, so you should be able to obtain a good, long supply.

✍ Crop planner

Ideal for growing in a cool climate. Choose an open site with soil that is fertile and manured the previous autumn. Lime the soil if necessary. Spinach can be sown directly into the vegetable plot, and if you grow it in between rows of taller vegetables, they will shield the leaves from any harsh sunlight. About 2 weeks before sowing, rake in a general-purpose fertilizer.

A 3 m (10 ft) row will provide about 2.25–4.5 kg (5–10 lb). Approximate time from sowing to harvesting is between 8 and 14 weeks, depending on variety.

✿ Varieties
Summer spinach

Summer varieties are sown between March and the end of May, and are ready for harvesting in June to October. These varieties produce the broad, rounded leaf that we are most familiar with. Young leaves can be picked and tossed into salads, while mature leaves are better cooked. Varieties include:

'Bloomsdale': resistant to bolting; dark green, flavoursome leaves.

'Medania': popular variety, resistant to bolting; large leaves, and vigorous growth.

Winter spinach

Seeds for this hardy spinach are sown in August and September for picking between October and April. Pick young leaves for cooking – older ones soon become bitter and quite unpleasant. Varieties include:

'Monnopa': mild, fine-flavoured, thick, dark green leaves.

'Sigmaleaf': very hardy; good cropper; flavoursome leaves.

New Zealand spinach

Not actually a true spinach, it grows on bushy stems and the leaves are smaller and more pointed. It is a dwarf plant, but it is a rambler and takes up more space than other types of spinach. This variety is better for dry conditions where the soil is poor, but it is not hardy and will be killed by frost. Sow seeds (soaked overnight) in late May for picking from June to September. It can be used in the same way as summer spinach but it is milder in flavour – the mid-ribs of the mature leaves are not eaten. Usually sold under its common name.

❉ Tips and techniques

For summer and winter varieties, make a drill about 1 cm (½ in) deep in your vegetable plot and sow the seeds thinly. Set the rows about 30 cm (12 in) apart. As they grow, thin out the seedlings when they are large enough to handle. Water the day before and thin to stations about 15 cm (6 in) apart. Discard the thinnings.

For New Zealand spinach, sow three soaked seeds about 2 cm (¾ in) apart, spaced about 60 cm (2 ft) apart, and then thin to one seedling per station.

Keep the leaves well watered and do not let the soil dry out. Shelter from the sun if necessary. Birds may be a problem, so erect some netting or put in bird scarers. As winter approaches, protect overwintering varieties with cloches – these do not have to be so well watered. Hoe to keep the weeds down.

☙ Possible problems

Spinach can be susceptible to slugs and snail damage, also downy mildew and spinach blight (see page 39). Look out for resistant varieties.

☞ Harvesting and storing

With all types of spinach, harvest the leaves when they are ready. Pick a few outside leaves before they become tough, but avoid taking more than half of the plant otherwise it will be unable to regenerate. All spinach wilts quickly after picking, so pick to order and use straightaway while still crisp.

☗ Preparation and cooking

Immerse young leaves for eating raw in cold water to remove any soil, and then rinse and dry in the same way as for lettuce (see page 51). For cooking, mature leaves are best stripped from the stalks and any coarse mid-ribs, and then broken up or left whole. Immerse in cold water, several times, until the water is clear of soil and grit. Shake off the excess water but don't dry. Pack the wet spinach leaves into a saucepan and add a pinch of salt. You don't need to add any more water for cooking – the leaves will cook in the steam. Cover with a tight-fitting lid and cook over a gentle heat for 7–8 minutes until wilted. Drain in a colander, pressing out as much of the water as possible – a potato masher is a good tool to use here. Season with nutmeg and butter.

✱ **Freezing:** choose young spinach and prepare as above. Blanch in small quantities for 2 minutes. Drain well and press out the excess water. Allow to cool. Pack into rigid containers or freezer bags. Seal and store for up to 12 months. Cook from frozen with a small amount of water. Cover and cook for about 5 minutes, stirring occasionally to break up. Drain well and serve with butter.

🕐 Short recipe: serves 4
Warm spinach, bacon and egg salad

Hardboil 4 eggs, place in ice-cold water for 10 minutes and then peel. Set aside. Meanwhile, prepare 4 large handfuls of young spinach leaves as described above and pile on to serving plates. Finely chop a large, ripe tomato. When ready to serve, roughly chop 8 rashers of rindless streaky bacon and dry-fry for 4–5 minutes until crispy and scatter over the spinach while warm. Halve the eggs and arrange on top. Sprinkle with chopped tomato and chopped chives. Dress with a mustardy vinaigrette and serve immediately.

Swiss chard and Spinach beet
Beta vulgaris Cicla Group

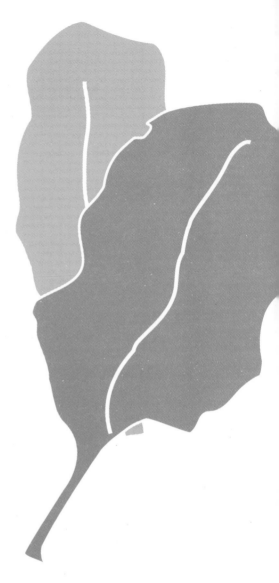

👁 At-a-glance

Plant: mid to late spring (depending on variety).

Ideal growing conditions: open site; fertile soil, manured the previous autumn.

Harvest: late summer to spring (depending on variety).

If you haven't had much luck with growing spinach (see page 54), yet like the leaves, you might have more luck growing one of these two plants. While spinach is susceptible to poor soil and dry weather, Swiss chard and spinach beet are much easier to grow, and they're a great-value crop. If you sow them in the spring, you'll be able to enjoy the leaves in mid- to late summer, and they keep going right through until the following spring.

Swiss chard has a number of other names – such as chard, ruby chard, seakale beet, silver chard and silver beet. It has succulent leaves and stalks and with so many varieties to choose from you can easily make a multicoloured display in your vegetable patch. The bright colours do dull down on cooking, but like spinach, small, young leaves make tasty salad additions and garnishes. For cooking, the larger green-leaved chard with its stunning white stems is regarded as the tastiest – the leaves and stems are usually cooked separately, the stems treated like asparagus – but on the whole, the flavour is less pronounced than spinach and the nutritional content is not as high. By sowing chards in different stages, you should be able to grow an all-year-round supply.

Spinach beet, also called Perpetual spinach, produces a succession of leaves over a long period and is probably easier to grow. It is similar to spinach but the leaves are larger, darker and more fleshy. The flavour can be more peppery than other spinach types, but it can be used in the same way. It doesn't keep long after picking, so must be used fresh.

✍ Crop planner

Choose an open site, in sun or light shade, with soil that is fertile and manured the previous autumn. Swiss chard and spinach beet can be sown directly into the vegetable plot, but 2 weeks before sowing, rake in a general-purpose fertilizer.

A 3 m (10 ft) row will provide about 3.15 kg (7 lb) leaves. Approximate time from sowing to harvesting is about 8–12 weeks, depending on variety.

✿ Varieties
Swiss chard

'Bright Lights': dark green leaves with orange, pinkish-red, cream and yellow stems – a real rainbow of colour.
'Charlotte': purple-red leaves and bright red stems.
'Lucullus': pale green, crinkled leaves with white stems; good flavour.
'Rhubarb Chard': purplish-green, crinkled leaves with deep red-pink stems.

Spinach beet

Usually sold under its common name or as 'Perpetual spinach' or 'Leaf beet'.

❋ Tips and techniques

For both varieties, make a drill about 1 cm (½ in) deep in your vegetable plot and sow the seeds thinly. Set the rows about 38 cm (15 in) apart. As they grow, thin out the seedlings when they are large enough to handle. Water the day before and thin to stations about 45 cm (18 in) apart for large leaves, and about 30 cm (12 in) for spinach beet. Discard the thinnings.

Keep the leaves watered and the plot weed-free. Birds may be a problem, so erect some netting or put in bird scarers. As winter approaches, if the weather is exceptionally cold, protect overwintering varieties with cloches – these do not have to be so well watered – but generally they are hardy enough to not need protection.

☠ Pests and diseases

On the whole, these are trouble-free plants but they can be susceptible to slug and snail damage (see page 39).

☛ Harvesting and storing

Neither Swiss chard or spinach beet stores well and should be cooked straight from the plant.

❙ Preparation and cooking

For chard varieties with large leaves, like Swiss, remove the green parts of the leaves and break off (not cut) the stalks and veins; remove the stringy parts. Break the stalks into sections about 5 cm (2 in) long, and rip the leaves into small pieces. Cook the leaves like spinach, and the stalks like asparagus. Traditionally chicken or vegetable stock is used instead of plain water because the vegetable is usually served with the cooking liquid made into a white sauce to add more flavour.

Spinach beet can be prepared and cooked as spinach (see page 55).

✱ Freezing: follow instructions for spinach (see page 55).

🕐 Short recipe: serves 4
Swiss chard with sweet spices

Prepare the leaves and stalks of 450 g (1 lb) Swiss chard. Wash the leafy part and pack into a saucepan while still wet. Cover and cook over a medium heat for 5–6 minutes, stirring occasionally, until just wilted. Drain well. Break the ribs into 2.5 cm (1 in) long pieces. Blanch in lightly salted boiling water for 3 minutes. Drain well. Heat 2 Tbsp of olive oil in a frying pan and gently fry 2 chopped garlic cloves with 1 tsp of crushed coriander seeds and 1 tsp of crushed cumin seeds for about 2 minutes until softened. Add the chard leaves and stalks and stir-fry for 2–3 minutes until heated through. Season and either stir in 3 Tbsp of double cream or leave plain. Serve sprinkled with chopped fresh tomato as an accompaniment to grilled fish, chicken or lamb.

Chapter 6
Peas and beans (legumes)

Legumes are some of the most beneficial crops you can grow in your garden because these pod vegetables need to be eaten soon after being picked, and produce that you grow yourself will always be so much more flavoursome than anything you can buy. All beans are easy to grow, but peas are more difficult. The crops take up quite a bit of space, but smaller varieties are available and are worth checking out if you are limited on space. Growing beans and peas need support because they are lanky, vinelike plants, so you'll need to erect canes or growing frames alongside your seedlings – you'll be amazed at the variety of structures you can buy. The frames themselves can add an ornamental feature to your garden, and once the beans and peas flower, you'll have an attractive display of foliage and colour on your plot.

Another good reason for growing legumes is that they are a natural soil fertilizer. After you've picked all the beans, dig the foliage into the soil to provide nutritious green manure, and the next lot of vegetables you grow on the site, will have a head start (see Rotation on page 10).

☠ Pests and diseases

Aphid: Black bean aphids are a major spring and summer pest. Large groups of **blackfly** stunt growth, eat flowers and distort the pods. Pinch out the tops of broad beans once four trusses have formed to discourage this pest. **Pea aphids** are **greenfly** and may be a problem in hot, humid weather. Insecticide sprays are available.

Birds and mice: erect netting over freshly planted pea and bean seeds, and young seedlings. Pin the netting down well to ensure there are no points of entry.

Chocolate spot: small brown patches appear on the leaves and pods and the disease can also affect the seeds inside. Lift and destroy affected plants; there are treatments available for the remaining plants if you choose to use them. To help discourage this disease, apply fertilizer before sowing and avoid growing plants too close together.

Mildew: Downy mildew appears as yellow blotches on leaves, with brownish mould on the underside. The pods can also appear distorted. This problem often occurs in damp, cool weather. Chemical sprays are available, otherwise burn or destroy the affected plants and practice crop rotation (see page 10).

Powdery mildew causes white patches to develop all over leaves and pods. It generally occurs in dry weather, in sheltered gardens. Chemical sprays are available, otherwise, burn or destroy affected plants and practice crop rotation (see page 10).

Pea and bean weevil: these little brown beetles eat 'U'-shaped sections around the leaf edge, retarding growth or destroying seedlings. Chemical sprays are available. Keep the plot well maintained and weed-free to cut down the risk of attack.

Pea moth: maggots form inside the pods rendering them unusable. There is no treatment. Preventative chemical sprays are available for applying after the start of flowering.

Pea thrip: very small black or yellow insects cause silver patches on the leaves and pods. The risk is worse in dry, hot weather. Chemical sprays are available, otherwise burn or destroy affected plants and practice crop rotation (see page 10).

Chapter 6: Peas and beans

58

Broad (Fava) bean
Vicia faba

👁 At-a-glance

Plant: late autumn; late winter; late spring (depending on variety).

Ideal growing conditions: open site; well-drained, fertile soil, manured the previous autumn.

Harvest: early–late summer (depending on variety).

Believed to have been introduced to Britain by the Romans, this legume has been around since Neolithic times. The broad bean is the most hardy of all beans and is one of the best home-grown vegetables as it tastes so much better straight off the plant. If you pick them young and fresh, you can eat the pods as well and they're deliciously sweet and a true culinary delight! You can even eat the shooting tops of the plants as well – they cook up like spinach and have an earthy-beany flavour. Broad bean plants can vary in size, from dwarf varieties of about 30–45 cm (12–18 in) tall to about 1.2 m (4 ft); the pod size varies accordingly. They have very fragrant, pretty flowers so are an attractive addition to any garden. For planting, varieties can be divided into overwintering beans for sowing in late autumn, and later bean types for a late winter to late spring sowing. Broad beans are usually grown from seed but you can purchase seedlings from nurseries and garden centres in the spring.

✍ Crop planner

Choose an open site with soil that is well drained, fertile and manured the previous autumn. Broad beans prefer a non-acid soil so lime the soil if necessary, but nearly every soil type will provide a good crop apart from waterlogged or very acid types. If you plan to grow taller varieties you will need to choose a sheltered area to prevent wind damage. Broad beans can be sown directly into the vegetable plot. Apply a general-purpose fertilizer about a week before sowing.

A 3 m (10 ft) double row of broad beans will provide about 9 kg (20 lb) beans. Approximate time from sowing to harvesting is about 26 weeks for autumn-planted, and 14 weeks for spring-planted beans.

✿ Varieties

'Aquadulce Claudia': popular bean for autumn growing. It is hardy, compact and grows well. The pods are long and contain white beans that are excellent for freezing.

'Red Epicure': another long-podded variety, but the beans are reddish-brown and turn yellow when cooked. They have a distinct flavour. The plant develops lovely scarlet flowers.

'The Sutton': a popular dwarf, compact variety that is great for small gardens or for a less-sheltered site. The beans are white and have an excellent flavour.

'Witkiem' varieties: 'W. Manita' is one of the earliest spring varieties, it is quite compact and yields are high; 'W. Major' and 'W. Vroma' are other spring varieties you may come across, these are ready for picking in the early summer.

♀ Tips and techniques

Broad beans are usually planted in a double row. Either dig a trench about 4 cm (1½ in) deep and 23 cm (9 in) wide, or use a dibber to make suitable holes. Plant the bean seeds about 23 cm (9 in) apart down the row and across from each other. Prepare other double rows about 60 cm (24 in) apart as required.

Tall varieties will require support with string tied to canes. Place the canes at intervals along each side of the double row.

When the plants are in full flower, pinch out about 8 cm (3 in) from the young top shoots to reduce the chance of black bean aphid infestation (see page 58) and to allow the beans to develop fully. Hoe to keep the weeds down and water during dry periods.

After you've picked all the beans, dig the foliage into the soil to provide nutritious green manure (see Rotation on page 10. Also see page 58).

☙ Possible problems

Relatively trouble-free, apart from blackfly. Reduce the risk of an attack by following the instructions above. Chocolate spot is another potential problem (see page 58).

⚬ Harvesting and storing

The earliest crops are ready in May. You can start to pick them when the pods are no more than 5 cm (2 in) long and cook them whole. Otherwise, pick the beans as required, feeling the pods to get an idea of the size of the beans inside – ideally the bean should not get beyond 2 cm (¾ in) diameter for the best flavour and texture. Older beans become tough skinned and floury textured; they take longer to cook and are best peeled before eating.

ⵦ Preparation and cooking

Young beans, no thicker than 2 cm (¾ in) and no longer than 7 cm (3 in) have the best flavour and texture and are the most delicious. Allow 225–350 g (8–12 oz) beans in pods per person. Wash and cook in the pods in lightly salted water for 5–6 minutes until just tender. Shell larger beans before cooking in boiling salted water: 8–10 minutes for smaller beans and 10–20 minutes for larger, older beans – these are better peeled after cooking and served mashed with butter.

✱ Freezing: depending on the size of the bean, blanch for 2–3 minutes. Drain and cool before packing in freezer bags or rigid containers. Keep for up to 12 months. Cook from frozen in boiling salted water for 5–8 minutes.

🕒 Short recipe: serves 4
Fresh broad bean salad for tuna

Shell 900 g (2 lb) beans and cook in lightly salted boiling water for 5–10 minutes, depending on size. Drain well and rinse under cold running water to cool. Peel and finely chop a shallot and place in a bowl. Drain the beans and pat dry with kitchen paper. Toss into the shallots along with 4 Tbsp of freshly chopped parsley, freshly ground black pepper, a little salt, 1 Tbsp of balsamic vinegar and 2 Tbsp of good-quality olive oil. Mix well, cover and stand at room temperature for a few minutes before serving as an accompaniment to freshly grilled tuna.

French (Green) bean
Phaseolus vulgaris

French beans are the best legume crop to grow for the impatient bean-lovers among us, because they are ready for picking 2–3 weeks earlier than runner beans and are a real treat when picked young. In spite of their name, it appears that the beans originated in Peru, although they have long been loved in France. If you leave the beans on the plant they will mature into flageolet beans, which require shelling before cooking, and finally into haricot beans, for drying and storing. You'll find dwarf types, as well as climbers that require poles for support. Pods come in a variety of colours – from yellow to green to purple. French beans are usually grown from seed but you can purchase seedlings from nurseries and garden centres in the spring. Look out for disease-resistant varieties.

✍ Crop planner

French beans aren't able to tolerate frosts so plant out when there is no danger of extremely cold weather and the soil is warmer. Choose an open site with soil that is well drained, fertile and manured the previous autumn. If you plan to grow taller varieties you will need to choose a sheltered area to prevent wind damage. French beans can be sown directly into the vegetable plot. Apply a general-purpose fertilizer about 2 weeks before sowing.

A 3 m (10 ft) double row of French beans will provide about 3.6–5.4 kg (8–12 lb) beans, depending on variety. Approximate time from sowing to harvesting is about 8–12 weeks, depending on variety.

✿ Varieties

'Annabel': this high-yielding dwarf variety has slim, green, stringless pods.
'Brown Dutch': a special haricot bean variety with brown beans.
'Hunter': long, wide, flattish pods containing white beans are produced by this high-yielding, popular climber.
'Mont d'Or': this dwarf variety yields a yellow bean, it has rounded pods with waxy flesh and black seeds. The pods can be cooked whole.

'Purple Queen': one of the best purple-coloured beans. It yields well and has long, slim pods of good flavour – they do turn green on cooking. Another dwarf variety.

۵ Tips and techniques

French beans need warm soil to germinate, so most gardeners sow directly into the soil in early summer. They can be sown in a single or double row (see Broad beans on page 59), about 5 cm (2 in) deep and 8 cm (3 in) apart, with rows set about 45 cm (18 in) away from each other. Climbing French beans require the same supports as runner beans (see page 63). Hoe to keep the weeds down and water during dry periods.

☄ Possible problems

Not prone to many problems. Slugs and snails are attracted to young foliage but will eat the pods as well. Black bean aphids and fungal diseases may also be a possibility (see page 58).

☛ Harvesting and storing

The plants will start to crop within 8 weeks of sowing, and may produce pods for a couple of months afterwards. The more you pick them the more they will produce. Pick the young beans carefully as you may pull out the whole plant – hold the stem with one hand and pull the pod downwards with the other. Young beans wither quite quickly after picking so they must be cooked or preserved as soon as possible. However, you can keep them wrapped in damp kitchen paper in the fridge overnight if you don't have the time to freeze them.

If the pods are left on the plants to develop further, you'll see that the beans inside begin to bulge. These 'flageolet' beans are more like peas, and can also be picked and should be used as fresh as possible.

For haricot beans, leave the pods on the plants until they have turned white – this means they are ripe – usually in about September/October. Wait until they are dry and then pull out the whole plants and hang them in a dry, airy place. When the pods feel crisp and dry, shell the beans and spread them out on trays to dry thoroughly.

ⵏ Preparation and cooking

Simply nip off the stalk end, and the tail if preferred, and cook whole in boiling salted water for 5–8 minutes. Young, thin beans cook very well in about 8 minutes in a steamer. Shell flageolet beans and cook as for broad beans (see page 59) – they will take about 10 minutes.

Dried haricot beans need soaking before cooking. Place in a pan and cover with cold water. Bring to the boil and cook for 2 minutes. Remove from the heat and stand covered for 1 hour. Drain well and rinse, then cook in a well-flavoured stock for about 40 minutes until tender.

✱ **Freezing:** young French beans are the best for freezing. Top and tail, leave small beans whole, larger ones should be cut into 2.5–5 cm (1–2 in) lengths. Blanch for 2 minutes. Drain and cool, before packing into freezer bags or rigid containers. Keep for up to 12 months. Cook from frozen for 5–7 minutes.

🕐 Short recipe: serves 2
French bean tortilla

Prepare a large handful of young French beans as above, cut in half and blanch in boiling water for about 2 minutes. Drain well. Beat 3 eggs together and mix in 2 Tbsp of freshly chopped tarragon. Season well. Heat a knob of butter in a small omelette pan until bubbling, add the beans and mix in the butter for 1 minute. Arrange the beans evenly over the bottom of the pan and pour in the egg mixture. Heat gently for about 5 minutes until almost set. Carefully turn over and cook for a further 2 minutes until lightly golden. Serve hot or cold.

Runner (String) bean
Phaseolus coccineus

👁 At-a-glance

Plant: early summer.

Ideal growing conditions: open site; non-acid, fertile soil, manured the previous autumn.

Harvest: late summer until the first frost.

Runner beans are a true symbol of the summer. Originating from Mexico, they are larger and coarser than the French variety but have much more flavour and a juicier texture than any other bean. It really is worth the effort to grow your own as shop-bought beans simply don't compare. Runner beans are a firm favourite, providing a good crop throughout the summer and into the autumn. The plant looks great too with its scarlet or white flowers and vinelike greenery that traditionally grows up wigwam-shaped canes. You will find dwarf varieties as well as the traditional climbers. Runner beans are usually grown from seed but you can purchase seedlings from nurseries and garden centres in the spring.

✍ Crop planner

Runner beans aren't able to tolerate frosts so plant out when there is no danger of extremely cold weather and the soil is warmer. Very cold weather can stunt their growth. Choose an open site with soil that is well drained, fertile and well manured the previous autumn. Lime the soil if necessary. If you plan to grow the traditional varieties you will need to choose a sheltered area to prevent wind damage. Runner beans can be sown directly into the vegetable plot. Apply a general-purpose fertilizer about 2 weeks before sowing.

A 3 m (10 ft) double row of runner beans will provide about 27 kg (60 lb) beans, so you may not want to plant a full row. Approximate time from sowing to harvesting is about 12–14 weeks.

✿ Varieties

'Desiree': this traditional climber produces a high yield of stringless, narrow pods with white seeds. Good flavour.
'Painted Lady' (or 'York and Lancaster'): this is the oldest variety of runner bean and is a traditional climber. The plant develops white flowers with bright red 'lips' and shortish pods.
'Pickwick': a shortish, curved stringless bean grows on this bushy dwarf variety that does not need support.
'Polestar': lots of scarlet-red flowers bloom on this high-yielding, well-known variety. The beans are long, straight and stringless.
'Scarlet Emporor': another traditional, old favourite, that yields long, straight beans that are regarded as having one of the finest flavours.

⚙ Tips and techniques

Before planting traditional climbing beans, you need to erect some supports. You can choose to grow your beans in a single or double row, and you'll need to place canes at intervals along each side of the single or double row. You can also provide strings for them to climb up. Alternatively, you can train them to climb up a wigwam of about five tall canes tied at the top. The distance between canes or strings should be about 25 cm (10 in) for easy picking.

Plant or sow one bean at each cane, making a 5 cm (2 in) hole with a dibber. You'll need to encourage young seedlings to climb up the right pole until they get established. Once they have reached the top of the canes, pinch out the growing tops.

For dwarf varieties, plant beans 15 cm (6 in) apart in single rows with about 45 cm (18 in) between them. Pinch out any long shoots.
Hoe to keep weeds down and water to prevent drying out. After you've picked all the beans, dig the roots and stem bases into the soil to provide nutritious green manure (see Rotation on page 10).

🌢 Possible problems

Slugs and snails will be attracted to young seedlings so take relevant precautions. Otherwise, runner beans are usually problem-free, but they may be affected by black bean aphid, chocolate spot or powdery mildew. (See page 58.)

↝ Harvesting and storing

Pick the beans while they are still tender and young, before the seeds begin to swell in the pods. The more the plants are picked, the more they will produce. For this reason large, oversized beans are better removed to encourage new growth – the larger and older the bean, the tougher and more tasteless it becomes. Once the beans are picked, any that can't be used straightaway can be stored in a jug of water, stem end in the water, in the fridge for 2–3 days.

⫼ Preparation and cooking

Wash the beans well when ready to cook them. Cut off the tops and tails and trim away any stringy edges. If you have a specialist bean shredder, you'll be able to cut the beans into long, thin shreds, otherwise cut into thin diagonal slices. Cook in a small amount of salted boiling water for 5–7 minutes. Drain well before serving.

✱ **Freezing:** prepare the beans as above, but cut the beans more thickly if you want a firm texture when the beans are cooked. Blanch for 2 minutes then drain and cool before packing into freezer bags or rigid containers. Keep for up to 12 months. Cook from frozen for about 5 minutes.

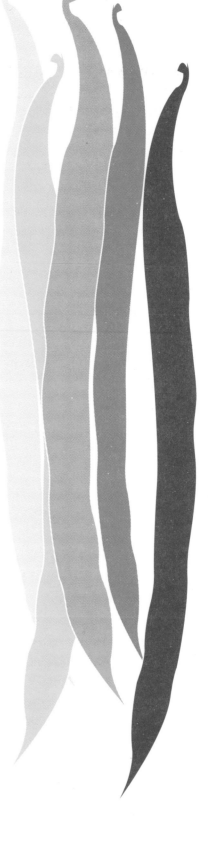

> ### 🕐 Short recipe: serves 4
> ### Sweet and sour dressed runner beans
>
> Prepare 450 g (1 lb) runner beans by cutting into long thin shreds. Cook in lightly salted boiling water for about 5 minutes until just tender. Drain well and return to the saucepan. Add a large knob of butter, a few shakes of balsamic or fruit vinegar and a sprinkling of brown sugar. Mix well to coat and serve warm as a side dish for fish or chicken, or allow to cool and serve as a salad to accompany smoked fish.

Pea
Pisum sativum

Plant: late autumn, late winter, early spring, early summer (depending on variety).

Ideal growing conditions: open site; non-acid, fertile soil, manured the previous autumn.

Harvest: early summer, midsummer, early autumn (depending on variety).

Of the members of the legume family, peas are considered to be quite a difficult crop to grow, and they do take up a lot of space. But, if you are prepared to persevere, peas are one of the most rewarding vegetables to grow – a freshly picked pea eaten just after picking is deliciously sweet and tastes like nothing else. If you don't have much space, then grow a couple of rows of an early variety that can be picked at the same time as the first carrots, French beans and turnips. You'll then have the space for leeks and cabbages to develop afterwards.

If you have more space, varieties can be planted to give you a supply from May to October. Remember to water well at the flowering stage to improve the crop. As well as the traditional, round garden pea, there are the very small petits pois, flat-podded mange touts and sweet sugarsnaps. Young pea shoots have a distinctly sweet, pea flavour and can be snipped off and eaten as a delicious salad leaf.

Look out for disease-resistant varieties. Peas can be planted from seed straight into the ground or from seedlings raised in the nursery or garden centre.

✍ Crop planner

Choose an open site with soil that is well drained, fertile and well manured the previous autumn. Lime the soil if necessary. Avoid adding too much fertilizer – too much nitrogen will do more harm than good – use only a light dressing just before sowing. Early varieties are planted in autumn and then overwintered, but should be covered to protect them. Crops can be planted successively until early summer.

A 3 m (10 ft) row of peas will provide about 4.5 kg (10 lb) beans. Approximate time from sowing to harvesting is about 32 weeks for autumn-planted peas and 12–16 weeks for spring peas.

✿ Varieties
Peas
'Early Onward': an early variety with good disease resistance, that produces plump pods of well-flavoured peas.
'Hurst Greenshaft': elegant-looking pea pods with fine flavoured peas result from this main crop variety that has good disease resistance.
'Kelvedon Wonder': a traditional favourite, this dwarf-type plant produces large, plump pods that are mid-green in colour. It is a good choice for successive sowing and is resistant to mildew.
Petits pois
These are not simply immature peas gathered early from small pods, but are a variety of dwarf pea with a very sweet flavour.
'Darfon' and 'Minnow' are both short-podded main crop varieties.
Mange touts
'Edula': quite compact plants, so ideal for a small garden. Produces high yield.
'Oregon Sugar Pod': this plant has good disease resistance. The long, flat pods are best picked when young and stringless.

Sugarsnap

'Delikett Dwarf': a compact variety, the pods are stringless when young, but flavour and juiciness develops as the pods mature.

'Sugar Anne': this early-to-mature, high-yielding variety produces light-coloured pods with excellent sweet flavour.

Ω Tips and techniques

The easiest way to plant peas is to make a trench about 15–20 cm (6–8 in) wide, 5 cm (2 in) deep, and plant the peas 5 cm (2 in) apart. Sow the peas in pairs, one on either side of the trench. Alternatively, plant in a single row at the same intervals. Rows of peas should be spaced about 60–90 cm (2–3 ft) apart, and supports should be added once the peas produce tendrils. Keep the plot weed-free.

Cover the newly sown seeds to protect them from birds and keep covered until the plants mature. Water during dry spells, especially once the flowers form. Applying a mulch can help conserve moisture during excessively dry weather.

✎ Possible problems

Peas are prone to several pests and diseases. Birds and mice will eat the seeds and seedlings, so protection is important. Aphids and pea thrips can also be a problem. Mildew is another hazard (see page 58).

⌁ Harvesting and storing

When the pods seem to have reached the desired length, check them daily to feel if the peas are swelling inside. Aim to pick when well developed but not overly large. For all varieties, carefully pull the pod upwards with one hand while holding the stem with the other. Pick garden peas regularly and eat as fresh as possible. Approximately 900 g (2 lb) pea pods will yield 450 g (1 lb) shelled peas.

Mange touts and sugarsnaps are ready to be picked when you can just see the peas forming in the pod – if you don't catch them at the right time they will go on to develop into a garden pea and can be harvested and used as such. If insufficient mange touts or sugarsnaps are ready at one time, pick the few that are ripe and keep in the fridge for a few days until others are ready for harvesting.

⦚ Preparation and cooking

For full-size garden peas and petits pois, prise off the stalk of the pod and carefully open the pod. Gently run your thumb up the pod to remove the peas. Boil garden peas in lightly salted boiling water for 8–15 minutes – adding a teaspoon of sugar will help to preserve their colour. Petits pois only need blanching in boiling water for 2 minutes and are then best drained and steamed in a covered pan with a little butter for a further 2–3 minutes.

Peas are often bottled and salted to be enjoyed in the winter months (see page 182).

Top and tail sugarsnaps and mange touts as you would French beans (see page 62). They should not need stringing. Rinse in cold water and cook in lightly salted water for 4–5 minutes for sugarsnaps and about 3 minutes for mange touts. Both varieties are good additions to stir-fries and can be used whole or sliced diagonally.

Young garden pea pods can be cooked in butter for about 5 minutes and served as a vegetable in their own right – break the pod at the blossom end and pull away the thin, waxy covering. Larger pods can be used to flavour stock for soups and casseroles.

Pea shoots require a simple rinse and shake dry before eating.

✳ Freezing: shell garden peas, blanch for 1 minute, drain, cool quickly in cold running water or iced water and dry, then pack into freezer bags. Top and tail mange touts and sugarsnaps. Blanch for 1 minute, then cool and pack as for peas. Freeze for up to 12 months. Cook from frozen for 5–7 minutes.

◔ Short recipe: serves 4
Pea crush

Shell 900 g (2 lb) fresh peas. Bring a saucepan of lightly salted water to the boil. Add the peas, 1 tsp of caster sugar, 2 peeled garlic cloves and a small bunch fresh mint. Cook for 8–10 minutes until tender. Drain well, reserving 6 Tbsp of cooking water, and return the peas to the saucepan. Discard the mint. Add the reserved cooking water and 2 Tbsp of olive oil. Mash until smooth and creamy. Pile into a heatproof dish and sprinkle with fresh mint to serve with fish or chicken. Can be served cold as a dip.

Chapter 7 Fruiting and flowering vegetables

This group of plants produces some of the most colourful and interesting vegetables you can grow in your garden. Not only is the foliage bushy and lush, the flowers are attractive and once the fruits form they offer a riot of colour and ornamental interest to any plot. While there are other varieties of vegetables that would fit into this chapter, I'm concentrating on the hardier varieties that are suitable for outdoor planting. If you have a greenhouse, you will be able to grow less hardy and more heat-loving varieties of these vegetables.

☠ Pests and diseases

Birds and mice: see page 58.

Blackfly: see page 58.

Corn smut: in hot and dry weather, galls containing black spores appear on the cobs and stalks. Cut off and destroy the galls before they burst. Burn or destroy all plants and avoid growing sweetcorn on this site for three years.

Cucumber mosaic virus: common and serious disease spread by greenfly. The leaves become puckered and mottled with yellow and dark green patches, and eventually the plant withers and dies. Destroy all affected plants, and wash hands and tools thoroughly to prevent transmission. Take relevant greenfly precautions to prevent an attack (see page 58).

Frit fly: maggots burrow into the seedlings and cause stunted growth and development. Plants should be removed and destroyed. Some preventative preparations are available, but this is quite a rare condition.

Potato blight: see page 21.

Potato (cyst) eelworm: see page 21.

Slugs and snails: see page 39.

Courgette, Marrow and Summer squash
Cucurbita pepo

👁 At-a-glance

Plant: early summer.

Ideal growing conditions: sheltered, sunny site; rich, well-manured, well-drained soil; lots of water.

Harvest: midsummer onwards.

All members of the cucurbit family, courgettes are simply small marrows, (although there are special marrow varieties that produce small fruit). This means you can get two different crops from the same plant if you let a few mature to full size. Both courgettes and marrows should be eaten fresh as they are very watery, soon dehydrate and don't store well. You'll find several types of summer squash to choose from – their growing habits and culinary uses match courgettes and marrows. These plants are half-hardy and need sunshine and shelter, and a good supply of water and nutrients. The trailing stalks and foliage produce lovely flowers before the fruit forms, and they make an attractive addition to any plot. In fact, the flowers are tasty too, and are often dipped in batter and deep-fried as a delicacy in their own right. You can grow all these cucurbits from seed – either in modules or directly into the soil – or you will find ready-sprouted seedlings in the nursery or garden centre.

✐ Crop planner
Choose a sunny site, protected from strong winds. Make sure the soil is rich in organic matter and well drained. No variety is hardy, so they should be planted out when there is no danger of a frost.

Most households will only need a few plants, so prepare only a few planting stations. Expected yield per plant is about 16 courgettes or small squash, or 4 marrows or large squash. Approximate time from sowing to harvesting is 12–14 weeks.

✿ Varieties
Courgette
'Defender': dark green, lightly flecked with paler green; has good disease resistance.
'Jemmer': bright yellow, high-yielding variety with a sweet flavour.
'Rondo di Nizza': small, round, striped Italian variety.
Marrow
'Green Bush': well-known variety; suitable for courgettes, but will grow to a large, striped marrow.
'Long Green Trailing': traditional pale- and green-striped fruit form on a trailing vine of leaves and stems.
Summer squash
'Patty Pan': a pretty mini squash variety, with yellow, white or pale green skin, and shaped like a flying saucer. Attractive to look at.
'Vegetable Spaghetti': pale yellow squash, cylindrical in shape, with unusual flesh that cooks like spaghetti.

✇ Tips and techniques
Plants can be raised in modules in late spring, but for sowing directly into the soil wait until the danger of a frost has passed. Soak the seeds overnight to speed up germination. Make a hole about 2.5 cm (1 in) deep and plant three seeds close together. Cover with soil and then place a large jam jar or small cloche on top until the seeds have germinated. Allow 60–90 cm (2–3 ft) between stations depending on variety. Scatter slug pellets around or similar deterrent. When the first true leaves have formed, thin out to leave the strongest seedling. Discard the thinnings. Renew slug pellets (or whatever deterrent you have used).

Keep weeded and water generously around the seedlings, not on them.

Bush types can be allowed to spread themselves, while trailing varieties may need trimming and training; if they begin to sprawl and take over, simply peg at regular intervals to hold in shape.

Once the fruits start to swell, feed with a high potash feed every 2 weeks. Rest marrows and large squash on upturned terracotta plant saucers or ceramic tiles to prevent them rotting and being attacked by slugs.

♦ Possible problems
Generally trouble-free. Can be prone to slug damage, but cucumber mosaic virus is the most common disease (see page 67).

Chapter 7: Fruiting and flowering vegetables

Harvesting and storing

All fruits can be harvested by cutting them off the stalks using a sharp knife about 2 cm (¾ in) away from the fruit. For courgettes, cut when the fruits are still young or about 10 cm (4 in) long. They are best cut and used straightaway, although they will keep for a few days in the fridge. Marrows are best eaten in the summer, when about 23–30 cm (9–12 in) long. When ready, the skin will yield to gentle pressure when gently squeezed. A few late marrows can be left until early October, but should be harvested before the frosts start. If left this long on the plant, marrows will store for several weeks hung in nets in an airy, frost-free place.

Large varieties of summer squash should be ready for picking in July – look for the stem beginning to split as an indicator that they are ready to pick. The skin should be soft enough to be pierced easily with a round-bladed knife. Use as soon as possible, but they can be stored for a couple of weeks in a cool, dark place. Mini varieties should be treated like courgettes.

Preparation and cooking

Courgettes and mini squash, like 'Patty Pan', require washing and trimming before cooking. They can be sliced or diced and pan-fried. Mini squash look attractive cut in half widthways, and baby courgettes lengthways. To boil, cook in a minimal amount of lightly salted boiling water for about 5–8 minutes depending on size and thickness. They also steam well and will take about 10–15 minutes – this cooking method retains their colour and delicate flavour.

Peel older marrows before cooking, remove the seeds and fibre and cut into rings or chunks. The pieces will take about 7–8 minutes to cook in lightly salted boiling water, or 15–20 minutes to steam. Younger marrows don't need peeling, simply halve lengthways and scoop out the seeds and fibres. These are good for stuffing, either as rings or whole. Larger varieties of summer squash can be prepared in the same way as older marrows.

✱ Freezing: watery vegetables are not very suitable for freezing, but if firm and young the result will be satisfactory. Do not peel, and cut into 1 cm (½ in) thick slices. Blanch for 1 minute, drain and cool and pack in rigid containers between sheets of freezing paper. Keep for up to one year. Partially thaw and then fry in butter. Alternatively, cook the slices in butter before freezing, then thaw completely before reheating in a frying pan for 3–4 minutes until piping hot.

⏱ Short recipe: serves 4
Curried marrow fritters

Prepare a small marrow as described above. Remove the skin if preferred. Cut into 1 cm (½ in) thick slices and scoop out the seeds from each slice. Dust in plain flour seasoned with mild curry powder and salt and pepper. Pour vegetable oil into a deep frying pan, until it is about 2.5 cm (1 in) deep, heat and fry a few slices of marrow at a time for 2–3 minutes on each side until crisp and golden. Drain well and keep warm while cooking the other slices. Ideal served with mango chutney.

Chapter 7: Fruiting and flowering vegetables

Cucumber and Gherkin
Cucumbis sativus

Cucumbis sativus is a wild plant originating from India that has been cultivated, and now no salad is complete without it. You can grow greenhouse varieties that are longer and smoother skinned, but for the purposes of this book, I have looked at the hardier, tougher ridged-skin cucumbers that grow outdoors. Gherkins are small, ridged cucumbers that are ideal for pickling, but can be used as a vegetable in their own right. Apart from the usual dark green-skinned varieties, you may also find yellow or white cucumbers. Cucumber and gherkins can be raised from seed or from ready-sprouted seedlings.

✎ Crop planner

Choose a sunny site, protected from strong winds. Make sure the soil is rich in organic matter and well drained. No variety is hardy, so should be planted out when there is no danger of a frost.

Most households will not need more than a few plants so prepare only a few planting stations. Expected yield per plant is about 10 cucumbers. Approximate time from sowing to harvesting is 12–14 weeks.

✿ Varieties
Cucumber

'Burpless Tasty Green': a Japanese variety considered to be one of the best outdoor varieties, that is more like a greenhouse cucumber. Disease resistant and has a smooth skin, crisp, juicy texture and good flavour.
'Bush Champion': compact variety, good for limited space; pale, faint yellow stripe. Grows quickly and has good disease resistance.
'Crystal Lemon': round, lemon-like cucumber, with good flavour.
'Marketmore': dark green, ridge-type fruit that is suitable for for cooler climates. Good disease resistance.
Gherkin

'Fortos': good for an even-sized crop, making it the perfect choice for pickles.
'Gherkin' : fast-growing, high-yielding plant with lots of small, pimpled fruits.

ℚ Tips and techniques

Plants can be raised in modules in late spring, but for sowing directly into the soil wait until the danger of a frost has passed. Soak the seeds overnight to speed up germination. Make a hole about 2.5 cm (1 in) deep and plant a seed in the centre. Cover with soil and then place a large jam jar or small cloche on top until the seeds have germinated. Allow 75 cm (30 in) between stations. Scatter slug pellets around or similar deterrent. When the first six leaves have formed, pinch out the top to encourage the plant to bush out. Renew slug pellets or similar.

Keep weeded and water generously around the seedlings, not on them. Once the fruits start to swell, feed with a high-potash feed every 2 weeks.

♦ Possible problems

Relatively trouble-free, but slugs and snails can be devastating if they chew through the stems. Cucumber mosaic virus may be a possibility (see page 67).

⚬┥ Harvesting and storing

If left alone cucumbers will grow to huge sizes, but the flavour will deteriorate. Therefore, they are best cut when they reach the recommended size – depending on the variety – and this will usually be from the end of July to the middle of September. Pick gherkins when they are about 5–8 cm (2–3 in) long. If you pick cucumbers and gherkins frequently, you will encourage more fruit to form. As with all watery vegetables, they are best cut and used immediately. Large cucumbers will keep for 2–3 days in the fridge, but gherkins start to become rubbery quite quickly, so are best preserved or eaten the day they are picked.

🍴 Preparation and cooking

Cucumbers are usually eaten in salads. Wash and dry and trim off either end. Outdoor varieties of cucumber tend to have a coarser skin than greenhouse-grown crops, so you may need to peel off the skin using a vegetable peeler. If the cucumber is particularly seedy, cut in half lengthways, scoop out the seeds, then slice or dice. For cooking, the skin often becomes bitter, so remove before cooking. Prepared chunks of cucumber cook in lightly salted boiling water for 5–7 minutes, or will steam in about 10 minutes. Alternatively, peel and slice, and add to a stir fry for the last 2–3 minutes of cooking. Gherkins are perfect for pickling, or look great sliced in dainty salads or garnishes.

✳ Freezing: not suitable.

Pumpkin and Winter squash
Cucurbita maxima

👁 At-a-glance

Plant: late spring to early summer.

Ideal growing conditions: open, sunny site, protected from wind; rich soil, manured the previous autumn; plenty of water.

Harvest: autumn.

Closely related to the marrow, pumpkins and winter squash develop a hard skin when left to mature. They can be grown as a bush or trailing plant, but do take up quite a bit of space, and some varieties of pumpkin can reach 100 kg (220 lb) in weight, so read the variety description carefully! Winter squashes come in all shapes and sizes and will certainly be the talking point of any patch, but the plants do tend to sprawl so are not really suitable if space is an issue. Pumpkins and winter squash can be grown from seed or from ready-grown seedlings.

✍ Crop planner
Choose a sunny site, protected from strong winds. Make sure the soil is rich in organic matter and well drained; manure the previous autumn. No variety is hardy, so they should be planted out when there is no danger of a frost.

Most households will only need a few plants so prepare only a few planting stations. Expected yield per plant is about two–four pumpkins or squash, depending on size. Approximate time from sowing to harvesting is 12–14 weeks.

✿ Varieties
Pumpkin
'Atlantic Giant': the name speaks for itself! You'll need plenty of space for this huge, orange variety.
'Mars': pretty, small, rounded pumpkin with good flavour and dense yellow flesh. Gives a good crop and stores well.
'Triple Treat': smaller, orange, classic-shaped pumpkin with tasty flesh. Makes a good jack-o'-lantern for Halloween.

Winter squash
'Butterball': grows quickly and has sweet, soft-cooking, buttery, orange flesh.
'Crown Prince': greyish skin, has flesh that is nutty, sweet and delicious.
'Turk's Turban': has a multicoloured skin with splashes of orange, green and cream and is turban-shaped. Grown for its eye-catching, ornamental appeal.

❡ Tips and techniques
Plants can be raised in modules in late spring, but for sowing directly into the soil wait until the danger of a frost has passed. Soak the seeds overnight to speed up germination. Water sowing positions well. Make a hole about 2.5 cm (1 in) deep and plant three seeds close together. Cover with soil and then place a large jam jar or small cloche on top until the seeds have germinated. Allow 90 cm (36 in) between stations, or more if you are growing a large variety (check seed merchant's instructions). Scatter slug pellets around or similar deterrent. When the first true leaves have formed, thin out to leave the strongest seedling. Discard the thinnings. Renew slugs pellets or similar.

Keep weeded and water generously around the seedlings, not on them. Pumpkins need frequent watering in order to help the fruits develop. Once the fruits start to swell, feed with a high-potash feeder every 2 weeks. Stop watering and feeding once the fruit is mature.

Keep the plants well trained by staking the stems in a spiral round the plant, pinning the stem with wire pegs. For large pumpkin varieties, limit to one or two fruits per plant.

💣 Possible problems
Usually trouble-free, although cucumber mosaic virus can be a problem (see page 67). Slugs and snails are the most common pest.

Chapter 7: Fruiting and flowering vegetables

☛ **Harvesting and storing**

Allow to ripen on the ground until they have reached their mature colour. They will sound hollow when tapped and the stems will begin to split. Harvesting time is usually between September and October, depending on the variety. Cut with about 5 cm (2 in) of stem and make sure you've harvested the fruit before the first frosts. Before storing, place in a sunny position for about a week in order to harden the skin. For winter keeping, store in a dry, frost-free shed for later use.

Preparation and cooking

Traditionally pumpkin flesh is made into a purée and used as a mash, soup or sweet pie filling, but as with squash, it does make a colourful and earthy vegetable accompaniment. Depending on the size of the beast, you'll probably need quite a heavy-duty knife or cleaver to cut the pumpkin or squash in half. Scrape out the seeds and stringy membranes and cut into chunks (skin on) for slow-roasting around a meat joint – this will take about an hour.

Alternatively, slice off the skin and cut into small chunks. Cook in lightly salted water for 8–10 minutes before draining well and serving as a vegetable, or mashing with butter and a little nutmeg or passing through a sieve to make a purée. You can also roast chunks of pumpkin and squash without the skin, seasoned and sprinkled with olive oil and a little butter for about 40–50 minutes at 200°C/400°F/gas 6 until tender and slightly charred.

✱ **Freezing:** not recommended for freezing as the flesh tends to be too soft and watery on thawing. Best frozen in purée form for using as a pie filling or soup base. Store for up to 12 months and thaw and drain before using.

⏱ **Short recipe: serves 4**
Pumpkin, apple and blue cheese tarts

Preheat the oven at 200°C/400°F/gas 6. Spread four 13 cm (5 in) rounds of ready-rolled puff pastry, each seasoned with 3 Tbsp of thick pumpkin or squash purée. Place on a baking sheet. Arrange ½ thinly sliced eating apple on top of each round along with 50 g (2 oz) blue cheese. Sprinkle with a pinch of ground nutmeg and bake for about 25 minutes until crisp. Serve sprinkled with freshly chopped parsley.

Sweetcorn
Zea mays

👁 At-a-glance

Plant: early summer.

Ideal growing conditions: warm, sunny, sheltered position; well-drained soil, slightly acid, well manured the previous autumn.

Harvest: autumn.

This much-loved vegetable is a variety of the cereal, maize, which is able to cope with the cooler British climate. As well as producing a fine crop of succulent, sweet vegetables, the plant is easy to grow. It is tall with long, draping leaves and fine, feathery flowers that make an attractive display, although it does take up quite a bit of space. Corn cobs can be yellow, cream, brown, even black, and there are varieties to plant throughout the year, ranging from supersize cobs to mini corns suitable for stir-frying. Apart from being popular with humans, birds and mice are also partial to the crop, so you'll need to take appropriate precautions. Sweetcorn can be raised from seed or you may be able to buy seedlings from a nursery or garden centre.

✍ Crop planner
Choose a warm, sunny site that is sheltered from the wind. Make sure the soil is rich in organic matter and well drained. Manure the previous autumn and dig in fertilizer 2 weeks before sowing or planting. Sweetcorn is best planted in a block formation of shorter rows, in a square plot. This provides the best chances of pollination in the breeze.

Each plant normally produces one or two cobs. Approximate time from sowing to harvest is about 14–16 weeks.

✿ Varieties
'Conquest': an early variety that yields medium-sized yellow cobs that are supersweet in flavour. Has good cold weather resistance.
'Dickson': early to mature, medium-sized yellow cobs with excellent supersweet flavour. Tall growing plant.
'Minisweet F1': minature variety with supersweet corn cobs.
'Sundance F1': a traditional stockier variety, that is quick growing and crops in early to mid-season. Ideal for a cool climate.

✆ Tips and techniques
You can sow seeds indoors in mid-spring as directed on the seed packet. Subsequent seedlings should be hardened off before planting out in early summer. Plant out in a block formation about 30 cm (12 in) apart.

You can sow seeds directly outdoors in late spring or once the threat of frost has passed, but they will need protecting under cloches. Make drills about 2.5 cm (1 in) deep in a block formation, and plant two seeds about 30 cm (12 in) apart. Lightly cover with soil and place a cloche or other protective covering on top. Once large enough to handle, remove the weaker seedling of the two and discard. Cloches and coverings can be removed once the seedlings have five true leaves. Keep watered in dry weather, especially during flowering. Protect seedlings from birds by erecting netting or other devices.

Weed by hand, rather than using a hoe, in order to protect the shallow roots. In exposed areas, earth-up the bottoms of the stems with soil to increase stability. Remove any side shoots that form. Once the cobs start to swell, water with a high potash fertilizer every 2 weeks.

☄ Possible problems
Mice and birds may try to steal the seed. Frit flies and corn smut are other problems, but are uncommon (see page 67).

☛ Harvesting and storing
Cobs are ready for picking about 6 weeks after the silvery, silky tassels appear. The aim is to pick them before the sugar turns to starch to ensure they will be sweet and tender. The tassels will shrivel and turn brown as the seeds or kernels develop and change colour from light to deep yellow. Carefully pull back the covering leaves from the cob and gently press a fingernail into one of the kernels – if it exudes a milky liquid the cobs are perfectly ripe, and if there is no liquid, the cob is well past its prime. Twist the cobs or snap them off from the stems. Use quickly to prevent drying out and flavour loss.

Preparation and cooking

Strip off the outer leaves and silky strings. Cook whole in unsalted water for about 8 minutes – you can season lightly halfway through, but do not add at the beginning as this will toughen the kernels. You can also add a teaspoon of sugar to the water to develop the sweetness. Test for 'doneness' by pricking carefully with a skewer to see if the kernels are tender. Drain well and serve with black pepper and butter. You can either insert specially designed small forks at either end of the cob for easy picking up or use dessert forks. The kernels are simply bitten or gnawed off the cob to eat.

To strip the cobs you can remove the kernels before or after cooking: before cooking, strip them off with a knife. After cooking, you should be able to run a fork down the cob to remove them. Kernels add extra 'bite' to relishes and chutneys and they bottle well to be enjoyed in the winter months (see method on page 182).

✱ **Freezing:** sweetcorn freezes well. Select young cobs and prepare as above. Blanch for about 4 minutes, cool and dry. Either wrap whole and pack into containers or freezer bags, or strip kernels from the cobs as described above. Freeze for up to 12 months. Thaw whole cobs thoroughly before cooking for 6–7 minutes. Kernels can be cooked from frozen for about 5 minutes, or added directly to your recipe.

Sweetcorn and cheese flats

Cook and strip the kernels from a whole sweetcorn cob as directed above. Sift 150 g (5 oz) self-raising flour into a bowl and make a well in the centre. Gradually mix in 25 g (1 oz) grated Parmesan cheese, 1 medium egg yolk and the sweetcorn. Gradually blend in 250 ml (9 fl oz) whole milk and 50 g (2 oz) melted butter to form a thick, smooth batter. Whisk a medium egg white and fold into the batter. Brush a large frying pan with oil and heat until hot. Spoon tablespoonfuls of batter on to the pan and cook for about 2 minutes on each side. Keep cooked flats warm while using up all the batter.

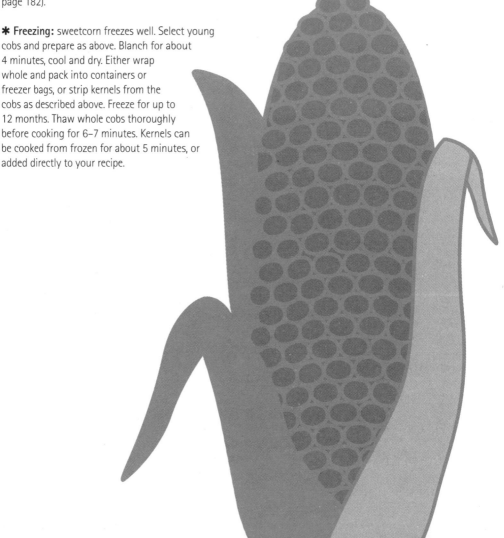

Tomato
Lycopersicon esculentum

👁 At-a-glance (outdoor varieties)

Plant: mid-spring.

Ideal growing conditions: very sunny (preferably south facing), sheltered site; light, slightly acid, well-drained soil, manured the previous autumn/ winter.

Harvest: late-summer onwards.

Like the home-grown carrot, a tomato fresh off the vine has a marked difference in flavour compared to a shop-bought one. The fresh smell and the juicy sweetness of the fruit just isn't the same if you haven't grown it yourself. While some varieties of tomatoes will only grow in the heat of a greenhouse, there are plenty that will grow outdoors. They come in all shapes, sizes and colours – large beefy ones, tiny sweet cherry-like, plum-shaped, pear-shaped, indented like pumpkins or smooth and rounded, and green, yellow, orange, red, purple and even striped in colour. Vine tomatoes grow off a sturdy main stem and need supporting on a frame or a cane. Bush varieties don't need supporting and are sprawling in habit, which makes them ideal for a restricted area; they are perfect for pots and planters. You can raise your plants from seed but it is easier to buy small plants from a nursery or garden centre.

✍ Crop planner

Outdoor tomatoes are a tender crop so choose the warmest, sunniest position for growing them. The soil should be well drained and hummus rich – they prefer soil slightly on the acid side (pH 5–7, see page 9). Just before planting, rake in a general-purpose fertilizer. The plants will need plenty of watering and feeding.

When choosing your potted seedlings, select ones with dark green foliage and sturdy stems about 20 cm (8 in) tall. Keep the seedlings well watered and in a warm, sheltered place to acclimatize them before planting out.

Each tomato plant should yield 900 g–1.8 kg (2–4 lb) fruit depending on variety and conditions. Approximate time from planting to fruiting is about 8 weeks if conditions are right.

✿ Varieties

'Gardener's Delight': a traditional cherry tomato variety that's been popular for many years. Heavy-cropping, bite-sized sweet tomatoes with a tangy flavour.

'Outdoor Girl': recommended as one of the best outdoor tomatoes. It ripens early, yields well and the fruit are slightly ribbed with a good flavour.

'Tornado': a bush tomato that produces lots of small–medium red fruit with good flavour.

'Yellow Perfection': a popular, traditional variety of sweet-tasting juicy yellow tomatoes. Excellent yield.

🌶 Possible problems

Outdoor tomatoes are usually trouble-free but they can be subject to potato blight, eelworm and mosaic virus (see pages 21 and 67).

❋ Tips and techniques

Usually, June is the right time for planting out, but if the weather is still on the cool side, wait a couple of weeks longer. Your tomato plants are ready to plant outside when the flowers of the first truss are beginning to open. Water the seedling just before planting, remove from the pot and make a hole in the ground just larger than the size of the soil ball.

Ensure that the top of the soil ball is set just below the soil surface. Plant each tomato at a distance of about 45 cm (18 in) apart depending on variety, in rows about 75 cm (30 in) apart, depending on variety.

If you are growing the traditional vine (or cordon) varieties, you will need to add a 1.5 m (5 ft) support for each plant, and tie the stem loosely to the cane. Continue to tie in the stem as it grows and remove any side shoots that appear. Once the plant reaches the top of the cane, pinch out the top. Bush tomatoes do not require support and you do not need to remove any shoots.

Keep tomatoes well watered and feed with a high-potash feed every 10 days once the fruit begins to swell.

⚬ Harvesting and storing

Outdoor tomatoes will be ready for picking from August through to October. Pick as they start to ripen. If tomatoes are left on the plants to ripen, the flavour is slightly better, but they will ripen successfully after picking. Hold the tomato in your hand and press the stalk with your fingers to break it neatly at the joint just above the fruit. Some recipes call for tomatoes still on the vine, so in these circumstances, snip off a few tomatoes still attached to the stalk.

Tomatoes will keep in the fridge for a few days once ripe, but as with most produce, they are best enjoyed as fresh as possible. If they have been chilled, allow them to come back to room temperature before eating.

Gather all the tomatoes if frost threatens and put them on a sunny windowsill to ripen them indoors. You can also put them in a paper bag or even in a drawer.

⫯ Cooking and preparation

Just before serving, wash, pat dry and remove the calyx and stalk. Fresh tomatoes are delicious served simply with a sprinkling of salt and black pepper, or a dressing of balsamic vinegar and olive oil; fresh basil and crusty bread would complete the meal. They also dry well. Tomatoes make great bases for soups, casseroles and sauces, and they can be grilled or baked. Green and red tomatoes are traditionally made into chutneys and ketchups (see pages 187 and 188).

🕐 Short recipe: serves 4
Fragrant honey-roasted tomatoes

Preheat the oven at 200ºC/400ºF/gas 6. Choose a selection of individual tomatoes or a few on the vine, about 450 g (1 lb) in weight. Wash and pat dry. Place in a baking dish (prick large tomatoes with a fork), season generously and drizzle with olive oil, honey and balsamic vinegar. Top with a few sprigs of rosemary, thyme and a few bay leaves. Roast for 10–15 minutes until the skin bursts and the fruits are tender. Serve with pork or sausages.

Chapter 8
Orchard fruit

When you think of an orchard, you think of quite a large area planted with mature trees, but it is possible to grow some orchard fruits on a small scale. You'll have to do a bit more research with these types of fruit and check exactly what variety you're buying in order to make sure you get the right specimen for your garden. Look at the rootstock as an indicator of tree size, and above all else, if in doubt, ask a specialist at the nursery or garden centre.

You also need to know that you often can't have just one tree. Quite a few varieties need at least one companion tree that flowers at the same time in order to pollinate it and bear fruit. My 'Lord Derby' cooking apple tree is partially self-fertile and has fruited by itself every year so far. Sometimes a neighbouring garden can have an appropriate variety, so it's worth asking around or having a look over the fence.

Quite a few novice gardeners feel a bit nervous about pruning, and fruit trees do require some routine maintenance. I remember the first time we tackled our old tree; it had been a bit neglected and I was convinced we'd killed it after the first pruning, but of course we hadn't, and it fruited even better the following year. Take some time to think about what you're trying to achieve by pruning before you start snipping – some pruning techniques simply keep the tree in shape or remove damaged branches, while others encourage new growth and a new crop. You'll need to know on which wood – old or new – the fruit forms, otherwise you may cut off the wrong branches and be deprived of a season's fruit. I've only been able to include a little information about pruning. It is worthwhile asking a specialist for advice or sourcing further information.

☠ Pests and diseases
Aphids: see page 59.
Brown rot: a fungus that affects most tree fruits and forms brown, bruised patches with white rings of fungus on the fruit. Common in summer and during storage. Discard all damaged fruit and remove dead shoots when pruning. Store only the soundest of fruit.
Canker: there are two types of canker: the first attacks the trunks and branches of apple and pear trees causing the bark to shrink and expose the inner

wood. Destroy infected spurs and small branches, and pare away diseased areas on larger branches, then seal with an appropriate medium (seek expert advice). The second type, bacterial canker, is a very serious disease that can affect cherries, plums, gages and damsons, causing affected areas to ooze a gumlike substance. It usually strikes in autumn and winter, but it can occur at any time. Destroy infected branches and seal the wood. Chemical treatments for both cankers are also available.
Fire blight: a serious bacterial disease that can affect most orchard fruits, causing the leaves to brown and wither, and the shoots to die around about flowering time. Always seek professional advice if an attack occurs. Usually branches have to be removed to 90 cm (3 ft) below the infection or the whole tree may have to be destroyed.
Moths: Codling moths: in July and August the moth's caterpillars are the main cause of 'maggot-ridden' apples and pears, causing damage around the core and into the flesh. Traps are available to catch the moths before they lay their eggs, or preventative sprays can also be found. **Winter moths** affect apple foliage, flowers and tiny fruit in spring. Can be sprayed with Derris, or chemical sprays are also available.
Pear midges: these can affect the same tree time after time. Small, orange-white maggots eat away at the tiny fruits causing them to malform and drop. Destroy infected fruit to reduce the risk of another attack.
Scab: a fungal disease of pears and apples where dark greenish-brown patches appear on leaves, causing them to fall; the fruits develop cracking and dark brown scabs. It can occur during the growing season, especially in wetter areas. Burn diseased leaves and destroy affected fruit. Seek professional advice.
Silver leaf: a fungal disease of many fruits but especially plums, gages and damsons. The leaves turn silvery and the upper surface peels away. Infected branches show a brownish stain. Cut branches to at least 15 cm (6 in) behind where the stain ceases and seal the wound with a protective sealant. To reduce the risk of infection, never prune during the dormant season.
Wasps: there's not very much you can do to stop wasps attacking your fruit apart from pick it before it over-ripens and remove any rotting or decaying fruit that will attract them. Try setting 'honey traps' in another part of the garden to keep them away.

Apple
Malus domestica

◉ At-a-glance

Plant: October–March.

Ideal growing conditions: open, sunny position; well-prepared, fertile soil.

Prune: in summer – July and August; in winter – November–March.

Harvest: August–October.

Apples like a good balance of sun, rain and cool temperatures in order to develop the perfect taste, texture and colour. There are over 700 varieties ranging from apples with soft, sweet flesh ready for eating straight from the tree, through to the crisp and sour, more ideally suited to cooking. The earliest apples are ready for picking and eating in August, and the later ones can be stored right through until the following spring. I have an old 'Lord Derby' apple tree in my garden. The apples are quite big, green skinned with a mild flavour (similar to a 'Granny Smith'). The apples hold their shape very well when cooked and after freezing – sadly they don't seem to store very well. Apple trees are usually raised from saplings available from nurseries and garden centres.

✍ Crop planner

It can be daunting choosing a variety to grow, but if you go to a specialist nursery it is often possible to taste some of the different types available. You must think about pollination, because most apple trees need at least one other variety to pollinate them – you'll need other varieties that flower at the same time. There are also different rootstocks to look at. This determines how large the tree will grow; for example a tree with M27 rootstock will grow to about 1 m (3½ ft), an M26 tree to 3 m (10 ft), while the largest varieties have a rootstock of MM111 and can grow to at least 4 m (13 ft). If you have a small garden, you might want to consider a cordon that will need a wall to grow up, or you can grow dwarf varieties in large pots. For small trees in pots or cordons, it may be possible to protect blossoms with fleece if there is chance of a late frost. Large trees are difficult to protect – choose a late-flowering variety if the weather in your area is extreme. If you are unsure, seek advice from the nursery before purchasing.

When choosing your site, remember that the tree will be in the same position for several years, but an open, sunny site is preferable. Prepare the soil well by digging in plenty of organic matter.

✿ Varieties

'Blenheim Orange': ready for picking in early October, suitable for eating and cooking. Has pale greenish-yellow skin with crisp, dry, distinctively flavoured flesh. Requires two pollinators.

'Bramley's Seedling': this much-loved cooking apple has greenish-white flesh that cooks to a pulp and has a delicious acidic flavour. The apples are often irregular in shape and the skin is greenish-yellow, flushed with brownish-red. Ready for picking in mid-October, it then stores well. Needs two pollinators.

'Cox's Orange Pippin': the only self-fertile apple, this eating apple favourite has a sweet, fresh flavour and dullish green skin with faint red stripes and red flush on one side. The skin is aromatic and is also delicious to eat.

'Discovery': ready to pick in mid-August to mid-September. A crisp-textured eating apple with yellow skin flushed all over with bright red. These apples keep quite well.

'Fiesta': harvest from mid-September; good yielding, well flavoured eating apple with fruit that keeps well. The fruit is yellow skinned with a bright red blush.

'Lord Lambourne': harvest in late September to mid-November. Juicy eating apple with greenish-yellow skin, striped with red. Heavy cropping.

'Reverend W. Wilks': a cooking apple that's ready for harvest in early September. The fruit is large, green and has pale cream flesh with a crisp texture and acid flavour. Crops well and is a popular choice for small gardens.

๑ Tips and techniques

Plant young trees with bareroots between autumn and early spring, when the weather is favourable. Container-grown trees may be planted at any time unless the ground is frozen or waterlogged. Dig a hole one-third wider than the tree's root system and push in a stake firmly, just off-centre – it is advisable to stake young trees, especially if it is windy. If the tree is to be trained into a cordon, fit supports and wires securely before planting. Spread out the roots and carefully fill in with soil, firming to make sure the tree is stable. Using the soil mark as a guide, continue filling with soil until you have reached the correct depth. Apply a spacer to the stake and attach the tree to this using a buckle so that the cushion is between the stem and the stake. Make sure your newly planted tree doesn't dry out, and mulch around the bottom of the trunk each spring with organic matter.

Once the apples form, thin them out if the tree is overcropping – try to thin them so that none of the apples are touching. This can be done in spring and midsummer.

When it comes to pruning, some trees develop fruit on the tips. In winter, cut back the long, thin branch leaders to a strong growth bud. Other trees fruit on older wood and produce spurs. For these trees, winter pruning involves cutting out weaker stems or dead branches, and keeping a good shape. Larger, older trees, like mine, only require pruning in winter. More vigorous growing varieties or those in a confined growing pattern need a summer pruning as well. Always follow the aftercare advice and maintenance routine that is supplied with your tree for the best results.

☙ Possible problems

Apple trees can be susceptible to several ailments but the most common are wasps, birds and codling moths, along with canker disease (see page 77).

☙ Harvesting and storing

To pick an apple, put the palm of your hand underneath it and then lift and gently twist the apple at the same time; if it is ripe it should come away easily with the stalk attached. Fruit for storage should not be over-ripe, bruised or marked with insect or bird damage, and should be handled carefully.

Apples for immediate use are best stored in the fridge for up to 2 weeks or in a cool, airy place, as they will deteriorate in warm conditions. They produce ethylene gas that will spoil other fruit, so store on their own. Another reason for storing apples separately is that they also give off an odour that may flavour other food. Only late-season apples will store over the winter months, mid-season varieties will only keep for a few weeks. When storing, the apples must be in perfect condition to start with – remember the saying that one bad apple can ruin a whole box – it's true! Wrap each apple individually in newspaper or specialist oiled paper (available from horticultural suppliers) and lay in a single layer, paper folds downwards, on aerated shelves or in a ventilated box. Keep in a cool, dark place – 7°C (45°F) minimum is ideal – and check regularly. Avoid putting different varieties in the same box.

Apples can also be stored in open fibre trays, like big egg boxes, unwrapped. These can be purchased from specialists or you may be able to get hold of some from your greengrocer. The advantage of this method is that the trays can be stacked one on top of the other, saving space and making it easier to check for signs of deterioration. Keep as for boxed apples above. You can also store apples in plastic bags ventilated with several holes – make the holes before you put the apples in the bag to avoid damaging

them! – and loosely tie the top to allow air to circulate. Try to store as flat as possible on ventilated shelves as above.

⫶ Preparation, cooking and serving suggestions

Apples for eating whole should be washed and dried just before serving. For other uses, peel, if preferred, then slice out the core using a special coring tool, or quarter and cut out with a small knife. Cut into chunks, wedges or slices depending on purpose, and sprinkle with lemon juice to prevent browning.

Cooking apples should be peeled, cored and cut up, depending on usage. A little lemon juice sprinkled over will help preserve the colour during cooking.

To bake cooking apples whole, preheat the oven to 200°C/400°F/gas 6. Carefully slit the skin all the way round the middle of the apples, then core and fill with butter, mixed spices and sugar. Put in a dish with a little water or mulled wine, cover with foil (make a vent to allow steam to escape) and bake for 45 minutes–1 hour, depending on size, until tender. Serve with custard.

To pulp cooking apples, peel and core them and cut into chunks. Put in a saucepan with a the juice of 1 lemon and a little water (approximately 2 Tbsp for 900 g (2 lb) apples). Bring to the boil, then simmer gently until the apples have softened and thickened to a pulp – how long you cook them for depends on how much texture you want in the finished dish. To serve hot, stir in sugar and a knob of butter to taste – approximately 75 g (3 oz) caster sugar per 450 g (1 lb) apples. To serve cold, add the butter while the apple is still warm and then allow to cool before sweetening. Push through a nylon sieve to make a smooth purée or apple sauce to go with roast pork or gammon.

✳ **Freezing:** peel, core and slice. Put the slices in cold water containing 1 Tbsp of salt to every 1.2 L (2 pt) cold water to prevent discolouration. Rinse before blanching in boiling water for 30 seconds, drain well and cool. Open-freeze on lined trays until frozen and then pack into freezer bags or containers. Keep for up to 12 months. Can be used straight from the freezer in pies, compôtes, etc.

To freeze cooked stewed or puréed apple, allow it to cool and then pack into freezer containers. It will keep for up to 12 months. Defrost in the refrigerator overnight and use in strudels, pies, puddings, sauces, etc.

Cherry
Prunus species

👁 At-a-glance

Plant: October–March.

Ideal growing conditions: very sunny (preferably south facing) site; light, well-drained, fertile soil.

Prune: sour cherries – spring and summer; sweet cherries – summer.

Harvest: July–September.

I can remember a huge cherry tree at the bottom of the garden in our first family home. It was covered in billows of pink blossom, and while I can't remember the flavour of the cherries, I do remember the heartbreak one year when the birds got there before my parents did! Cherry trees are big and for this reason have not been so popular of late, and it is difficult to protect the fruit from the birds. However, there are now several varieties of smaller trees that take up less space and can be netted. You'll find sweet cherry varieties for eating (it is best to choose a self-fertile variety because it is more complicated trying to pollinate a cherry tree than other orchard fruit), and sour varieties for cooking and preserving. The latter are self-fertile so you'll only need one tree, they are more hardy and are most often the smallest trees – the best choice for a garden with limited space. Cherry trees are usually raised from saplings available from nurseries and garden centres.

✍ Crop planner

Both sweet and sour varieties of cherry trees like the sun and warmth, so a south-facing spot is ideal. The soil needs to be well drained but able to retain some moisture – however it should not be waterlogged. Mulch with organic matter to help improve moisture levels in the soil and provide the tree with nutrients. The soil needs to be deep as well, especially if you're planting a large cherry variety – the roots will need to grow a long way down to give good anchorage.

Look out for different rootstocks: 'Colt' is a semi-dwarfing stock suitable for bush or fan training and is the choice for a small garden, while 'Malling F12/1' will provide the standard vigorous growing tree for planting where there is plenty of space. If you are unsure, seek advice before purchasing.

✿ Varieties

'Morello': the most well known of the sour or acid cherries. Perfect for cooking, the dark red, rounded, large fruits are ready to harvest in August–September. Self-fertile.

'Stella': a dark red, sweet cherry with an excellent flavour; it is self-fertile and fruits from late July.

'Sunburst': a good-quality, black eating cherry with large fruits. It is self-fertile and fruits from late July.

⚘ Tips and techniques

The preparation and planting instructions are the same as for apples (see page 78). Cherry trees also have the same watering and mulching requirements as apple trees, but they do not need to be thinned. As the fruits begin to colour, protect the tree from birds by draping netting over the tree if possible, otherwise you'll have to get your timing exactly right and harvest the cherries before the birds flock down.

Sweet cherry trees require little pruning apart from removing dead or damaged wood or crossing branches. The fruit forms on spurs on two-year-old and more mature wood. Mature trees require summer pruning to restrict foliage and encourage fruit buds to form. When being trained as a fan, the new growth should be cut back to five leaves each summer. Take out all the new shoots that prevent the tree fitting snugly against the wall and that shoot out towards you.

Sour cherries grow on one-year-old wood, so remove wood each year to encourage new growth. Once the fruit is harvested, cut back the branches where the fruit has been to a suitable point near its base. Cut back dead or damaged wood or crossing branches. In early summer, reduce the number of new shoots to about one every 7 cm (3 in).

Always remove any shoots from the main trunk or the bottom of the tree – these shoots are called 'water shoots'.

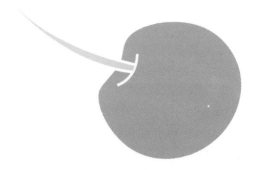

Possible problems

Birds are the biggest pest, while aphids may also attack. Canker, silver leaf and brown rot are the most common diseases (see page 77).

Harvesting and storing

Sweet cherries can be easily pulled off the stalks by hand – for the most successful harvest, try to choose a cool time of the day so that the leaves aren't wilting and dropping over the fruit. Sour cherries should be cut off with the stalk intact to prevent damage. Both types should either be eaten or used in cooking on the same day as picking for best results, but will keep unwashed for 2–3 days in the fridge if necessary.

Preparation, cooking and serving suggestions

A bowl of sweet, ripe cherries, with their delicious flavour, makes a truly summery dessert. Just wash and pat dry. To add them to fruit salads and punches and to make a topping for summer desserts, pit using a cherry stoner (do this over a bowl to catch the fruit and the juice so that nothing gets wasted). Cherries go very well with soft cheeses, chocolate, almonds and berry fruits.

Sour cherries are used for cooking and preserving. Prepare as above, then remove the stalks and the stones if appropriate to the recipe – for bottling it is better to leave the stone in so that the shape is retained. Sour cherries make wonderful jams and preserves, and can be poached in red wine with spices and sugar, then served hot or cold with whipped cream for dessert. Preserved in sugar syrup and alcohol such as brandy, cherries will keep well into the winter months and can be spooned over ice cream, rice pudding or crêpes for an indulgent reminder of the summer.

✱ Freezing: cherries can be frozen in the same way as raspberries (see page 92), but they do lose some of their texture once thawed. Cooked cherries can be frozen successfully like stewed apple (see page 79).

Pear
Pyrus communis

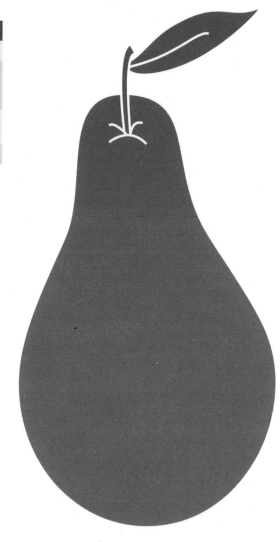

👁 At-a-glance

Plant: November–March.

Ideal growing conditions: warm, sunny, sheltered position; well-drained soil but moisture retentive and well manured.

Prune: in summer – July; in winter – November–February.

Harvest: August to October.

Pears need more sun and water than apples. They flower earlier so are best located in a sheltered position in case of a late frost, but it is best to choose a late-flowering variety for good results. Pears like to be pruned much more than apples, but, like apples, they can be trained into any shape; they will grow flat against a wall or in a tub if space is short. Pears are not self-fertile, so you must make sure that you have at least two compatible trees that flower at the same time in order to make them fruit. Different varieties fruit from August through to the end of December. Pear trees are usually raised from saplings available from nurseries and garden centres.

✍ Crop planner

The same considerations about pollination apply as for apple trees (see page 78). When it comes to rootstock, pear trees are much more vigorous than apple trees, and are usually grown on quince rootstock that makes smaller trees. For example, 'Quince C' rootstock gives the smallest trees and 'Quince A' is semi-vigorous in growing habit. It is best to seek specialist advice with regards to suitability and growing habit for your garden.

When choosing your site, remember that the tree will be in the same position for several years. An open, sunny site is preferable, and the soil should have good drainage, but be moisture retentive. Prepare the soil well by digging in plenty of organic matter.

✿ Varieties

'Beth': pale yellow-skinned pear with flecks of russet brown. Small to medium-sized with a rich, sweet flavour and creamy soft flesh. Crops well from mid- to late September.

'Concorde': pale green, medium to large, classic-shaped fruit with excellent flavour and firm texture. Crops well from late September –January.

'Conference': long, thin distinctive-shaped pear; firm flesh and stores well. It is reliable and partially self-fertile. Crops late October–December.

'Doyenne du Comice' or 'Comice': means 'top of the show'. Broad, blunt pear with greenish-yellow skin marked with russet brown to red. Juicy, sweet and aromatic. Needs to be pollinated by two other varieties for a good crop. Crops mid-October to December.

'Williams Bon Chretien': pale yellow-skinned with a faint red blush. Medium-sized, squat-shaped pears with white, soft and juicy flesh. A poor storer with short cropping season from September.

✪ Tips and techniques

The preparation and planting instructions are the same as for apples (see page 78). They require the same watering, mulching and thinning also.

When it comes to pruning, most pear trees produce spurs, so they fruit on wood older than 2 years, and new growth can be cut back by about a third of its original length in the first winter. Once the tree is established you'll need to prune in order to maintain its shape. In the summer, new growth at the ends of permanent branches can be cut back to five or six leaves, and the small stems or 'laterals' coming from these branches can be cut back to three leaves. During winter, cut out any areas that become intertwined with spurs and remove weak, dead or damaged growth. Always follow the aftercare advice and maintenance routine that is supplied with your tree for best results.

✪ Possible problems

Pear trees are susceptible to several pests and diseases such as aphids, codling moths and pear midges, along with fire bright, canker, scab and brown rot (see page 77).

✪ Harvesting and storing

Most pears ripen off the tree. Cut early varieties from the tree when the fruit is mature but still hard. Mid- and late-season fruits can be picked when the stalk comes away easily after gently twisting it from the tree.

Unlike apples, pears don't need wrapping. Arrange them in a single layer, not touching, on a shelf or tray. As with all produce for storing, they should be in perfect condition. They need frequent checking, and once the fruit begins to soften at the stalk end, bring indoors and store at about 16°C (61°F) for 2–3 days to complete the ripening.

✪ Preparation, cooking and serving suggestions

Dessert pear varieties simply need to be washed and patted dry. If the skin is tough, it is better peeled. Once the flesh is cut it is best eaten quickly before it discolours, otherwise, brush lightly with lemon juice to keep for a short while. For cooking, peel using a stainless steel knife or vegetable peeler and brush with lemon juice if necessary.

To poach whole pears, remove the blossom end but leave the stalk end intact – simply scrape the stalk area to remove the skin. Alternatively, cut in half and scoop out the core using a teaspoon and pull out the woody strings that run up to the stalk. Whole pears will take about 25 minutes to cook through, and halves about 15 minutes.

Pears can be baked in the same way as apples (see page 79), although they are better cut in half. Use pears in chutneys, jams, pickles and wine-making. They can also be dried.

✱ **Freezing:** uncooked pears are not recommended for freezing as they discolour and are very watery after thawing. Best made into a purée or cooked in sugar like apples (see page 79).

Plum, Gage and Damson
Prunus species

◉ At-a-glance

Plant: November–March.

Ideal growing conditions: sunny, sheltered site; non-acid, fertile and moisture-retentive soil, but can tolerate drier soil better than other orchard fruits.

Prune: summer.

Harvest: end of July–October.

These rich-flavoured fruits can be grown in much the same way as pears. In general, they like sun, warmth, shelter and good drainage. They flower early so choose a late variety suitable for a more extreme climate if you have late frosts – consult your local nursery or have a look round to see which varieties your neighbours grow.

Plums and gages are mainly grown as trees or bushes of different shapes (e.g. a pyramid), and there are many varieties suitable for a small garden. There are self-fertile specimens as well as ones that need pollination from another variety. The damson is the hardiest variety and will thrive in the wettest areas, where other plums will find it difficult; it is also self-fertile. Damsons make the bushiest tree and are often grown as hedges to save space. Plums and gages can be rich red to purple in colour, or green to golden yellow depending on variety. Plum, gage and damson trees are usually raised from saplings available from nurseries and garden centres.

✍ Crop planner

Choose an open sunny site, but not in an area where there is chance of a late frost. In a cooler climate it would be better to choose a site next to a sunny wall for more protection. Make sure the soil is fertile and moisture retentive by digging in plenty of organic material. As with apples and pears, there are different rootstocks to consider when thinking about the size of tree you plant. For example, 'Pixy' rootstock gives a dwarf tree suitable for a small garden, and 'St Julien A' is a medium-sized tree of around 2.2–4 m (7–13 ft), while trees over 4.5 m (15 ft) come from 'Brompton' and 'Myrobalan B' rootstock.

✿ Varieties

'Cambridge Gage': deliciously flavoured, small, yellow-green juicy fruit for eating or cooking; moderate cropping in late August–early September. Partially self-fertile.

'Czar': deep purple cooking plum with good, acidic flavour, which ripens early in August. Self-fertile.

'Marjorie's Seedling': a plum for eating and cooking, ready to pick towards the end of September–mid-October. Purple skin with deep yellow flesh and a good balance of sweet/acidic flavour. Self-fertile.

'Merryweather Damson': – dark blue, juicy acidic fruit with excellent flavour for cooking. It fruits in late July and is self-fertile.

'Oullins Golden Gage': dessert gage with sweetly flavoured, large, yellow, round fruits with green spots. Ripens in mid-August. Self-fertile.

'Victoria': the foodie's favourite. The most well-known plum with pale red skin and juicy golden flesh suitable for eating and cooking. It crops well in late August–September and is self-fertile.

❈ Tips and techniques

The preparation and planting instructions are the same as for apples (see page 78). They require the same watering and mulching also. If the fruit yield is heavy, start thinning the fruit as soon as the stones form until about 5 cm (2 in) apart.

Prune in the summer to lower the risk of infection by silver leaf (see page 77), especially in cooler climates. Plum trees produce fruit at the base of one-year-old shoots, as well as on wood and spurs that are 2 years old. Once they have been trained, they require less pruning than pears or apples, and simply need to be kept in shape. Cut back any retained new growth to six leaves. Remove crossing or overcrowded branches along with any diseased or damaged wood by taking it back to healthy wood.

Fan-shaped trees growing against a wall need a bit more attention. Take out all the new shoots that prevent the tree fitting snugly against the wall and that shoot out towards you. After the tree has fruited in the autumn, cut back the leaves of all the side shoots that were shortened to six leaves earlier in the summer.

🍸 Possible problems

Wasps and birds can be a problem, as well as aphids and winter moths. More problematical diseases are silver leaf, canker and brown rot (see page 77).

☞ Harvesting and storing

Harvest time for plums and greengages is August–September. Pick them for cooking, preserving and freezing before they are fully ripe. For eating, leave them on the tree to ripen and they will be sweeter for it. If the weather is excessively wet, it is advisable to pick the fruit to avoid the skins splitting. Pull the fruit away from the tree with the stalk intact. Damsons should be ready to harvest in late August/September through to October. Pick by the stalks to avoid bruising. All of these fruits are best used as soon after picking as possible.

🍴 Preparation, cooking and serving suggestions

Sweet juicy plums and gages are delicious eaten as a fresh fruit dessert. Wash and wipe dry before eating.

For cooking, cut along the indented part of the fruit and twist the halves apart; prise out the stone with the tip of a knife. Stew in a little water with some sugar to taste for about 10 minutes until soft. They can be halved and poached submerged in a wine or sugar syrup by covering and cooking gently for 7–8 minutes. Plums and gages are particularly suited to be paired with cream and soft cheese, and with the flavours of almond and cinnamon.

Damsons require cooking as they are less sweet and juicy. They are traditionally used in making jams and preserves, but do make a rich and fruity pie filling or compôte. Prepare as for plums, but if the damsons are small you will have to use them whole and skim off the stones before serving. If you are unable to stone the fruit first, use 450 g (1 lb) damsons, which will take about 15 minutes to cook down in 600 ml (1 pt) water. Otherwise, cook the damsons in just enough water to prevent them drying and sticking for about 15–20 minutes for a good rich, compôte. They will need quite a bit more sugar than plums and greengages. If using more water, once you have removed the stones, thicken the juice with a cornflour or arrowroot paste to make a more substantial mixture. Temper the flavour by mixing with stewed apple if preferred.

❉ **Freezing:** avoid dry-packing plums, greengages and damsons as the skin will be tough once thawed. They are best prepared in halves with a heavy sugar syrup with added lemon juice or in cooked or puréed form (see page 79). Pack in rigid containers and freeze for up to 12 months.

This chapter includes some of the most delicious and attractive varieties of fruit that can be grown in the garden. I'm currently growing strawberries, alpine strawberries, raspberries, tay berries, redcurrants, blackcurrants and gooseberries and am looking forward to a wonderful harvest of flavours and jewel-like colours – providing I can get to them before the birds do! These fruits are, of course, delicious eaten fresh, but they freeze well and can be preserved by bottling or jam-making for enjoyment later in the year when fresh fruit is scarce.

Soft fruit species are relatively easy to grow providing they have sunshine, although partial shade will still offer some success. They prefer a cool climate and well-drained soil with plenty of water to help swell the fruits. Cane and bush fruits require pruning in order to establish and maintain a good cropping nature, and the actual wood cutting depends on whether the fruit forms on one-year-old wood or on older wood.

☠ Pests and diseases

Birds (and squirrels): see page 58.

Blackcurrant gall mite: a tiny mite that feeds inside the buds causing them to swell to the size of peas and prevents fruit setting. Pick off and destroy swollen buds. Always buy certified stock to try to prevent infestation in the first place.

Grey mould (*Botrytis cinerea*)**:** can affect all berries – they become covered in a dense grey mycelium that causes the fruit to rot. More prevalent in wet conditions and where excessive amounts of fertilizer have been used. Fungicide can be applied as a matter of routine from flower to ripening if desired.

Powdery mildew: affects gooseberries, raspberries and strawberries. Purple spots appear on the upper surfaces of the leaves, and underneath a white fungus forms. This can then spread to the fruit. Chemical treatments are available if desired. Remove diseased shoots in the autumn.

Raspberry beetle: small, pale brown beetles appear on raspberry, blackberry and hybrid berry bushes in late May and feed on new leaves and then on the flowers. Insecticide treatments are available, or spray with Derris.

Red spider mite: affects all types of fruit, but on strawberries and other soft fruits it sucks the sap from the leaves, leaving white spots. Eventually the leaves turn brown. Attacks are more prevalent in hot weather. Natural predators usually provide adequate control unless excessive amounts of other chemicals have been used.

Slugs: see page 58.

Blackberry and other hybrid berries
Rubus fruticosus and Rubus hybrids

👁 At-a-glance

Plant: November–March.

Ideal growing conditions: sunny spot; rich, fertile soil.

Prune: September–October.

Harvest: late summer/early autumn.

Often not as popular as other fruits to grow in the garden because blackberries are believed by many (including myself) to be better flavoured if they come wild from the hedgerows. Blackberries will grow in sun or partial shade, and although the plants are prolific and bushy, they produce fewer fruits than raspberries. They are easier to grow but more difficult to control – thornless varieties do not have such a vigorous growth habit and take up less space. Hybrids have been developed by crossing blackberry and raspberry plants to produce an assortment of berries of good flavour – loganberry, tay berry and boysenberry, to name only three. The loganberry is one of the most popular and successful of the hybrids; it has large, elongated fruits, with a drier texture and a delicious, slightly acidic flavour. The loganberry and tay berry are my preferred choice, and grow well in my garden. Blackberries and hybrids are grown from canes available from nurseries and garden centres.

✍ Crop planner
Prepare the site, soil and frame support structure as for raspberries (see page 92). Planting three blackberry or loganberry bushes should provide sufficient fruit for the average family.

✿ Varieties
'Fantasia': large, shiny black berries that have a good flavour. The stems are very thorny, and the season is late August–September.
'Loch Ness': elongated, shiny black berries, with thornless stems. Less flavour but juicy and makes good jam.

⍰ Tips and techniques
Plant during winter, or early spring if the weather is severe. Some hybrids will not survive winter planting, so check local advice for planting timings. Plant the canes about 3–5 m (10–16 ft) apart depending on how vigorous the variety. Don't plant the roots too deeply, spread them out in a shallow hole and cover with soil. Once planted, immediately cut the canes down to a bud about 23 cm (9 in) above ground. Keep mulched during spring and water in dry weather. Protect from birds as fruit forms.

In autumn, cut out all the old fruiting stems and tie in the new growth. This can be done in a variety of ways, but a fan shape is the easiest: fruiting canes (stems) are temporarily tied individually to the left and right of the main plant, while new canes are allowed to grow up the centre. Any excess canes are removed and once fruiting is over, these old canes are taken out and the new ones are tied in their place.

💣 Possible problems
See Raspberries on page 92.

⟿ Harvesting and storing
Blackberries fruit from July–September, according to variety, until the first frost comes, when superstition has it that the Devil spits on the berries. The best fruits form on the previous season's shoots. Pick carefully to avoid bruising and use quickly as the fruit soon deteriorates after picking. They will keep unwashed, loosely covered in the fridge for 24 hours if necessary.

Loganberries and tay berries ripen in August, midway between raspberries and blackberries. Pick when dry and deep dark red. Use them quickly whether eating fresh, preserving or cooking.

⍓ Preparation, cooking and serving suggestions
Unlike the raspberry, the whole blackberry fruit is eaten. When a raspberry is harvested, the white, conelike central core remains behind on the plant; with the blackberry, it comes away with the rest of the berry. Simply remove any hulls that remain and rinse the fruit carefully before eating or cooking. Traditionally, blackberries are mixed with apples to temper their intense flavour. They make wonderful pies, crumbles and tarts. Blackberry jam, jelly, cordial and vinegar are excellent ways to preserve their flavour all year round. Loganberries and tay berries are prepared and used in the same way as raspberries (see page 92).

✳ **Freezing:** see Freezing on page 92.

Blueberry
Vaccinium corymbosum

Plant: November–March.

Ideal growing conditions: sunny site; acid, free-draining, rich, fertile soil.

Prune: November–March.

Harvest: July–September (depending on variety).

The native wild bilberry, or blaeberry, has grown for years in the British Isles, but over the last decade or so, the American 'high bush' blueberry has become popular. A cultivated relative of the wild fruit, the plant produces bigger fruit in greater quantities and is an attractive addition to any garden. The blueberry plant needs lots of moist, acid soil to grow, and for this reason, it is often suggested that the plants are grown in pots. You will need to protect the plants from the birds, who will otherwise get to enjoy them instead of you! Blueberries are raised from plants available from nurseries and garden centres.

✐ Crop planner

Choose a sunny site, although light shade can be tolerated. The soil must be acidic (pH 4–5.5, see page 9) so add ericaceous compost to your soil as necessary. Fertilize the soil with sulphate of potash or sulphate of ammonia, and avoid those containing lime or calcium.

Blueberry bushes take a while to crop well, but after about five years an established bush can yield approximately 2.25 kg (5 lb) fruit.

✿ Varieties

'Bluecrop': most commonly grown and popular variety; it is a reasonably compact plant, ideal for limited growing space and pots. Lightish blue berries with good flavour ripen in early to mid-season.
'Colville': vigorous growing, spreading bush with good yields of large, light blue berries with good flavour, late in the season.
'Herbert': one of the best flavoured varieties; large, mid-blue berries that ripen in August. The bush grows vigorously but upright.

☯ Tips and techniques

Plant from late autumn to late winter when conditions are favourable, spacing bushes about 1.5 m (5 ft) apart, covering the roots with about 5 cm (2 in) soil. Mulch with acid compost or leaf mould. Do not allow the soil to become dry, and water with rain water for best results. Protect with netting to keep birds away from the fruit.

Blueberries grow on the second- or third-year wood stems, so do not prune until the first crop is complete. Then, in the following winter or early spring, cut out any dead or weak wood and take out up to one-third of the oldest stems to help promote new growth.

💣 Possible problems

Apart from birds, blueberries are usually trouble-free.

⌖ Harvesting and storing

Berries should be ready to pick from mid-July to September. Harvest over a few weeks when they are evenly blue and have a slight bloom. They will not ripen after harvest, so avoid any with a green tinge or reddish colour near the stem as this indicates that they are unripe. You'll need to go over each plant several times in order to make sure you harvest all the berries. As with all berries, eat them as soon after picking as you can. Otherwise, store unwashed in the fridge for 24 hours, if required, and wash just before using.

🍴 Preparation, cooking and serving suggestions

Perfect for eating raw, and only take a little light cooking in a minimal amount of liquid (about 3 minutes) to serve stewed. Delicious raw served with soft cheeses or clotted cream, and they are complemented by the flavours of lavender and rose. Ideal mixed with other berries, or can easily be added whole to batters and cake mixes. Blueberries make delicious preserves and are good for bottling or preserving in alcohol. They also make a pretty bluish-purple fruit vinegar.

✳ **Freezing:** blueberries freeze like raspberries (see page 92) and can be cooked straight from frozen; they do soften on defrosting if using uncooked.

Currant: Red, White and Black
Ribes sativum and Ribes nigrum

👁 At-a-glance

Plant: November–March.

Ideal growing conditions: sunny spot; rich, moisture-retentive, fertile soil.

Prune: winter and summer (depending on variety).

Harvest: June–August.

Rich in vitamin C and strongly flavoured, the hardy blackcurrant does well in any part of the country. It is easy to grow and lives for a long time. Blackcurrants like to be free-standing and are quite bushy, whereas red- and whitecurrants can be trained, making them a better choice if you are short on space, and they are just as easy to grow as blackcurrants. Currants are raised from bushes available from nurseries and garden centres.

✎ Crop planner

Choose a sunny site with rich, moisture-retentive soil. Blackcurrants will tolerate a light shade. The soil should be well prepared with plenty of well-rotted organic material added to it.

✿ Varieties
Blackcurrants
'Ben Lomond': popular variety, ripening in late July. The bushes are compact and require little pruning; they have a good resistance to the cold. The berries are well flavoured.
'Ben Sarek': good yields in late July from small compact bushes. The branches spread and require support from canes and strings. The berries are very large, glossy and have good flavour.
Redcurrants
'Laxton's No. 1': popular variety that fruits early; medium-sized bright red berries on long trusses with fair flavour.
'Rovada': good yields from early August of large scarlet berries on long trusses, and has good flavour.
Whitecurrants
'White Versailles': not so many varieties available, but this one has large, light yellow fruits that are juicy and sweet, and ripen in early July.

⚙ Tips and techniques
Plant the bushes between autumn and early spring when the weather is favourable. Set at intervals of between 1.2–1.5 m (4–5 ft) depending on variety. After planting blackcurrants, cut down all shoots to one bud to encourage new growth. For red- and whitecurrants, if there are any side shoots after planting, cut them back to one bud. Red- and whitecurrants produce suckers as they grow – these should be pulled off (not cut) the stem or root in June or July while the wood is soft.

Mulch all currants in spring with well-rotted organic matter as well as potassium (and nitrogen for blackcurrants) fertilizers. Water in dry weather but not as the fruit ripens as this may cause it to split. Protect currants with netting once the fruit forms.

Regular pruning is essential to maintain high yields. Red- and whitecurrants are usually grown in open-centre bushes but can be trained on wires as cordons or fans (for pruning see Gooseberry on page 91). The first winter after planting blackcurrants, remove any weak wood. Continue removing dead wood each winter along with up to one-third of the older wood so that new growth is encouraged. As a guide, new shoots are beige in colour, while older wood is grey and mature wood is black. Never reduce the length of shoots.

☄ Possible problems
Apart from birds, aphids, blackcurrant gall mite and grey mould may be a problem (see page 86).

⚘ Harvesting and storing
Pick blackcurrants when they are fully ripe – this will be about a week after they turn black. The ones at the top of the stems will be the ripest. Red- and whitecurrants need picking as soon as they ripen; they spoil quickly and do not keep for long, and will become difficult to pick cleanly if too ripe. Currants should be used as soon after picking as possible.

🍴 Preparation, cooking and serving suggestions
Like all soft fruits, handle currants as little as possible and only wash just before using. If you are making a purée then the currants can be cooked on the stalks, otherwise the best way to remove them is by running a fork down the length of the cluster. Carefully rinse the currants in a sieve or colander dipped in cold water and then drain well. Currants need little water to cook with, and sugar should be added to taste; blackcurrants are the most acidic of the currants and will require more sugar.

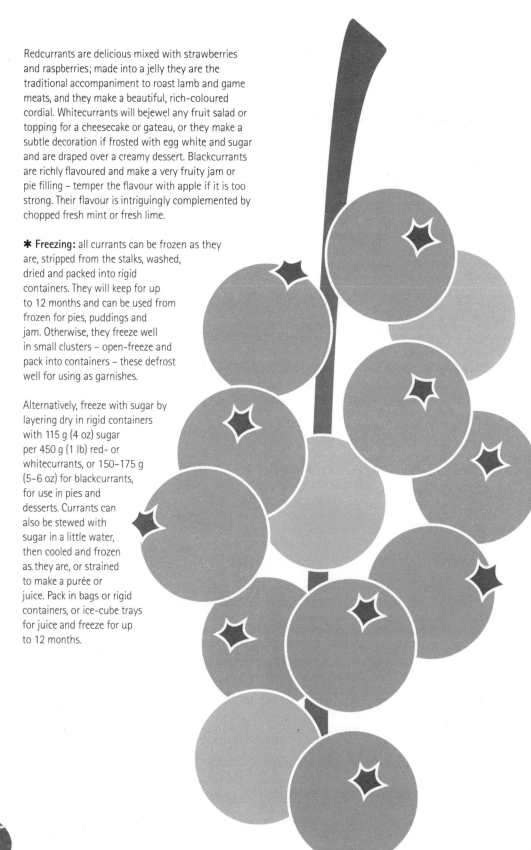

Redcurrants are delicious mixed with strawberries and raspberries; made into a jelly they are the traditional accompaniment to roast lamb and game meats, and they make a beautiful, rich-coloured cordial. Whitecurrants will bejewel any fruit salad or topping for a cheesecake or gateau, or they make a subtle decoration if frosted with egg white and sugar and are draped over a creamy dessert. Blackcurrants are richly flavoured and make a very fruity jam or pie filling – temper the flavour with apple if it is too strong. Their flavour is intriguingly complemented by chopped fresh mint or fresh lime.

✷ **Freezing:** all currants can be frozen as they are, stripped from the stalks, washed, dried and packed into rigid containers. They will keep for up to 12 months and can be used from frozen for pies, puddings and jam. Otherwise, they freeze well in small clusters – open-freeze and pack into containers – these defrost well for using as garnishes.

Alternatively, freeze with sugar by layering dry in rigid containers with 115 g (4 oz) sugar per 450 g (1 lb) red- or whitecurrants, or 150–175 g (5–6 oz) for blackcurrants, for use in pies and desserts. Currants can also be stewed with sugar in a little water, then cooled and frozen as, they are, or strained to make a purée or juice. Pack in bags or rigid containers, or ice-cube trays for juice and freeze for up to 12 months.

Gooseberry
Ribes uva-crispa

Plant: October–March.

Ideal growing conditions: open, cool/sunny site (needs shelter if very hot); rich, fertile soil.

Prune: winter and summer.

Harvest: May–August.

A native plant to northern Europe that's only really enjoyed in the UK. Dating back to Tudor times, gooseberry recipes for pies, tarts, fools and jellies can be found in abundance. They are one of the first berry fruits of the season. Gooseberries are easy to grow in bush form or can be trained more formally into cordons or standards. There are several varieties to choose from, some with sweet or sour berries, large or small in size, and white, yellow, green and red in colour. Some are more suited to jam- and wine-making, while others are better for eating fresh. Gooseberries are raised from small bushes.

✍ Crop planner
Choose an open sunny site, although they will tolerate light shade. The soil should be richly fertilized with well-rotted manure or compost.

✿ Varieties
'Careless': traditional, widely grown, large, whitish-green cooking berry; a mid-season plant that crops well. The flavour of the fruit is excellent.
'Leveller': greenish-yellow dessert berries, suitable for cooking. The berries are large and are one of the best for flavour.
'Whinham's Industry': a popular purplish-red dessert variety that also cooks well. The berries are large, hairy, sweet and juicy.

❋ Tips and techniques
Plant the bushes between autumn and early spring when the weather is favourable. Set the bushes about 1.5 m (5 ft) apart. Any side shoots should be cut back to one bud. Suckers should be pulled off (not cut) the stem or root in June or July while the wood is soft.

Take care when weeding around gooseberry bushes, because they are shallow rooted and easily damaged. Gooseberries require high potassium levels and regular mulching with well-rotted manure. New shoots are prone to bird damage and also need protecting from strong winds. Water in dry weather but not as the fruit ripens as this may cause it to split.

Gooseberry bushes require pruning to keep them in shape. In winter, aim to make an open framework of branches in a vase shape, by removing all shoots from the base, leaving just the main stem. Cut back the main shoots in the first and second years by about a third to left- and right-facing buds. After this, each year follow the same procedure to increase the number of branches in the main frame. Cut back new growth on the main stems by about half in winter, and reduce the side shoots on the remaining stems down to two buds. Remove damaged wood or crossing branches. Any central or other unwanted vigorous shoots that grow should be cut out from June onwards.

✦ Possible problems
Apart from birds, powdery mildew can be a problem (see page 86).

⚘ Harvesting and storing
Heavy-cropping plants should start to be thinned out from May onwards. The unripe picked fruit needn't be wasted as it will still be suitable for jam-making. The main harvesting depends on the variety but is usually from June–August; carefully pick the berries when they are beginning to yield to gentle pressure.

❘ Preparation, cooking and serving suggestions
To prepare the fruit for eating or cooking, top and tail (snip off the flower and stalk end) with scissors. Put in a colander and wash by dipping in cold water several times. Drain well and dry the berries. Cook in a small amount of water, covered, for 5–6 minutes until soft. If you plan to purée and strain gooseberries, it is unnecessary to top and tail the fruit before cooking. Gooseberries are traditionally mixed with custard and cream to make a fool. They make delicious jellies or cheesecakes, and are complemented by cooking with elderflowers.

❄ Freezing: gooseberries can be successfully frozen in different ways. Without sugar: prepare as for eating. Freeze on trays and then pack into freezer bags or rigid containers. Keep for up to 12 months. Cook from frozen for use in pies and puddings. With sugar: prepare as for eating, then layer dry in rigid containers with 115 g (4 oz) sugar per 450 g (1 lb) cooking gooseberries. To stew with sugar: cook the gooseberries in a little water with sugar to taste. Cool and freeze as is, or strain to make a purée; pack in freezer bags or rigid containers and freeze for up to 12 months.

Raspberry
Rubus idaeus

Raspberries grow well throughout the cooler parts of the northern hemisphere. Full sun will produce the best crop, but partially shaded sites are also suitable. Raspberries give a good yield and they freeze well. Different varieties fruit at different times: summer-fruiting from July and August, and autumn-fruiting from September to October. Raspberries take up space and need a supporting structure to keep them upright; you will also need to protect them from the birds. Raspberries are raised from canes.

✍ Crop planner

Choose an open sunny site, but unlike most fruits, partially shaded areas are also suitable. The soil should be fertile and moisture retentive but not waterlogged. Permanent supports need to be erected, and there are various systems you can adopt. A single row of posts and wires is the most straightforward: set a single row of stout posts, about 3 m (10 ft) apart, and run three lengths of wire or nylon string horizontally between them, about 75 cm (30 in), 1.1 m (3 ½ ft) and 1.5 m (5 ft) from the ground. The strings need to be taut and the posts secure in order to support the plants and prevent wind damage.

A 3 m (10 ft) single row of 6 canes will eventually yield between 2.7 kg (6 lb) and 4.5 kg (10 lb) raspberries.

✿ Varieties

'Autumn Bliss': a late-fruiting raspberry with large, pinkish-red fruit that has a firm texture and good flavour. The plants are sturdy and in a sheltered spot, may not require support.

'Glen Moy': a summer raspberry that crops heavily in July and is resistant to greenfly. The berries are quite large with a downy bloom. They have a good flavour.

'Malling Admiral': one of the best varieties with large, conical berries of excellent flavour and all-round usage. Lower-yielding but disease-resistant.

'Malling Jewel': increasingly popular variety with firm, dark red, conical berries. Slower to ripen but packed full of flavour. Grows in a compact shape, so good for container gardening.

✪ Tips and techniques

Plant dormant canes in autumn or early winter so that they establish quickly. Space them about 38–45 cm (15–18 in) apart, and in rows about 2 m (6 ft) apart. Spread out the roots evenly at a depth of 5–7 cm (2–3 in), and gently firm them in. After planting, immediately cut the canes to within 25 cm (10 in) of the ground. Pull off any suckers that appear out of the ground; mulch each spring either side of the canes, taking care not to bury them, and water in dry weather. Protect from birds as the fruit forms.

In autumn, cut all fruiting canes to the base. Tie in new canes to the wires. In late winter, cut off the tip of each cane to a bud about 18 cm (7 in) above the top wire. For autumn fruiting varieties, cut the fruiting canes to the ground in late winter.

⬥ Possible problems

Birds are the biggest problem, but also raspberry beetle and grey mould (see page 86).

⚭ Harvesting and storing

Pick raspberries when they are evenly and richly coloured. They should come away easily, leaving the white core behind on the stalk. Once picked, they won't keep very long, so eat or freeze as soon as possible after harvesting. Will keep unwashed in the refrigerator for 24 hours if required.

🍴 Preparation, cooking and serving suggestions

These fruits bruise easily so handle with care. Place in single layers in a colander and dip in cold water to rinse. Drain well and pat dry with kitchen paper before serving. Eat fresh with a squeeze of lemon juice, coarse white sugar and thick cream. To remove the seeds, whiz in a blender or food processor and then push through a nylon sieve using a wooden spoon, into a bowl. Sweeten with icing sugar, maple syrup, sugar syrup or honey. If serving hot, raspberries require minimal poaching in a little liquid and sugar before they go mushy; 2–3 minutes is all it takes to heat them through for a compôte. They go well with apples and pears for a pie filling. Use raspberries for mousses, creamy desserts, ice creams and sorbets, and jams, jellies and other preserves.

✳ Freezing: to freeze, wash and carefully pat dry as soon as possible after picking. Either pack straight into freezer bags or rigid containers, or open-freeze in single layers, with the berries side by side, on trays for packing later. Keep frozen for up to 12 months. Can be used straight from frozen, but they do hold up quite well once defrosted.

Chapter 9: Soft fruit

Strawberry
Fragaria x ananassa

👁 At-a-glance

Plant: late summer or early autumn.

Ideal growing conditions: open, sunny, site; fertile, well-drained soil.

Prune: none required.

Harvest: end of May–October (depending on variety).

Probably the favourite soft fruit to grow because it's so easy to maintain. There are many varieties that offer crops of berries from the end of May right through to October. Strawberry plants grow to form ground-covering mounds and can be used to make an informal edging to a plot, particularly alpine varieties which spread prolifically. Mid-season strawberries give a good crop in the first year, while early and late varieties need to be held back to crop in the second year. There are also perpetual varieties that fruit in the summer, then have a break, and fruit again in the autumn. Runners should be removed to conserve the plant's energy, but if you like, keep a few and pot them up for use next year. Strawberries are usually grown from plants bought from a nursery or garden centre or from runners obtained from mature plants. Alpine strawberries can be raised from seed and usually self seed to multiply.

✐ Crop planner

Choose an open sunny site where strawberries haven't been grown in the last three years. The soil should be richly fertile and well drained. Before planting, weed the area thoroughly and dig in plenty of well-rotted manure or compost and fork in a general-purpose fertilizer to finish. Slightly acidic soil with pH 6–6.5 is ideal (see page 9).

Yield per plant will vary depending on when the strawberries have been planted. For the heaviest cropping, about 450 g (1 lb) per plant, put in the ground the previous winter.

✿ Varieties

'Aromel': a perpetual variety with well-flavoured, large fruits.
'Cambridge Favourite': a widely grown, well-known, reliable variety. Mid-season, heavy-cropping, medium-sized, juicy, bright fruits with a fair flavour.
'Hapil': mid-season, good yield with excellent flavour.
'Honeoye': early crop with firm, glossy, well-flavoured, slightly acidic fruits.

ℚ Tips and techniques

In a cooler climate, plant strawberries in late summer or early autumn to give a better yield the following year. For later planting, take off flower heads in spring to allow the plants to establish before they bear fruit.

Using a trowel, make a 'V'-shaped hole in the ground about 15 cm (6 in) deep. Make holes at intervals of about 40 cm (16 in), and in rows spaced about 75 cm (30 in) apart. Put in the soil with the base of the central crown at soil level. As the plants begin to fruit the following year, place clean straw under the leaves and fruiting stems to keep the fruit off the ground.

Water regularly and keep the patch weed-free. If frost threatens during flowering, cover with polythene or cloches. Remove runners as they form and keep as new plants if desired. After fruiting, cut off all the old leaves and remove the straw.

● Possible problems

Birds, red spider mite, squirrels and slugs are the most common problems, but grey mould can occur (see page 86).

⚬ Harvesting and storing

Pick strawberries by the stalk to avoid bruising. Eat as soon as possible after picking, although they will keep unwashed in a dish for 2–3 days. Leave alpine strawberries to ripen fully to develop flavour, and eat on the same day as picking. Pick regularly to encourage more fruits to form.

ꭍ Preparation, cooking and serving suggestions

Unless using as a decoration or a dipper, remove the green calyx and stalk by carefully pulling it out (hulling). Rinse carefully in cold water, drain and pat dry before serving. Strawberries are best eaten fresh as they tend to go soft if cooked, but if you do want them hot, poach in a little sugar syrup for 4–5 minutes and serve warm spooned over ice cream.

Alpine strawberries can be prepared in the same way. Mix into other berries and currants and serve with thick cream and sugar. All varieties of strawberries make excellent jams, preserves and syrups, and perfectly combine with cream in ices, mousses and custards; they can also be dried.

✳ **Freezing:** freeze as for raspberries (see page 92), but strawberries do go very soft after defrosting and their flavour changes; they are best used up in sauces or folded into mousses and creams.

Recipes

Chilled beetroot and sour cream soup (p 128)

Recipes: Soups, starters, light meals and salads

Bejewelled smoked chicken summer salad (p 131)

Deep-dish spinach and goat's cheese omelette (p 132)

Midsummer mezze (p 133)

Primavera vegetable pizza tarts (p 134)

Carpaccio of fennel with fresh herbs and seafood (p 138)

Slow-cook, Indian-style lamb with beetroot (p 139)

Pork and sweetcorn patties with apple salsa (p 140)

Cheesy leek- and polenta-crusted fish (p 141)

Salmon with fennel and cucumber gremolata (p 143)

Potato pilau cake (p 145)

Chicken pad thai (p 146)

Courgette and squash with eggs and chorizo (p 150)

Kale and 'tattie' scones (p 151)

Pumpkin and apple mash (p 152)

Mixed root 'stovies' (p 154)

Roast new potatoes with baby vine tomatoes (p 156)

Broad beans and peas in the pod (p 158)

Courgette and squash 'crisps' (p 160)

Recipes: Desserts, puddings and bakes

Chocolate beetroot muffins (p 163)

Cherry pithiviers (p 165)

Blueberry soup (p 167)

Poached rhubarb with blackcurrant syrup (p 170)

Strawberry syllabub (p 171)

Rhubarb and raspberry crump (p 173)

Recipes: Desserts, puddings and bakes

Berry cake with sugar crunch topping (p 176)

Pickled cauliflower and shallots in spiced vinegar (p 180)

Bottled peas (p 182)

Whisky and raspberry cordial (p 183)

Loganberry 'marmalade' (p 184)

Autumnal chutney (p 187)

Tomato ketchup (p 188)

Salad-in-a-glass

A few years ago I wrote a book on healthy fruit and vegetable juices and up until that point I was a vegetable juice virgin. I admit that I'm still not a huge fan – they're just not my thing – but this is one I do make when I'm feeling virtuous. Juices are a great way to enjoy fresh produce from your plot. You will need a juicer to make this.

Serves 1

115 g (4 oz) radishes, trimmed
1 large carrot, scrubbed
2 medium ripe tomatoes
2 spring onions, trimmed
1 small cucumber
Dash of Tabasco sauce (optional)
Pinch of salt (optional)

1. Wash and roughly chop each vegetable and then taking each vegetable in turn, push them through a juicer.

2. Mix the juices together well and either drink as it is, or add a few drops of Tabasco sauce and a little salt to taste. Always drink freshly prepared juices as soon as possible after making so that you get maximum benefit from the nutritional content.

🍴 Cook's note

You can add other vegetables to the mix. Try a small beetroot (washed, unpeeled and trimmed) for an earthy flavour or a handful of wild rocket for a peppery edge; fresh herbs will also add other flavours. For a slightly sweeter mixture, push an apple through the juicer or add a little pressed apple juice to taste.

✳ Freezing: not suitable.

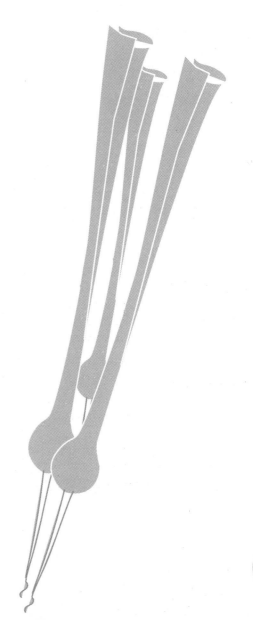

Chilled beetroot and sour cream soup

This has to be one of the prettiest soups you will ever make. If you're not into cold soups, try serving it over ice in a glass and drinking it as a savoury smoothie.

Serves 6

50 g (2 oz) butter
1 onion, peeled and chopped
1 garlic clove, peeled and crushed
1 tsp caraway seeds, lightly crushed
1 tsp coriander seeds, lightly crushed
350 g (12 oz) carrots, peeled and chopped
450 g (1 lb) beetroot
1.5 L (2½ pt) vegetable stock
150 ml (5 fl oz) sour cream
Small beetroot leaves, to garnish

1. Melt the butter in a large saucepan and add the onion, garlic and spices. Cook, stirring, for about 5 minutes until softened but not browned. Add the carrots and remove from the heat. Set aside.

2. Wash the beetroot well, then carefully peel (you may want to wear latex gloves because the juice will stain your fingers) and cut into small pieces. Stir into the saucepan and return to the heat. Cook, stirring, for 1 minute until well incorporated into the oniony butter.

3. Pour over the stock, bring to the boil, half-cover and simmer for about 1 hour until very tender. Set aside to cool completely.

4. Put the cooled soup mix in a blender or food processor with the sour cream and blend until smooth. Taste and season, then cover and chill for at least 2 hours.

5. Serve in small soup bowls and garnish with small beetroot leaves. Serve with griddled bread.

✱ **Freezing:** not suitable.

FOR PICTURE, SEE PAGE 95

Recipes: Soups, starters, light meals and salads

Potato, garlic and sage soup

A humble-sounding combination of ingredients that blend together to make a very tasty meal. The fritters add an extra herby dimension to the finished dish.

Serves 4

FOR THE SOUP
25 g (1 oz) butter
3 garlic cloves, peeled and finely chopped
900 g (2 lb) main crop potatoes
   (such as King Edward), peeled and diced
1 L (1¾ pt) chicken or vegetable stock
2 sprigs fresh sage
150 ml (5 fl oz) double cream
Salt and white pepper

FOR THE SAGE FRITTERS
Sunflower oil, for shallow-frying
50 g (2 oz) + 1 Tbsp plain flour
1 medium free range egg yolk
100 ml (3½ fl oz) soda water
16 large leaves fresh sage

1. Melt the butter in a large saucepan and cook the garlic for 2–3 minutes until softened but not browned. Add the potato and pour over the stock. Add the sprigs of sage, bring to the boil, cover and simmer for 25–30 minutes until tender. Remove from the heat and cool for 10 minutes. Discard the sage sprigs.

2. Transfer to a blender or food processor and blend for a few seconds until smooth. Return to the saucepan and stir in the cream and season to taste. When ready to serve, reheat until piping hot.

3. For the sage fritters, pour sufficient oil into a deep frying pan or saucepan to a depth of about 2.5 cm (1 in), and heat the oil to 180°C (350°F). Put 50 g (2 oz) plain flour in a bowl and blend in the egg yolk. Gradually blend in the soda water to make a smooth batter.

4. Wash and pat dry the large sage leaves. Dust in the remaining flour and then, holding the stalk, dip the leaf into the batter. Fry a few leaves at a time for 1–2 minutes until crisp, puffed and golden. Drain on kitchen paper and keep warm while frying the other leaves. Serve four fritters floating on the top of each portion of soup.

🍴 Cook's note

You can make this soup using Jerusalem artichokes instead of potatoes, or half and half. Jerusalem artichokes will give a sweeter, slightly smoky flavour to the soup.

✴ Freezing: make the soup as below but omit the cream. Allow to cool then pack into freezer soup bags or a freezer container. Seal and label. Freeze for up to 3 months. Allow to defrost overnight in the fridge. Reheat in a saucepan for about 10 minutes until piping hot, stir in the cream and continue with the recipe above. The fritters should be made fresh and do not freeze.

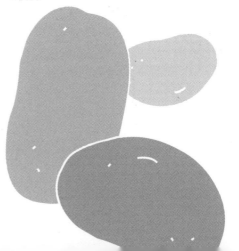

Twice-cooked broccoli and cheese soufflés

Unless you're very organized, cooking and serving a hot soufflé can be quite stressful. Since I discovered this version, I have few qualms about serving soufflés to my guests.

Serves 4

75 g (3 oz) butter, softened
150 g (5 oz) broccoli curds or small florets (no thick stalks)
25 g (1 oz) plain flour
150 ml (5 fl oz) whole milk
2 tsp wholegrain mustard
50 g (2 oz) mature Cheddar (or similar) cheese, grated
3 large free range eggs, separated
Salt and freshly ground black pepper
2 Tbsp freshly grated Parmesan cheese
Freshly chopped parsley, to garnish

1. Preheat the oven to 190°C/375°F/gas 5. Grease four 200 ml (7 fl oz) large ramekins or ovenproof dishes thickly with a little of the butter and place a small circle of baking parchment in the bottom of each. Place on a baking sheet and set aside.

2. Finely chop the broccoli along with any small stalks until it resembles finely chopped herbs. Melt 25 g (1 oz) butter in a frying pan and gently fry the broccoli, stirring, for 3–4 minutes until just softened. Remove from the heat.

3. Melt another 25 g (1 oz) butter in a saucepan and stir in the flour. Cook, stirring, for 1 minute, then remove from the heat. Gradually stir in the milk, then return to the heat and continue to cook, stirring, until the mixture boils and thickens. Remove from the heat.

4. Stir in the broccoli, mustard, grated Cheddar cheese and egg yolks and mix well. Season to taste. Whisk the egg whites until stiff and fold carefully into the broccoli mixture.

5. Divide between the four prepared ramekins and bake for about 25 minutes until well risen and browned. Allow to cool (and watch them sink!) for 10 minutes then carefully turn out on to a board lined with baking parchment. Leave to cool completely, then cover and chill until ready to serve.

6. When ready to serve, preheat the oven to the same setting. Transfer the soufflés to a baking tray lined with baking parchment. Melt the remaining butter and brush all over. Sprinkle with grated Parmesan and bake in the oven for about 20 minutes until warm and lightly crisp. Serve hot sprinkled with chopped parsley.

✱ **Freezing:** follow the recipe to the end of Step 5, then pack into a rigid freezer container and freeze for up to 6 months. Allow to defrost overnight in the fridge and then continue with the recipe above.

Recipes: Soups, starters, light meals and salads

Bejewelled smoked chicken summer salad

You don't just have to save your berry harvest for pudding, try adding them to a salad for an extra tart/sweet flavour. It's up to personal taste which ones you use, but this is my favourite combination.

Serves 4

FOR THE DRESSING
4 Tbsp raspberry or other berry vinegar
2 Tbsp cold-pressed rapeseed oil or
    extra virgin olive oil
1 Tbsp wholegrain mustard
2 tsp clear honey
Salt and freshly ground black pepper

FOR THE SALAD
350 g (12 oz) assorted berries and currants
    (such as small strawberries, redcurrants
    and raspberries)
125 g (4½ oz) radishes, trimmed
Large handful of salad leaves
    (such as wild rocket, mizuna or corn salad)
450 g (1 lb) skinless, boned, smoked chicken,
    sliced
Few sprigs of fresh tarragon

1. First prepare the dressing. Put the vinegar, oil, mustard, honey and seasoning in a small screw-top jar and shake well to mix. Set aside until ready to serve.

2. Carefully rinse and dry the berries and currants. Remove the tops of the strawberries and cut in halves or quarters depending on size. Strip the redcurrants from the stalks and place in a bowl. Mix in the raspberries. Set aside. Thinly slice the radish.

3. When ready to serve, put a few salad leaves on each serving plate and sprinkle with radish and the berries. Top with a few slices of smoked chicken and spoon over the berry dressing. Sprinkle with a few leaves of tarragon and serve at room temperature.

> **♟ Cook's note**
>
> The secret of this salad is to serve it unchilled. While you can prepare the various elements in advance, let them stand at room temperature for about 10 minutes to allow the flavours to develop before serving.

✱ Freezing: not suitable.

FOR PICTURE, SEE PAGE 96

Recipes: Soups, starters, light meals and salads

Deep-dish spinach and goat's cheese omelette

This thick, eggy mixture is oven baked and makes a delicious supper served either hot or cold. Served cold it makes a great picnic treat too.

Serves 4

50 g (2 oz) butter, softened
500 g (1 lb 2 oz) spinach, trimmed and shredded
1 large leek, trimmed and shredded
1 tsp cumin seeds, lightly crushed
6 large free range eggs, beaten
225 g (8 oz) firm goat's cheese, crumbled
Salt and freshly ground black pepper

1. Preheat the oven to 180°C/350°F/gas 4. Use about 2 teaspoons of butter to thickly grease a 23 cm (9 in) round pie dish, at least 5 cm (2 in) deep, and place on a baking sheet.

2. Melt the remaining butter in a large saucepan and add the spinach, leek and cumin seeds. Cook, stirring occasionally, for about 5 minutes, until the vegetables have wilted and softened. Drain well, pressing against the side of the colander. Transfer to a heatproof bowl and set aside to cool.

3. Mix the eggs into the cooled spinach mixture and carefully mix in the goat's cheese. Season well and then transfer to the prepared dish. Level off the top and bake in the oven for about 35 minutes until just set. Stand for 10 minutes before slicing to serve hot. Alternatively, allow to cool before serving in wedges.

✱ Freezing: not suitable.

FOR PICTURE, SEE PAGE 97

Midsummer mezze

My favourite type of food is Middle Eastern. I love all the mellow spices used to season and the colourful and tasty vegetable dishes you get served as part of a mezze meal. Serve these salads with warm flatbread.

Serves 4

FOR THE BROAD BEAN HUMMUS
Salt
450 g (1 lb) shelled broad beans
3 garlic cloves, peeled and halved
2 tsp ground cumin
Small bunch of fresh thyme
2 Tbsp cold-pressed rapeseed oil or extra
   virgin olive oil
Salt and freshly ground black pepper

FOR THE CHILLI-GARLIC TOMATOES
350 g (12 oz) ripe tomatoes
1 tsp coriander seeds, crushed
2 garlic cloves, peeled and crushed
1 small red chilli, deseeded and finely chopped
2 Tbsp cold-pressed rapeseed oil or extra
   virgin olive oil
2 Tbsp freshly chopped coriander
Salt and freshly ground black pepper

FOR THE SWEET MINT CUCUMBER
1 cucumber
1 small onion, peeled and very finely chopped
Few sprigs of fresh mint
2 Tbsp cider vinegar
2 tsp caster sugar
Whole milk yoghurt, to serve

1. For the hummus, bring a saucepan of lightly salted water to the boil. Add the beans, garlic, cumin and a few sprigs of thyme. Cook for 5–6 minutes until tender. Drain well, reserving 6–8 tablespoons of cooking water, and cool for 10 minutes. Discard the thyme.

2. Transfer the cooked beans and garlic to a blender. Add the reserved cooking water and oil. Blend for a few seconds until smooth and creamy. Season well. Pile into a heatproof dish and allow to cool. Garnish with more thyme to serve.

3. For the tomatoes, chop the tomatoes and place in a shallow bowl. Mix in the remaining ingredients and season well. Allow to stand at room temperature for 30 minutes before serving to allow the flavours to develop.

4. For the cucumber, thinly slice the cucumber and arrange on a serving platter. Sprinkle with the chopped onion.

5. Reserving a few leaves for garnish, chop the remaining mint finely and mix with the vinegar and sugar. Spoon over the cucumber. Allow to stand at room temperature for 30 minutes before serving to allow the flavours to develop. Sprinkle with mint leaves and serve with yoghurt.

✱ **Freezing:** not suitable.

FOR PICTURE, SEE PAGE 98

Primavera vegetable pizza tarts

This is an idea that you can adapt using any combinations of your favourite vegetables, but cut them into small pieces and blanch them first otherwise they will dry rather than cook in the oven.

Serves 4

150 g (5 oz) shelled peas
100 g (3½ oz) shelled young broad beans
1 small leek, trimmed and shredded
4 ripe tomatoes
1 garlic clove, peeled and crushed
Salt and freshly ground black pepper
2 Tbsp sun-dried tomato purée
Few sprigs of fresh basil
350 g (12 oz) ready-made puff pastry
175 g (6 oz) mini mozzarella or small pieces
   block mozzarella, drained
2 Tbsp cold-pressed rapeseed oil or olive oil
Handful of wild rocket

3. On a lightly floured surface, roll out the pastry to form a 30 cm (12 in) square. Cut out four 15 cm (6 in) circles and arrange on a large baking sheet lined with baking parchment.

4. Spread the tomato mixture equally over each pastry circle and bake in the oven for 15 minutes until starting to puff up and brown slightly.

5. Divide the vegetables between the tarts and arrange the mozzarella on top. Brush each lightly with oil and season with black pepper. Return to the oven and continue to bake for a further 10 minutes until the pastry is crisp.

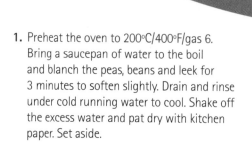

1. Preheat the oven to 200°C/400°F/gas 6. Bring a saucepan of water to the boil and blanch the peas, beans and leek for 3 minutes to soften slightly. Drain and rinse under cold running water to cool. Shake off the excess water and pat dry with kitchen paper. Set aside.

2. Meanwhile, finely chop the tomatoes and put in a bowl. Mix in the garlic, seasoning and tomato purée. Tear the basil into small pieces and mix into the tomatoes.

6. Serve the tarts while still warm, topped with wild rocket leaves.

✱ **Freezing:** not suitable.

FOR PICTURE, SEE PAGE 99

Buckwheat crêpes with chard and nutmeg sauce

Chard is a very versatile leaf as it can be cooked or eaten raw, like spinach. If you use one of the coloured stalk varieties, it will lose some colouring on cooking.

Serves 4

125 g (4½ oz) buckwheat flour
125 g (4½ oz) plain flour
Salt and freshly ground black pepper
225 ml (8 fl oz) light continental beer or lager
300 ml (10 fl oz) whole milk
2 Tbsp cold-pressed rapeseed oil or olive oil
1 free range egg, beaten
65 g (2½ oz) butter
1 large onion, peeled and finely chopped
600 g (1 lb 5 oz) Swiss chard
½ tsp ground nutmeg
6 Tbsp extra thick double cream

1. Sift the flours with a pinch of salt into a bowl and make a well in the centre. Pour in the beer, milk and add 1 tablespoon of oil and the egg. Gradually mix together to form a smooth, thick batter. Stand for 30 minutes.

2. Heat a large frying pan (25 cm / 10 in in diameter) and add a small knob of the butter. When bubbling, ladle in one-eighth of the batter – approximately 100 ml (3½ fl oz) – quickly swirling it around to cover the base of the pan. Cook over a medium heat for about 2 minutes. Carefully turn over and cook for a further 2 minutes until cooked through and lightly golden. Turn on to a wire rack and cover with baking parchment and a clean tea towel while making another seven crêpes. Keep warm.

3. For the filling, melt the remaining butter with the remaining oil in a large saucepan or wok and cook the onion gently for about 10 minutes until just softened but not too browned. Rip off the leaves from the chard stalks and break into small pieces. Break the stalks into 5 cm (2 in) pieces and remove stringy parts. Add the leafy bits to the frying pan. Raise the heat and stir-fry for about 5 minutes until wilted. Add the nutmeg and cream, and heat through for about 2 minutes until hot. Season to taste.

4. Meanwhile, bring a small saucepan of lightly salted water to the boil and cook the stalks for 4–5 minutes until just tender. Drain well.

5. To serve, place a few of the chard stalks down the length of the centre of each crêpe and top with a spoonful of the creamed chard leaves. Roll up and serve two per person whilst still warm.

✱ **Freezing:** the crêpes will freeze unfilled. Allow the crêpes to cool then fold in half and layer between sheets of baking parchment. Place in a freezer bag and seal well. Freeze for up to 3 months. Defrost for a few hours in the refrigerator. To reheat, place on a baking tray lined with baking parchment, cover with foil and place in a preheated oven at 190ºC/375ºF/gas 5 for about 5 minutes until piping hot.

👕 Cook's note

The filling will not freeze and is best made fresh.

Cauliflower and macaroni cheese

A combination of my two favourite childhood suppers. Broccoli tastes just as good in this dish, as do chopped green beans and peas.

Serves 4

45 g (1½ oz) butter
45 g (1½ oz) plain flour
600 ml (1 pt) whole milk
1 Tbsp wholegrain mustard
4 Tbsp freshly chopped chives
150 g (5 oz) mature Cheddar cheese, grated
Salt and freshly ground black pepper
1 small cauliflower, broken into small florets
225 g (8 oz) macaroni
50 g (2 oz) granary breadcrumbs
4 Tbsp freshly grated Parmesan cheese
25 g (1 oz) butter

1. First make the sauce. Melt the butter in a saucepan and stir in the flour. Cook for 1 minute. Remove from the heat and gradually stir in the milk. Return to the heat and cook, stirring, until the mixture comes to the boil and thickens. Cook for a further minute then remove from the heat and stir in the mustard, 3 tablespoons of chives and the grated Cheddar cheese. Taste and season. Cover the surface with a piece of greaseproof paper and set aside to cool.

2. Meanwhile, bring a saucepan of lightly salted water to the boil. Add the cauliflower, bring back to the boil and add the macaroni. Cook for about 5 minutes until just tender. Drain well and put in an ovenproof dish.

3. Preheat the oven to 190°C/375°F/gas 5. Spoon over the sauce, spreading it evenly over the cauliflower and macaroni. Mix the breadcrumbs and Parmesan together and then sprinkle on top. Dot with butter and bake in the oven for 25–30 minutes until bubbling and golden. Serve hot sprinkled with the remaining chives.

✳ **Freezing:** before baking but after assembling in an ovenproof and freezer-proof dish, cover and seal well. Freeze for up to 3 months. Defrost in the refrigerator overnight and proceed with the recipe at Step 3.

Recipes: Soups, starters, light meals and salads

Sweet spiced marrow and chickpea salad

I usually make this dish with aubergine, but marrow and courgettes work just as well. The spice gives it a fragrant flavour that is more pronounced when you serve the dish cold with a dollop of hummus on top.

Serves 4

500 g (1 lb 2 oz) young marrow
2 Tbsp cold-pressed rapeseed oil or olive oil
1 onion, peeled and chopped
1 garlic clove, peeled and crushed
½ stick cinnamon
150 ml (5 fl oz) vegetable stock
450 g (1 lb) ripe tomatoes, chopped
2 Tbsp tomato purée
2 tsp caster sugar
400 g (14 oz) tin chickpeas, drained and rinsed
Small bunch fresh coriander, finely chopped
Salt and freshly ground black pepper
Crisp salad leaves, warm bread, hummus and
   lemon wedges, to serve

1. Unless the skin is particularly tough you don't need to peel the marrow. Slice in half lengthways and scoop out the seeds, then cut into small pieces.

2. Heat the oil in a saucepan and gently fry the onion, garlic and cinnamon for about 5 minutes until softened. Add the marrow and cook, stirring, for about a minute until well coated in the onion mixture.

3. Pour in the stock and mix in the tomatoes, tomato purée and sugar. Bring to the boil and simmer gently, uncovered, for about 20 minutes until tender. Remove from the heat and stir in the chickpeas. Set aside to cool. Discard the cinnamon stick.

4. Stir in the chopped coriander and season well. Cover and chill for at least 1 hour before serving. Serve with crisp salad leaves, warm bread, hummus and lemon wedges.

✳ **Freezing:** follow the recipe to the end of Step 3. Pack into a rigid freezer container. Seal and freeze for up to 3 months. Defrost in the refrigerator overnight before serving and continuing with the recipe above.

Carpaccio of fennel with fresh herbs and seafood

The mild, fresh aniseed flavour of Florence fennel is the perfect accompaniment to sweet, succulent seafood. Slice it as thinly as you can for best results. Accompany with freshly buttered brown bread.

Serves 4

1 small bulb Florence fennel
Juice of 1 lime
1 Tbsp cold-pressed rapeseed oil or extra virgin olive oil
Few sprigs of fresh tarragon
Few sprigs of fresh dill
450 g (1 lb) assorted cooked seafood, thawed if frozen
6 Tbsp ready-made mayonnaise
2 Tbsp Pernod
Lime wedges, to serve

1. Trim the fennel, reserving the green fronds for garnish. Using a sharp knife, slice the fennel downwards , in wafer-thin slices and arrange in a shallow dish. Mix the lime juice and oil together and drizzle over the fennel. Cover and chill for at least 2 hours – in this time the fennel with soften and absorb the lime juice.

2. When ready to serve, break up the tarragon and dill leaves. Drain the fennel and arrange it with the herbs on four serving plates.

3. Rinse the seafood and pat dry with kitchen paper. Put in a bowl. Mix the mayonnaise and Pernod together and mix into the seafood. Pile on top of the fennel. Garnish with reserved fennel fronds and serve with wedges of lime to squeeze over.

✱ **Freezing:** not suitable.

FOR PICTURE, SEE PAGE 100

Recipes: Soups, starters, light meals and salads

Slow-cook, Indian-style lamb with beetroot

This is one of the most delicious ways I have ever eaten beetroot. Its earthy, sweet flavour absorbs the warming spices and it turns the lamb a stunning colour. It looks great served with saffron rice.

Serves 6

900 g (2 lb) lean cubed lamb, trimmed
Salt and freshly ground black pepper
2 tsp each of cumin, coriander and black onion
  seeds, lightly crushed
50 g (2 oz) butter
8 shallots, peeled and halved
675 g (1½ lb) small beetroot
2 bay leaves
300 ml (10 fl oz) lamb or chicken stock
150 ml (5 fl oz) whole milk natural yoghurt
4 Tbsp freshly chopped coriander

1. Preheat the oven to 170°C/325°F/gas 3. Season the lamb and mix in the spices.

2. Melt the butter in a large frying pan and fry the lamb and shallots for 5–6 minutes, stirring frequently, until lightly browned all over. Remove from the heat, keep in the pan and set aside.

3. Carefully peel the beetroot. Cut small beetroot in half and larger ones into small chunks. Place in a large, ovenproof casserole dish. Transfer the lamb and all of the cooking juices to the casserole dish and push in the bay leaves. Pour over the stock. Cover with a piece of foil across top of dish and set the lid on top. Bake in the oven for about 3 hours, stirring well after 2 hours, until tender.

4. To serve, ladle over freshly cooked saffron rice and serve with a dollop of yoghurt and a sprinkling of freshly chopped coriander.

🍳 Cook's note

Remember beetroot stains your fingers, so you may want to wear latex gloves when peeling it.

✱ **Freezing:** not suitable.

FOR PICTURE, SEE PAGE 101

Pork and sweetcorn patties with apple salsa

Juicy sweetcorn kernels and succulent pork make the perfect addition to any barbecue. The apple salsa is an up-to-date version of a classic apple sauce accompaniment.

Serves 4

FOR THE PATTIES
2 ripe corn cobs or 250 g (9 oz) kernels
1 tsp caster sugar
500 g (1 lb 2 oz) lean minced pork
4 spring onions, trimmed and finely chopped
75 g (3 oz) fresh white breadcrumbs
3 Tbsp freshly chopped sage
Salt and freshly ground black pepper
1 free range egg, beaten

FOR THE SALSA
2 eating apples
6 tsp caster sugar
3 Tbsp cider vinegar

Sage fritters (see page 129), to serve

1. Strip off the outer leaves and silky strings from the corn cobs. Bring a saucepan of water to the boil, add 1 teaspoon of sugar (but no salt, it toughens the kernels) and cook for about 8 minutes. Test for 'doneness' by pricking carefully with a skewer to see if the kernels are tender. Rinse in cold water to cool, then strip off the kernels by running a small sharp knife down the length of the cob, collecting the kernels as they are released. Set aside to cool.

2. Put the pork in a bowl and mix in all but 1 tablespoon of the chopped spring onion. Mix in the breadcrumbs, 2 tablespoons of sage and the sweetcorn. Season well and bind together with the egg. Divide into 12 balls and form each into a thin patty about 7.5 cm (3 in) in diameter. Place on a board lined with baking parchment, cover and chill for at least 30 minutes.

3. For the salsa, core the apples, then finely chop the flesh. Put in a bowl and stir in the sugar, and reserved spring onion and sage, along with the vinegar. Mix well, cover and chill for up to 30 minutes, before it starts to discolour.

4. Preheat the grill to a medium/hot setting. Cook the patties for about 5 minutes on each side. Alternatively cook on on the barbecue. Drain and serve hot with the apple salsa and sage fritters (see page 129).

✳ **Freezing:** cook the patties and allow to cool. Stack between layers of baking parchment and place in a freezer bag. Seal and freeze for up to 6 months. Allow to defrost in the refrigerator overnight. To reheat, place on a baking tray lined with baking parchment. Cover with foil and place in a preheated oven at 190°C/375°F/ gas 5 for about 25 minutes until piping hot. The salsa is not suitable for Freezing.

FOR PICTURE, SEE PAGE 102

Recipes: Main meals

Cheesy leek- and polenta-crusted fish

If you bake fish with a thick topping it helps to keep it from drying out. Leeks and chives have the subtlest flavour of all the onion family so are the best varieties to serve with fish.

Serves 4

200 ml (7 fl oz) water
Salt and freshly ground black pepper
50 g (2 oz) quick–cook polenta
2 large leeks
2 Tbsp freshly chopped chives
4 Tbsp freshly grated Parmesan cheese
2 Tbsp cold–pressed rapeseed oil or olive oil
4 x 150 g (5 oz) skinless chunky white fish fillets
   (such as pollock, haddock or cod)
Sunflower oil for shallow-frying

1. Preheat the oven to 200°C/400°F/gas 6. Pour the water into a saucepan and add a pinch of salt. Bring to the boil and stir in the polenta, beating with a wooden spoon. Cook for about 5 minutes, stirring, until very thick. Turn into a shallow, heatproof dish and allow to cool completely. Once cold, crumble the polenta into a bowl.

2. Trim the leeks, split lengthways and run under cold water to flush out any trapped earth. Shake well to remove excess water. Cut in half and then slice into thin ribbons. Take a small handful of leeks and finely chop. Mix into the polenta along with the chives, Parmesan cheese, oil and plenty of seasoning.

3. Wash and pat dry the fish fillets and season on both sides. Place on a baking tray lined with baking parchment. Top each piece with the polenta mixture to make a thick crust. Bake in the oven for about 20 minutes until cooked through.

4. Meanwhile, pour sufficient sunflower oil into a wok or deep frying pan to a depth of 5 cm (2 in), and heat until 190°C (375°F). Add half of the remaining leek ribbons and fry for 3–4 minutes or until shrivelled and crisp. Drain and keep warm while frying the remaining leek.

5. Preheat the grill to the hot setting. Grill the fish for about 3 minutes to crisp the top. Serve the fish with crispy leeks piled on top.

✱ **Freezing:** not suitable.

FOR PICTURE, SEE PAGE 103

Gormeh sabsi with lamb's liver skewers

This recipe is based on an Iranian dish of basmati rice with lots of chopped herbs and diced French beans. It makes a light meal on its own, but is also a good accompaniment for kebabs.

Serves 4

FOR THE GORMEH SABSI
250 g (9 oz) basmati rice, soaked for 2 hours
1 tsp salt
2 bay leaves
6 cardamom pods, lightly crushed
6 curry leaves or 1 tsp mild curry powder
4 Tbsp cold-pressed rapeseed oil or olive oil
350 g (12 oz) green beans, stalk removed
    and chopped
1 medium onion, peeled and finely sliced
4 Tbsp each of freshly chopped dill, parsley
    and coriander
50 g (2 oz) unsalted cashews, toasted

FOR THE LAMB'S LIVER SKEWERS
450 g (1 lb) lamb's liver, cut into 2 cm (¾ in)
    thick pieces
1 tsp each ground cumin and ground coriander
Freshly ground black pepper

1. Drain and rinse the rice. Bring a large saucepan of water to the boil. Add the salt and rice. Bring back to the boil and boil uncovered for 3–4 minutes until the rice is slightly tender but still opaque.

2. Drain and rinse in cold running water to remove excess starch. Shake off excess water and put back in the saucepan. Stir in the bay leaves, cardamom pods and curry leaves. Level off the rice and make indents into the rice with the end of a wooden spoon and drizzle in 2 tablespoons of oil.

3. Cover with a layer of foil across the top of the saucepan, cover with the lid and place over a very low heat to cook, undisturbed, for about 30 minutes until tender and the grains on the bottom are slightly crisp. Fork through to mix well. Discard all the leaves and cardamom pods.

4. Meanwhile, bring a saucepan of lightly salted water to the boil, add the beans and cook for 4–5 minutes until just cooked. Drain well and set aside.

5. Heat 1 tablespoon of the remaining oil in a small frying pan and cook the onion gently, stirring occasionally, for about 10 minutes until cooked through. Set aside.

6. Once the rice is cooked, mix the beans and cooked onion into it along with the chopped herbs and cashews. Cover and keep warm.

7. Just before serving, preheat the grill to a hot setting. Put the liver in a bowl and mix in the remaining oil, spices and black pepper. Thread on to eight medium skewers. Place under the grill and cook for 2–3 minutes on each side until tender, but still slightly pink. Serve the skewers on a bed of gormeh sabsi.

✱ Freezing: The gormeh sabsi freezes well. Follow the recipe until the end of Step 6. Allow to cool then pack into a rigid container. Cover and freeze for up to 6 months. Defrost in the refrigerator overnight. To reheat, place in a large saucepan, add 2 tablespoons of water, cover and put over a low heat, and heat, stirring occasionally, for about 20 minutes until piping hot.

Recipes: Main meals

Salmon with fennel and cucumber gremolata

Gremolata seems to be one of those recipes with lots of different variations. This is my version, using lots of fresh flavours as well as pickles. Serve with smoked mackerel if hot smoked salmon is not available.

Serves 4

FOR THE GREMOLATA
1 small bulb Florence fennel
1 small cucumber
2 garlic cloves, peeled and crushed
2 shallots, peeled and finely chopped
115 g (4 oz) pitted green olives, chopped
4 Tbsp capers, chopped
6 anchovy fillets, drained and chopped
4 Tbsp freshly chopped parsley

FOR THE SALMON
4 x 150 g (5 oz) pieces hot-smoked salmon
2 tsp cold-pressed rapeseed oil or olive oil
4 bay leaves
Freshly ground black pepper
2 Tbsp lemon juice
Parsley, to garnish
Fresh lemon wedges, to serve

1. Trim the fennel, reserving the leaves. Break up the fennel layers and wash well. Pat dry, then chop finely and place in a bowl. Chop the fennel leaves and add to the bowl.

2. Slice the cucumber in half lengthways and finely chop. Mix into the fennel along with the garlic, shallots, olives, capers, anchovies and parsley. Mix well, cover and chill for at least 30 minutes.

3. Preheat the oven to 190°C/375°F/gas 5. Place each piece of salmon in the centre of a square of lightly oiled foil. Lay a bay leaf on top and season with black pepper. Drizzle with lemon juice, seal the foil edges to make a parcel and place on a baking tray. Put in the oven for about 15 minutes until piping hot.

4. To serve, pile the gremolata on to serving plates, and lay a piece of salmon on top. Discard the bay leaf and serve garnished with parsley and wedges of fresh lemon to squeeze over.

✱ **Freezing:** not suitable.

FOR PICTURE, SEE PAGE 104

Recipes: Main meals

Tagine of chicken and autumnal vegetables

A tagine or stew is a great way to use root and dense-textured vegetables. All the flavours are retained in the cooking liquor, which can be soaked up with couscous or boiled rice.

Serves 4

1.3 kg (3 lb) free range chicken, quartered
Salt and freshly ground black pepper
2 Tbsp cold-pressed rapeseed oil or olive oil
2 small cinnamon sticks, broken
2 tsp cumin seeds, lightly crushed
1 tsp coriander seeds, lightly crushed
2 carrots, peeled
2 courgettes, trimmed
350 g (12 oz) pumpkin or squash,
    peeled and seeds removed
225 g (8 oz) small white turnips
225 g (8 oz) swede (yellow turnip), peeled
Pinch of saffron strands
2 Tbsp local honey
1.2 L (2 pt) fresh chicken or vegetable stock
4 Tbsp freshly chopped coriander

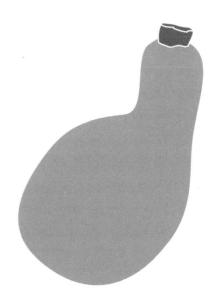

1. Wash and pat dry the chicken, then season all over. Heat the oil in a large saucepan and fry the spices for 1 minute. Add the chicken and cook for 2–3 minutes on each side until lightly browned. Remove from the heat and set aside.

2. Cut the carrots and courgettes into 7 cm (3 in) pieces and cut in half lengthways to reduce the thickness. Cut the pumpkin or squash into pieces of the same size.

3. Peel the white turnips if necessary then cut in half or quarters, depending on its size. Peel the swede and cut into 2.5 cm (1 in) thick pieces.

4. Mix the vegetables into the saucepan of chicken. Add the saffron and honey and pour over the stock. Bring to the boil, cover and simmer gently for about 1 hour until the chicken is falling off the bone.

5. Discard the cinnamon. Remove the chicken skin and serve the vegetables, chicken and cooking liquor spooned over freshly cooked couscous or rice, and sprinkle with chopped coriander.

✱ **Freezing:** allow to cool then pack into a rigid container. Cover and freeze for up to 6 months. Defrost in the refrigerator overnight. To reheat, place in a large saucepan, cover and place over a low heat, and heat, stirring occasionally, for about 25 minutes until piping hot.

Potato pilau cake

Once of the tastiest ways to serve potatoes I have ever made. It makes a very substantial main meal served with freshly cooked vegetables, or you can serve it as an accompaniment sliced into thinner wedges.

Serves 6

250 g (9 oz) basmati rice, soaked for 2 hours
1 tsp salt
1 cinnamon stick, broken
1 tsp coriander seeds, lightly crushed
50 g (2 oz) seedless raisins
50 g (2 oz) pine nuts, toasted
Freshly ground black pepper
450 g (1 lb) main crop potatoes
    (such as King Edward)
50 g (2 oz) butter
2 garlic cloves, peeled and finely chopped
2 Tbsp cold-pressed rapeseed oil or olive oil
2 Tbsp freshly chopped parsley

1. Drain and rinse the rice. Bring a large saucepan of water to the boil. Add the salt, rice, cinnamon and coriander seeds. Bring back to the boil and boil uncovered for 3–4 minutes until the rice is slightly tender but still opaque.

2. Drain and rinse the rice in cold running water to remove excess starch. Shake off the excess water and stir in the raisins, pine nuts and black pepper. Set aside.

3. Peel the potatoes and slice very thinly. Melt the butter in a 25 cm (10 in) frying pan with a lid and gently fry the garlic for 1 minute. Add the potato slices and cook, stirring, for 1 minute to coat in the garlic butter. Remove from the heat then arrange the potatoes in a neat layer over the bottom of the pan.

4. Pack the rice mixture on top. Make indents into the rice with the end of a wooden spoon and drizzle with the oil. Cover with a layer of foil over the pan and then the lid, and place over a very low heat to cook, undisturbed, for about 30 minutes until the potatoes are tender and the rice is cooked through. Raise the heat and cook for a further 2–3 minutes to crisp off the potatoes.

5. Turn off the heat and stand for 10 minutes. Turn on to a large serving platter, potato side up, and serve sprinkled with chopped parsley.

✱ **Freezing:** follow the recipe above then turn out on to a freezer-proof plate or board. Allow to cool, then wrap well and freeze for up to 3 months. Defrost overnight in the refrigerator. To reheat, transfer to a baking tray lined with baking parchment. Cover with foil and reheat in a preheated oven at 180°C/350°F/gas 4 for about 30 minutes until piping hot.

FOR PICTURE, SEE PAGE 105

Recipes: Main meals

Chicken pad thai

My favourite Thai dish. This version is a great way to incorporate some of the freshest flavours from the garden. Leave out the chicken if you prefer, or serve with cooked prawns or strips of stir-fried beef or pork.

Serves 4

115 g (4 oz) rice noodles
   (about ½ cm / ¼ in wide)
225 g (8 oz) small peas in pods or mange touts,
   topped and tailed
2 heads pak choi
1 small cucumber
2 Tbsp ground nut or vegetable oil
1 garlic clove, peeled and finely chopped
1 green or red chilli (optional), deseeded and
   finely chopped
8 spring onions, trimmed and finely chopped
225 g (8 oz) cooked skinless chicken, shredded
2 Tbsp fish sauce
2 Tbsp lime juice
1 Tbsp clear honey
2 Tbsp crushed roasted peanuts
Handful of pea shoots

1. Put the noodles in a large heatproof bowl and pour over sufficient boiling water to cover. Put aside to soak for at least 10 minutes.

2. Meanwhile, slice through each pea pod or mangetout lengthways but on the diagonal. Bring a small saucepan of water to the boil and cook for about 2 minutes until just cooked. Drain and rinse in cold water to cool. Set aside.

3. Shred the pak choi. Cut the cucumber in half lengthways and thinly slice.

4. Heat the oil in a wok or a large deep frying pan and stir-fry the garlic, chilli (if using) and all but 2 tablespoons of spring onions for 1 minute. Add the peas, pak choi and cucumber and stir-fry for a further 2 minutes.

5. Drain the noodles well and add to the wok along with the chicken, stir-fry for a further minute, then add the fish sauce, lime juice and honey and continue to stir-fry, mixing well, for another minute.

6. Pile on to warmed serving plates or bowls. Sprinkle with the remaining spring onions, the crushed peanuts and a few pea shoots to serve.

✱ **Freezing:** not suitable.

FOR PICTURE, SEE PAGE 106

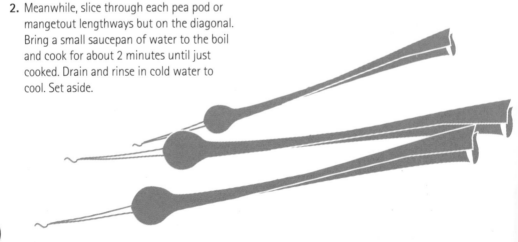

Guinea fowl with pears and black pudding

Not a widely used meat these days, but nonetheless worth checking out for flavour. Pears as an accompaniment help take the edge off the richness of the meat. Chicken or pork will also work as alternatives.

Serves 4

4 ripe pears
150 ml (5 fl oz) pressed pear or apple juice
4 boneless guinea fowl breasts
Salt and freshly ground black pepper
3 Tbsp cold-pressed rapeseed oil or olive oil
15 g (½ oz) butter
4 thick slices black pudding
2 Tbsp balsamic vinegar
1 tsp clear honey
Few sprigs of fresh chervil or lamb's lettuce

1. Peel and core the pears, and either cut in half or quarters depending on their size. Place in a saucepan and pour over the juice. Bring to the boil, cover and simmer gently for 5–7 minutes, turning occasionally, until tender. Set aside.

2. Meanwhile, remove any excess skin from the guinea fowl breasts, and take out the sinew from each piece. Wash and pat dry, then season all over.

3. Heat 1 tablespoon of oil with the butter until frothy and bubbling and add the breasts, skin-side down; fry gently for 7–8 minutes, browning slightly. Turn over and continue to cook for a further 7–8 minutes, or until cooked through and golden. Drain, reserving the pan juices, and keep warm.

4. Gently fry the black pudding in the reserved pan juices for 3–4 minutes on each side until cooked through. Drain well and keep warm.

5. Place the vinegar in a small screw-top jar with the remaining oil, honey and about 4 tablespoons of the pear cooking liquor. Season well, then seal and shake well to mix.

6. To serve, cut each guinea fowl breast into four or five thick slices. Arrange the pear slices on warm serving plates, then top with the black pudding and the guinea fowl. Spoon over the dressing to serve while meats are still warm and garnish with fresh chervil or lamb's lettuce.

✱ **Freezing:** not suitable.

Summer veg and pesto meatball pasta bake

Bursting with the colours and flavours of summer vegetables, the whole family will love this meal.

Serves 4

2 ripe corn cobs or 250 g (9 oz) kernels
1 tsp caster sugar
3 Tbsp cold-pressed rapeseed oil or olive oil
1 medium onion, peeled and chopped
350 g (12 oz) squash, peeled, seeds removed
 and diced
2 small courgettes, trimmed and diced
600 g (1 lb 5 oz) ripe tomatoes, chopped
200 ml (7 fl oz) dry white wine or vegetable stock
2 bay leaves
Salt and freshly ground black pepper
500 g (1 lb 2 oz) lean minced beef
1 garlic clove, peeled and crushed
6 Tbsp freshly grated Parmesan cheese
50 g (2 oz) fresh white breadcrumbs
4 Tbsp toasted pine nuts
Few sprigs of fresh basil
1 free range egg, beaten
250 g (9 oz) penne pasta
Crisp salad, to serve

1. Strip off the outer leaves and silky strings from the sweetcorn. Bring a saucepan of water to the boil, add the sugar (but no salt, it toughens the kernels) and cook for about 8 minutes. Test for 'doneness' by pricking carefully with a skewer to see if the kernels are tender. Rinse in cold running water to cool, then strip off the kernels by running a small, sharp knife down the length of the cob, collecting the kernels as they are released.

2. Heat 2 tablespoons of the oil in a large frying pan and gently fry the onion for 5 minutes until just softened but not browned. Stir in the squash, courgettes, sweetcorn and tomatoes and mix well. Pour in the wine or stock and add the bay leaves and plenty of seasoning. Bring to the boil, then cover and simmer gently for about 25 minutes until just tender. Allow to cool. Discard the bay leaves.

3. Meanwhile, make the meatballs. In a bowl, mix together the minced beef, garlic, half of the Parmesan cheese, the breadcrumbs and half of the pine nuts. Chop a few sprigs of basil and add to the mixture along with some seasoning. Bind together with the egg. Divide into 16 portions and roll into balls. Cover and chill until required.

4. Bring a saucepan of salted water to the boil and cook the pasta according to the manufacturer's instructions until 'al dente'. Drain well and set aside.

5. Preheat the oven to 180°C/350°F/gas 4. Heat the remaining oil in a frying pan, add the meatballs and cook gently for 5 minutes, stirring, until browned all over. Use a slotted spoon to transfer them to a large ovenproof dish. Carefully mix the pasta into the meatballs, then spoon over the prepared vegetable sauce. Cover with foil and bake in the oven for 30 minutes. Remove the foil, sprinkle with the remaining Parmesan cheese and cook for a further 20 minutes until golden and bubbling. Serve sprinkled with remaining pine nuts and a few fresh basil leaves. Accompany with a crisp salad.

✶ **Freezing:** follow the recipe using a freezer-proof and ovenproof dish, but omit the garnish. Allow to cool, then cover well and freeze for up to 3 months. Defrost overnight in the refrigerator. To reheat, cover with foil and place in a preheated oven at 190°C/375°F/gas 5 and reheat for about 30–40 minutes until piping hot. Garnish as above and serve.

Recipes: Main meals

Five-spice five veg stir-fry

The secret of this dish is to cut the vegetables into thin shreds so that they cook evenly. This does take time of course. You may find the julienne or coarse grating attachment on a food processor suitable for this.

Serves 4

1 head kohl rabi
115 g (4 oz) radishes, trimmed
1 small celeriac
Juice of 1 lemon
4 Tbsp ground nut or vegetable oil
12 spring onions, trimmed and sliced
4 Tbsp light soy sauce
2 tsp clear honey
1 tsp Chinese five-spice powder
1 small head Chinese leaves, shredded
4 Tbsp freshly chopped fresh chives
1 Tbsp toasted sesame seeds

1. Cut off the leafy tops of the kohl rabi and trim away the taproot. Scrub thoroughly in running water. Peel and cut into thin strips or grate coarsely. Slice the radishes thinly. Set aside.

2. Prepare the celeriac. Trim off the leaves – these can be used to flavour stocks and soups. Slice off the root end and scrub under cold running water. Cut into manageable pieces and remove the thick skin. Put it in a bowl of water with the lemon juice to prevent discolouring until required.

3. Just before cooking, drain and pat dry the celeriac, then cut into thin strips or grate coarsely. Heat the oil in a wok or large, deep frying pan until hot and stir-fry the spring onions and celeriac for 3 minutes. Add the kohl rabi and radishes and stir-fry for a further 2 minutes.

4. Add the soy sauce, honey and five-spice powder and carefully stir in the Chinese leaves. Continue to stir-fry for 2–3 minutes until the leaves are wilted and the vegetables are almost tender. Stir in the chives and serve immediately sprinkled with the toasted sesame seeds.

> ### 🍽 Cook's note
>
> Serve as an accompaniment to stir-fried or grilled fish or chicken. Add toasted cashew nuts or tofu pieces for a vegetarian meal.

✱ **Freezing:** not suitable.

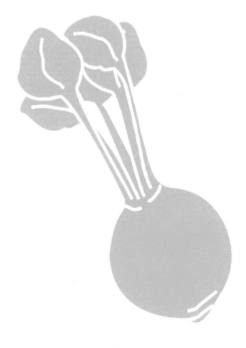

Courgette and squash with eggs and chorizo

I based this dish on a recipe I came across in Tunisia called chakchouka. It was hot and spicy and full of sweet peppers. This selection of vegetables works just as well and is not fiery hot, but add chillies if you want some more heat.

Serves 4

225 g (8 oz) chorizo sausage
3 Tbsp cold-pressed rapeseed oil or olive oil
1 onion, peeled and thinly sliced
2 medium courgettes, trimmed and diced
225 g (8 oz) squash, peeled, seeded and diced
6 ripe tomatoes, chopped
Salt and freshly ground black pepper
4 free range eggs
2 Tbsp freshly chopped parsley

1. Peel off the papery skin from the chorizo and slice. Place in a large frying pan and heat gently, stirring, until the juices begin to run. Turn up the heat and cook for 1 minute to brown all over. Remove from the pan using a slotted spoon and set aside.

2. In the same frying pan, reheat the chorizo juices along with the oil until hot, then add the onion and cook, stirring, for 5 minutes until softened. Add the courgettes, squash and tomatoes. Bring to the boil, cover and cook gently for about 15 minutes until softened slightly.

3. Return the chorizo to the pan, season lightly and mix well, then spread the mixture evenly across the pan. Make four slight indents in the mixture and break an egg into each. Cook gently for about 10 minutes or until the eggs have cooked to your liking. Serve straight from the pan sprinkled with chopped parsley.

🍲 Cook's note

Omit the chorizo if preferred. Serve with cooked rice or simply with warmed flatbread as part of a mezze meal.

* **Freezing:** not suitable.

FOR PICTURE, SEE PAGE 107

Recipes: Accompaniments

Kale and 'tattie' scones

A cross between a thick pancake and a flat scone, these Scottish treats can be served with soups or stews, and they're also delicious with sausages.

Makes 8

450 g (1 lb) main crop potatoes,
   (such as Maris Piper or King Edward)
1 tsp salt
150 g (5 oz) curly kale
1 small leek
50 g (2 oz) self-raising flour, plus extra
   for dusting
Vegetable oil for brushing

1. Peel the potatoes thinly and cut into small pieces. Place in a saucepan and cover with water. Bring to the boil, add a large pinch of salt and cook for 8–10 minutes until tender. Drain well and allow to air-dry in a colander or large sieve for 10 minutes.

2. Meanwhile, cut the curly kale leaves from the central stalks and chop roughly, wash thoroughly and place in a saucepan without drying so that the kale will cook in the steam produced by the wet leaves. Trim the leek and slice lengthways. Run under cold running water to flush out any trapped earth and shake to remove excess water. Shred finely and mix into the kale. Cover the saucepan and cook over a gentle heat for 10–12 minutes, stirring occasionally, until just tender. Drain well, chop finely and blot with kitchen paper.

3. Return the potatoes to the saucepan and mash well using a potato masher – if you have a ricer, you will get a finer texture if you push the potato through the machine.

4. While the mash is still fairly hot, add another pinch of salt, sieve in the flour and add the kale and leek mixture, then gradually work them into the mashed potato using a wooden spoon. The mixture should form a pliable dough.

5. Turn on to a lightly floured work surface and knead gently until smooth. Roll the dough to form an approximate 23 cm (9 in) square. Cut into quarters and then cut each on the diagonal to form two triangles.

6. Brush a large frying pan or griddle pan lightly with oil and heat until hot. Cook the scones in two batches for about 2 minutes on each side until lightly golden. Keep warm while cooking the remaining scones. Serve warm.

✳ **Freezing:** allow to cool, then layer between sheets of baking parchment. Wrap well and store for up to 6 months. Defrost individual slices, covered, at room temperature for 30 minutes. Reheat by placing under a preheated hot grill for about 1 minute on each side, or fry gently in melted butter for about 1 minute on each side.

FOR PICTURE, SEE PAGE 108

Recipes: Accompaniments

Pumpkin and apple mash

Americans traditionally serve a sweet pumpkin dish with their Thanksgiving turkey roast. This accompaniment is good with a rich, savoury mutton stew or game casserole.

Serves 4

500 g (1 lb 2 oz) pumpkin, deseeded, skinned and cut into small pieces
Salt
250 g (9 oz) cooking apples, peeled, cored and chopped
2 Tbsp maple syrup
2 Tbsp seedless raisins
1 tsp ground cinnamon
15 g (½ oz) toasted flaked almonds

1. Put the chopped pumpkin in a saucepan. Cover with water and add a good pinch of salt. Bring to the boil and cook for 5 minutes.

2. Add the chopped apples to the pumpkin, bring back to the boil, then cover and cook for a further 5–6 minutes until tender. Drain well and return to the saucepan.

3. Mash thoroughly using a fork or potato masher. Stir in the maple syrup, raisins and cinnamon. Taste and season well, then pile into a warmed serving bowl and sprinkle with flaked almonds to serve.

✱ **Freezing:** omit the raisins and almonds, allow to cool, then pack into a rigid freezer container. Seal and freeze for up to 3 months. Defrost in the refrigerator overnight. To reheat, place in a saucepan, cover and put over a very low heat for about 20 minutes, stirring occasionally, until piping hot. Stir in the raisins to serve as above.

FOR PICTURE, SEE PAGE 109

Three-bean gratin

The sweet earthiness of fresh beans in this recipe is complemented with a fresh tomato sauce and a creamy, lightly seasoned white sauce. Serve the gratin with fish or chicken, or as a vegetarian main course.

Serves 6 (as an accompaniment)

600 ml (1 pt) fresh tomato sauce
  (see Cook's note)
450 ml (15 fl oz) whole milk
4 cloves
1 bay leaf
Pinch of nutmeg
225 g (8 oz) runner beans
175 g (6 oz) French beans
225 g (8 oz) shelled broad beans
Salt and white pepper
25 g (1 oz) butter
25 g (1 oz) plain flour
1 free range egg yolk
Freshly chopped tarragon, to garnish

1. Make up the tomato sauce as described in Cook's note, and set aside. Meanwhile, pour the milk into a saucepan and add the cloves, bay leaf and nutmeg. Slowly bring to the boil, remove from the heat and cool for 30 minutes, then strain.

2. Meanwhile, top and tail the runner beans, and slice thinly. Top and tail the French beans – cut in half if quite long. Bring a saucepan of lightly salted water to the boil and cook all the beans for about 5 minutes until just tender. Drain well and set aside.

3. Melt the butter in a saucepan and stir in the flour. Cook for 1 minute. Remove from the heat and gradually stir in the seasoned milk. Return to the heat and cook, stirring, until the mixture comes to the boil and thickens. Cook for a further minute then remove from the heat. Taste and season if necessary. Stir in the egg yolk.

4. Preheat the oven to 180°C/350°F/gas 4. Transfer the beans to the bottom of a 1 L (1¾ pt) gratin dish. Spoon over the tomato sauce and then the white sauce. Put on a baking sheet and cook for about 40 minutes until lightly golden. Serve sprinkled with freshly chopped tarragon.

🍞 Cook's note

For 600 ml (1 pt) tomato sauce, place 1.25 kg (2 lb 12 oz) halved ripe tomatoes in the bottom of a large saucepan. Add 2 peeled garlic cloves and a couple of bay leaves. Cover with a lid. Cook over a low/medium heat for about 40 minutes until soft and collapsed – keep the heat quite low to prevent burning. Discard the bay leaves and push the pulpy tomato mixture through a nylon sieve to form a thick juice, leaving a dry residue of skins and seeds in the sieve. Return to a clean saucepan and add 1 teaspoon of caster sugar, ½ teaspoon of salt and 75 g (3 oz) unsalted butter. Heat gently until the butter melts, then simmer gently for about 20 minutes until thickened, but still thin enough to pour. Use as per recipe or allow to cool, cover and store in the fridge until required, for a maximum of 3 days. To freeze, ladle into small containers when cool, seal and freeze for up to 6 months. Thaw in the fridge overnight.

❄ **Freezing:** not suitable.

Mixed root 'stovies'

Until I moved to Scotland, I'd never had stovies before. Now, this crumbling mass of crushed potato is a firm favourite of mine. In this version I've added other roots, but try it with just potato for something more authentic.

Serves 6

450 g (1 lb) main crop potatoes
   (such as Maris Piper or King Edward)
1 parsnip
1 small swede (yellow turnip)
1 large carrot
50 g (2 oz) beef dripping, butter or vegetable oil
2 onions, peeled and chopped
300 ml (10 fl oz) beef or vegetable stock
225 g (8 oz) corned beef, mashed (optional)
Salt and freshly ground black pepper
2 Tbsp freshly chopped parsley

1. Peel all the root vegetables. Cut the potatoes into 5 cm (2 in) chunks and place in a large bowl. Cut the parsnip and swede into 2.5 cm (1 in) thick pieces and the carrot into smaller pieces still. Mix all the vegetables together in the bowl.

2. Melt the dripping or butter, or heat the oil until hot, in a large saucepan. Cook the onion gently for about 10 minutes, stirring occasionally, until tender and lightly golden. Mix in the prepared roots and pour over the stock. Bring to the boil, half-cover and simmer gently for about 20 minutes, stirring halfway through to help break them up a bit. Stir in the corned beef, if using, and heat through for 3–4 minutes.

3. The stovies are ready when the potatoes have started to break down and form a lumpy gravy. Taste and season as necessary, then sprinkle with parsley and serve with roast or grilled meats.

* **Freezing:** not suitable.

FOR PICTURE, SEE PAGE 110

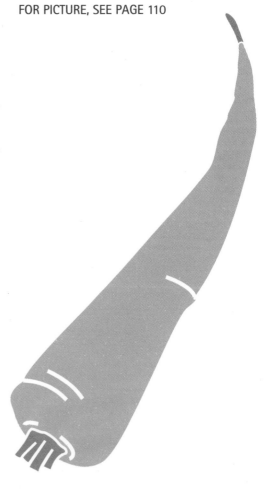

Balsamic and honey-glazed sprouts with bacon

It does take a bit of time to shred sprouts, but you can do it a few hours before you want to cook them and keep them covered in the fridge. This is a lovely alternative for a special occasion like Christmas Day lunch.

Serves 6

675 g (1½ lb) Brussels sprouts
1 large leek
1 Tbsp vegetable oil
175 g (6 oz) smoked streaky bacon,
   cut into thin strips
3 Tbsp balsamic vinegar
1 Tbsp clear honey
Pinch of ground nutmeg
Salt and freshly ground black pepper

1. Trim the Brussels sprouts and shred them finely. Trim the leek and cut in half lengthways. Rinse under cold running water to flush out any trapped earth. Shake to remove excess water and then slice very thinly. Set aside.

2. Heat the oil in a wok or large, deep frying pan and stir-fry the bacon for 2–3 minutes, then add the shredded sprouts and leek and continue to cook for 4–5 minutes.

3. Add the balsamic vinegar and honey and stir-fry over a high heat for a further 1–2 minutes until just tender. Stir in the nutmeg and season to taste. Serve immediately.

🍞 Cook's note

Replace all or half the sprouts with finely shredded dark green cabbage if preferred.

✱ **Freezing:** not suitable.

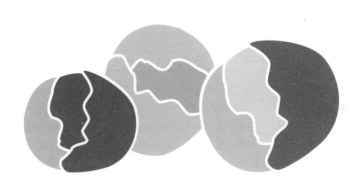

Roast new potatoes with baby vine tomatoes

Baby new potatoes have a certain sweetness to them and when seasoned with a smoked spice, the combination works very well together.

Serves 4–6

225 g (8 oz) shallots
4 garlic cloves
500 g (1 lb 2 oz) small potatoes in their skins, scrubbed and halved
4 Tbsp cold-pressed rapeseed oil or olive oil
2 tsp smoked paprika
1 tsp ground cumin
1 Tbsp clear honey
Few sprigs of fresh thyme and rosemary
Few bay leaves
Salt and freshly ground black pepper
225 g (8 oz) ripe cherry tomatoes on the vine

1. Preheat the oven to 200°C/400°F/gas 6. Peel the shallots, cut in quarters lengthways and place in a shallow roasting tin. Peel the garlic and cut into thick slices and toss into the shallots along with the potatoes.

2. Mix the oil with the spices and honey and brush thickly over the vegetables, reserving a tablespoonful for the tomatoes. Lay the herbs on top, season well and bake for about 30 minutes, basting occasionally.

3. Lay the vine tomatoes on top and brush with the remaining spiced oil. Continue to cook for a further 10 minutes until the vegetables are tender. Discard the herbs before serving.

Cook's note

Line the roasting tin with baking parchment in case the honey over caramelizes and burns on the bottom of the tin.

* Freezing: not suitable.

FOR PICTURE, SEE PAGE 111

Recipes: Accompaniments

French-style Jerusalem artichokes

I have to admit to not being very adventurous with Jerusalem artichokes, and I usually dice them up and add them to a roasting tin of other roots. Luckily, the French know several other ways to use them, and this is now one of my favourites.

Serves 4

1 unwaxed lemon, scrubbed
500 g (1 lb 2 oz) Jerusalem artichokes
25 g (1 oz) butter
2 garlic cloves, peeled and finely chopped
150 ml (5 fl oz) dry white wine
Salt and freshly ground black pepper
Few sprigs of fresh thyme

1. Finely grate 1 teaspoon of lemon zest and set aside. Cut the lemon in half and squeeze the juice into a large bowl. Half-fill with cold water. Peel the artichokes, putting them in the lemony water as you go, and then cut them into small chunks, placing them back in the lemony water, until required.

2. Melt the butter in a frying pan with a tight-fitting lid and gently fry the garlic for 1 minute until softened. Drain the Jerusalem artichokes well and pat dry with kitchen paper. Add to the pan and stir well to cover in the butter and cook, stirring, for 2 minutes.

3. Pour in the wine and season well. Bring to the boil then reduce to a gentle simmer. Sprinkle with the lemon zest and a few sprigs of thyme, cover and cook gently for about 45 minutes until very tender.

4. Discard the thyme, mix the artichokes in the pan juices and serve garnished with fresh thyme. Delicious served with roast chicken or pheasant.

✱ **Freezing:** not suitable.

Broad beans and peas in the pod

You need to use the smallest, well-formed pods for the best results. If the pods have grown too big, simply triple the quantity and shell the beans and peas.

Serves 4

225 g (8 oz) baby broad beans in the pod
225 g (8 oz) small pea pods
Salt and freshly ground black pepper
Large sprig of mint + 2 Tbsp freshly chopped mint
1 small cucumber
2 tsp caster sugar
150 ml (5 fl oz) whole milk natural yoghurt,
    at room temperature
1 Tbsp white wine vinegar

1. Top and tail the bean and pea pods, and pull away the string that seals the pod together. Slice the pods in half lengthways, on the diagonal.

2. Bring a saucepan of lightly salted water to the boil and cook the pods with a sprig of mint for 5 minutes until just tender. Drain well and discard the mint sprig.

3. Meanwhile, peel the cucumber. Cut in half lengthways and scoop out the seeds. Finely chop the flesh and place in a bowl. Mix in the remaining ingredients and season well.

4. Serve the freshly cooked pods with the cucumber dressing. Ideal to serve with smoked fish, cooked chicken or egg dishes.

✱ **Freezing:** not suitable.

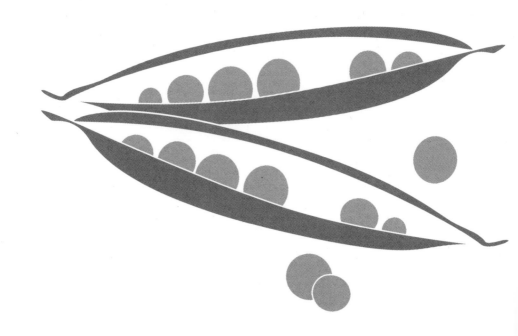

FOR PICTURE, SEE PAGE 112

Winter cabbage with anchovy butter

One of my favourite cabbage dishes is the sweet, spiced red cabbage that is often served with roast pork or sausages. I thought I'd create a more savoury white cabbage alternative.

Serves 4–6

50 g (2 oz) unsalted butter
1 medium onion, peeled and chopped
1 bay leaf
2 tsp cumin seeds, lightly crushed
2 tsp coriander seeds, lightly crushed
500 g (1 lb 2 oz) white cabbage, trimmed
  and shredded
3 Tbsp cider vinegar
3 Tbsp water
25 g (1 oz) caster sugar
Freshly ground black pepper
6 tinned anchovy fillets in oil, drained
4 Tbsp freshly chopped parsley

1. Melt half the butter in a large saucepan and gently fry the onion with the bay leaf and spices for 5 minutes, until softened but not browned.

2. Stir in the cabbage and mix well to thoroughly coat in the oniony butter. Add the cider vinegar, water, sugar and plenty of black pepper. Stir well, bring to the boil, cover and simmer very gently for about 40 minutes, stirring occasionally to prevent sticking, until tender. Discard the bay leaf before serving.

3. While the cabbage is cooking, mash or finely chop the anchovy fillets into a paste and mix into the remaining butter. Cover and chill until required.

4. Just before serving, mix the anchovy butter and chopped parsley into the cabbage, and serve to accompany pork, gammon or sausages.

✱ Freezing: without adding the anchovy butter and parsley, allow to cool then pack into a freezer bag. Seal well and freeze for up to 3 months. Defrost for a few hours in the refrigerator. To reheat, place in a saucepan and add 4 tablespoons of water. Heat until steaming, then cover and cook very gently, stirring occasionally, for about 20 minutes until piping hot. Add the butter and parsley as per recipe.

Courgette and squash 'crisps'

I remember having some lovely, lemon-flavoured courgette fritters in an Italian restaurant once. I'm not sure how authentic they were but they were very good, so much so that I thought I'd have a go at making my own.

Serves 4

2 medium courgettes
225 g (8 oz) squash
100 g (3½ oz) + 2 Tbsp plain flour
1 small unwaxed lemon
Sunflower oil, for deep-frying
1 free range egg
4 Tbsp freshly chopped basil
175 ml (6 fl oz) soda water
Sea salt and freshly ground black pepper

1. Trim the courgettes and cut in half to make shorter lengths. Using a vegetable peeler, shave off thin strips into a mixing bowl.

2. Slice off the skin from the squash and scoop out the seeds. Cut into pieces about the same length as the courgette, and pare strips of squash into the bowl.

3. Toss the vegetable strips in 2 tablespoons of plain flour to thoroughly coat. Grate the rind from the lemon and extract the juice.

4. Heat the oil for deep-frying to a temperature of 190°C (375°F). Put the remaining flour in a bowl and blend in the egg, 1 teaspoon of lemon rind and chopped basil. Gradually blend in the soda water and the juice of the lemon to make a smooth batter.

5. Pour over the vegetables and gently mix to make sure the slices are coated. Using tongs, lift out a few slices at a time and deep-fry for 3–4 minutes until crisp, puffed and golden. Drain on kitchen paper and keep warm while frying the rest of the vegetable strips. Serve the 'crisps', seasoned with sea salt and black pepper, as soon as possible after cooking.

🍞 Cook's note

If you fancy experimenting, courgette flowers taste delicious cooked in this way. Follow the method above with the still closed but fully formed flower heads. Just rinse, pat dry and they are ready to use.

✳ Freezing: not suitable.

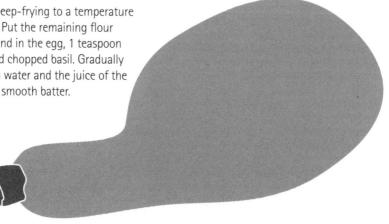

FOR PICTURE, SEE PAGE 113

Sweetcorn and polenta pudding

I really like cornbread served fresh out of the oven, and this recipe is a cross between a bake and something that needs a spoon. It's good for soaking up gravy or sauces, or eating on its own straight from the dish!

Serves 6

4 ripe corn cobs or 500 g (1 lb 2 oz) kernels
1 tsp caster sugar
2 Tbsp corn or vegetable oil
2 green chillies, deseeded and finely chopped
2 garlic cloves, peeled and finely chopped
8 spring onions, trimmed and finely chopped
250 g (9 oz) polenta or fine cornmeal
2 Tbsp plain flour
1 tsp salt
1 Tbsp baking powder
2 large free range eggs, beaten
200 ml (7 fl oz) whole milk
115 g (4 oz) mature Cheddar (or similar) cheese, grated

1. Preheat the oven to 200°C/400°F/gas 6. Strip off the outer leaves and silky strings from the sweetcorn. Bring a saucepan of water to the boil, add the sugar (but no salt, it toughens the kernels) and cook for about 8 minutes. Test for 'doneness' by pricking carefully with a skewer to see if the kernels are tender. Rinse in cold running water to cool, then strip off the kernels by running a small, sharp knife down the length of the cob, collecting the kernels as they are released.

2. Heat the oil in a frying pan and gently fry the chillies, garlic and spring onions, stirring, for about 3 minutes until just softened. Set aside.

3. In a bowl, mix together the polenta, flour, salt and baking powder. Make a well in the centre and add the eggs and milk. Gradually mix together to form a smooth batter. Stir in the sweetcorn and the chilli mixture, along with the pan juices.

4. Transfer to a greased 1 L (1¾ pt) ovenproof, round dish and place on a baking tray. Sprinkle with the cheese and bake for about 30 minutes until slightly risen, golden and firm. Best served warm.

✱ **Freezing:** make in an ovenproof and freezer-proof dish. Allow to cool then wrap well and freeze for up to 3 months. Allow to defrost overnight in the refrigerator. To reheat, cover with foil and place in a preheated oven at 190°C/375°F/gas 5 to reheat for about 25 minutes until piping hot.

The perfect chip

After dauphinoise, chips are the next best thing to do with potatoes as far as I'm concerned. I'm including a low-fat option as well.

Serves 4

900 g (2 lb) large, main crop potatoes
(such as Maris Piper or King Edward)
½ tsp salt
Corn oil for deep-frying
Sea salt
Mayonnaise, to serve

1. Peel the potatoes and cut into 1 cm (½ in) thick chips. Rinse in cold running water. Place in a large saucepan and cover with water. Add the ½ teaspoon of salt and bring to the boil. Cook for 6–7 minutes until almost cooked, but still firm. Drain well and set aside to air-dry in a colander or large sieve for 10 minutes, then return them to the saucepan, cover with a lid and shake a few times to 'rough up' the edges.

2. Heat the oil for deep-frying to 190°C (375°F). Fry the par-boiled chips for about 5 minutes until golden and crisp. Drain on kitchen paper and serve as soon as possible sprinkled with sea salt and accompanied with mayonnaise.

Low-fat variation

Preheat the oven to 240°C/475°F/gas 9. Using the same quantity of potatoes, follow Step 1 of the recipe. Put the chips in a large clean food bag and add 1 tablespoon of corn oil. Shake the bag to disperse the oil. Spread the chips out on a large baking tray lined with baking parchment and bake for 20–25 minutes, turning occasionally, until golden and crisp all over. Drain on kitchen paper and serve as above (but with reduced-fat mayo!).

✱ **Freezing:** blanch uncooked chips in boiling water for 1 minute. Drain and cool. Open freeze until solid, then pack into freezer bags. Freeze for up to 6 months. To use, defrost and cook as described in Step 2.

Chocolate beetroot muffins

Sounds a little weird, but really this mixture follows the same principle as a carrot cake. The beetroot simply adds moistness. Leave the icing colouring out if you prefer!

Makes 12

FOR THE MUFFINS
210 g (7½ oz) plain flour
40 g (1½ oz) cocoa powder
1½ tsp baking powder
1 tsp bicarbonate of soda
175 g (6 oz) dark muscovado sugar
150 g (5 oz) plain or milk chocolate chips
175 g (6 oz) unsalted butter, softened
2 medium free range eggs, beaten
100 ml (3½ fl oz) whole milk
250 g (9 oz) cooked beetroot, puréed

FOR THE ICING
175 g (6 oz) icing sugar
½ tsp good-quality vanilla extract
1–2 tsp beetroot juice

1. Preheat the oven to 180ºC/350ºF/gas 4. Line a 12 deep-bun muffin tray with 12 paper muffin cases. Sift the flour, cocoa, baking powder and bicarbonate of soda into a mixing bowl. Stir in the sugar and chocolate chips, and make a well in the centre.

2. Melt 75 g (3 oz) of the butter and mix into the eggs. Pour into the chocolate mixture along with the milk and blend together gradually to form a thick batter. Fold in the beetroot purée.

3. Divide between the muffin cases and bake in the oven for about 30 minutes until risen and firm to the touch. Transfer to a wire rack to cool completely.

4. Beat the remaining butter until soft and gradually sieve and beat in the icing sugar. Add the vanilla and beetroot juice to form a fluffy icing. Spread thickly over each muffin and serve.

🍲 Cook's note

Use this method with other vegetables, such as grated raw carrot or courgette, or cooked, smoothly mashed parsnip, potato, squash or pumpkin.

✳ Freezing: allow muffins to cool completely, then place uniced in a rigid freezer container. Seal well and freeze for up to 3 months. Thaw a few muffins at a time at room temperature. Make up icing as above.

FOR PICTURE, SEE PAGE 114

Recipes: Desserts, puddings and bakes

Pear and ginger loaf

If you ask me what my favourite cake is I'd be torn between a coffee and walnut sponge and a dense ginger cake. I'm always coming up with variations for the latter, and here's my latest.

Serves 8

4 small ripe pears
Juice of 1 lemon
115 g (4 oz) treacle
115 g (4 oz) golden syrup
115 g (4 oz) dark muscovado sugar
115 g (4 oz) butter
150 ml (5 fl oz) whole milk
225 g (8 oz) self–raising flour
1 Tbsp ground ginger
1 tsp ground mixed spice

1. Preheat the oven to 180°C/350°F/gas 4. Grease and line a 900 g (2 lb) loaf tin. Peel the pears, cut in half and carefully remove the core to leave the pieces whole. Place in a shallow dish and sprinkle with lemon juice.

2. Place the treacle, syrup, sugar, butter and milk in a saucepan, and heat gently, stirring, until melted together. Sieve the flour and spices in a bowl, and make a well in the centre and gradually stir in the melted ingredients until well mixed.

3. Drain the pears halves and pat dry with kitchen paper. Carefully arrange 4 pear halves in the bottom of the tin. Pour over half the ginger cake mixture and arrange the remaining pears on top.

4. Spoon over the remaining cake mixture and put the tin on a baking tray. Bake in the centre of the oven for about 1 hour until risen and firm to the touch. Leave to cool in the tin, then remove from the tin, wrap and store for 24 hours before slicing to serve.

✱ **Freezing:** allow to cool completely, then wrap and seal well. Freeze for up to 3 months. Defrost at room temperature, in the wrappings, for a few hours until ready to serve.

Recipes: Desserts, puddings and bakes

Cherry pithiviers

A lush dessert based on a traditional French recipe of rich almond paste encased in puff pastry. Cherries go so well with almonds, they make an ideal addition to this wonderful creation.

Serves 8

200 g (7 oz) ground almonds
125 g (4½ oz) caster sugar
1 tsp good–quality almond extract
2 medium free range eggs, beaten
500 g (1 lb 2 oz) pack puff pastry,
  thawed if frozen
250 g (9 oz) cherries, stoned
1 Tbsp icing sugar
Crème fraîche, to serve

1. Preheat the oven to 200°C/400°F/gas 6. Line a baking tray with baking parchment. Mix together the ground almonds, caster sugar and almond extract. Bind together well using one of the eggs to form a paste. Set aside.

2. Roll out half of the pastry on a lightly floured board to form an approximate 25 cm (10 in) square. Cut out a 25 cm (10 in) circle of pastry and transfer to the baking tray.

3. Form the almond paste into an approximate 20 cm (8 in) circle and place in the centre of the pastry. Pile the cherries on top, gently pressing them into the almond paste.

4. Brush the edges of the pastry with beaten egg. Roll out the remaining pastry to a 30 cm (12 in) square and cut out a 30 cm (12 in) circle.

5. Cover the cherries with the pastry circle and press down and score the edge to seal. Score the top all over in either a swirled pattern or a criss-cross design. Make a slit in the centre to allow steam to escape, brush with egg and bake in the oven for about 40 minutes until golden and crisp. Cool on the baking tray for 10 minutes then dust with icing sugar before slicing to serve. Best served warm with crème fraîche.

✱ **Freezing:** allow to cool completely then place on a freezer-proof plate or tray. Wrap well and freeze for up to 3 months. Defrost overnight in the refrigerator. To reheat, cover with foil and place on a baking tray in a preheated oven at 180°C/350°F/gas 4 for about 25 minutes until piping hot.

FOR PICTURE, SEE PAGE 115

Recipes: Desserts, puddings and bakes

Blackberry, oatmeal and honey ice cream

I prefer to cook down berries before I make them into ice cream, and I think brambles (blackberries) have more flavour if you serve them in this way. You can use this method with raspberries as well.

Serves 6

25 g (1 oz) medium oatmeal
200 ml (7 fl oz) boiling water
225 g (8 oz) blackberries
3 Tbsp unsweetened apple juice
300 ml (10 fl oz) whole milk
3 large free range egg yolks
40 g (1½ oz) caster sugar
50 g (2 oz) heather honey or other
    well-flavoured honey
150 ml (5 fl oz) double cream
Shortbread biscuits, to serve

1. Put the oatmeal in a small frying pan and heat, stirring, for 4–5 minutes until toasted. Transfer to a small heatproof bowl and pour over the boiling water. Set aside.

2. Meanwhile, put the blackberries in a saucepan with the apple juice. Heat gently, bring to the boil and simmer for about 5 minutes until soft. Allow to cool, then push through a nylon sieve to remove the seeds and to make a purée. Cover and chill until required.

3. Pour the milk into a saucepan and heat until hot but not boiling. In a heatproof bowl, whisk the egg yolks with the sugar and honey until pale, thick and creamy. Gently whisk in the hot milk.

4. Put the bowl on top of a saucepan of gently simmering water and cook, stirring occasionally, until thick enough to coat the back of a spoon – this will take about 25 minutes. Remove the bowl from the saucepan, cover with a layer of buttered greaseproof paper directly on the surface and set aside to cool, then cover and chill until required.

5. Whip the cream until softly peaking. Drain the oatmeal well and fold into the custard along with the blackberry purée. Turn into a freezer-proof container and put in the freezer for about 2 hours until just beginning to freeze round the edges. Beat well and return to the freezer for a further 40 minutes to 1 hour. Beat again and refreeze. Repeat this once more then allow to freeze solidly for at least 2 hours. If you have an ice cream maker, simply churn until firm.

6. To serve, stand at room temperature for 10–20 minutes before scooping and serving accompanied with shortbread biscuits.

✳ **Freezing:** has to be frozen. Keep well sealed in the freezer for up to 3 months. Stand at room temperature for a few minutes, to allow to soften enough to scoop, before serving.

Blueberry soup

You can serve this refreshing, deep purple berry soup as a light dessert or as an alternative starter. Replace the star anise with cinnamon for a different flavour if preferred. Use a vegetable peeler to pare off lemon rind.

Serves 4

550 g (1 lb 3½ oz) blueberries
115 g (4 oz) caster sugar
4 pared strips unwaxed lemon rind
2 star anise
600 ml (1 pt) freshly pressed apple juice
Juice of 1 lemon
4 Tbsp Greek yoghurt
Lemon wedges, to serve

1. Wash the blueberries and pat dry. Reserving a handful for decoration, put the rest in a saucepan.

2. Add the sugar, strips of lemon zest, star anise and apple juice. Bring to the boil, cover and simmer for 10 minutes until very soft. Allow to cool then push through a nylon sieve to make a smooth purée. Stir in the lemon juice, cover and chill for at least 2 hours or until ready to serve.

3. To serve, spoon into small dessert bowls and serve with a spoonful of yoghurt and a wedge of lemon. Sprinkle with the reserved berries.

✳ **Freezing:** follow the recipe up to the end of Step 2. Pour into a rigid freezer container, cover and freeze for up to 3 months. Allow to defrost in the refrigerator overnight before serving as above.

FOR PICTURE, SEE PAGE 116

Recipes: Desserts, puddings and bakes

Gooseberry îles flottantes

A combination of creamy custard marbled with tangy fruit purée topped with 'floating' soft, billowing marshmallow meringues, makes this a truly dreamy early summer dessert.

Recipes: Desserts, puddings and bakes

Serves 4

450 g (1 lb) green gooseberries, topped and tailed
Approx. 150 g (5 oz) caster sugar
Juice of ½ lemon
600 ml (1 pt) single cream
1 vanilla pod, split
4 large free range egg yolks
1 tsp cornflour
1 large free range egg white
Pinch of salt
600 ml (1 pt) whole milk for poaching

1. Place the gooseberries in a saucepan with 75 g (3 oz) caster sugar and 2 tablespoons of water, bring to the boil, cover and simmer for 8–10 minutes until soft.

2. Transfer to a blender or food processor and blend until smooth. Push through a nylon sieve to make a smooth purée – approximately 450 ml (15 fl oz). Mix in the lemon juice; taste and add more sugar if required. Set aside to cool. Then cover and chill for 1 hour or until ready to serve.

3. Meanwhile, make the custard. Pour the single cream into a saucepan and heat to just below boiling point. Remove from the heat and add the vanilla pod. Set aside to infuse for 30 minutes. Whisk the egg yolks with the cornflour and 25 g (1 oz) caster sugar in a heatproof bowl until pale and creamy. Pour the warm vanilla cream over the egg yolks, stirring all the time. Discard the vanilla pod.

4. Set the bowl over a saucepan of barely simmering water and cook, stirring frequently, until the mixture thickens sufficiently to coat the back of a wooden spoon – approximately 25 minutes. Remove the bowl from the saucepan, cover the surface of the custard with a layer of greaseproof paper and allow to cool.

5. For the meringue islands, whisk the egg white with the salt in a grease-free bowl until very stiff and dry. Whisk in the remaining caster sugar to form a thick, glossy mixture. Pour the milk into a deep frying pan and heat until just simmering. Drop tablespoonfuls of the meringue mixture onto the milk and poach for 3–4 minutes until just firm to the touch. Remove using a slotted spoon and set aside in a shallow dish while cooking the remaining mixture – you should be able to make 12 meringues in total.

6. To serve, gently marble the gooseberry purée into the custard and divide the custard between four shallow serving bowls. Arrange three meringues on top of each portion of custard and serve immediately.

* Freezing: not suitable.

Old-fashioned steamed fruit dumpling

A real 'rib-sticker' of a pudding. You can put just about anything in the middle, but orchard fruits work particularly well

Serves 6–8

350 g (12 oz) self-raising flour
½ tsp salt
175 g (6 oz) suet
Approx. 175 ml (6 fl oz) water
225 g (8 oz) cooking apples, peeled,
    cored and finely chopped
Juice and finely grated zest of 1 lemon
225 g (8 oz) plums or gages, stones removed
    and finely chopped
75 g (3 oz) granulated sugar
2 tsp ground cinnamon
Custard, to serve

1. Grease a 1.2 L (2 pt) pudding basin and place a small disc of baking parchment in the bottom.

2. Place the flour and salt in a bowl and mix in the suet along with sufficient water to make a light, elastic dough. Roll out two-thirds of the dough on a lightly floured surface, 2.5 cm (1 in) larger all round than the top of the prepared basin, and carefully ease the pastry into the basin to line it.

3. In a bowl, mix the apples with the lemon juice and zest. Stir in the plums, sugar and cinnamon, and mix well. Pack into the lined basin.

4. Roll out the remaining pastry to form a circle to fit the top of the basin. Dampen the edge with water and seal on the pastry lid. Top the pudding with a round of baking parchment, and then cover the top of the pudding basin with a layer of pleated foil. Secure with string.

5. Half-fill a large saucepan with water and bring to the boil. Either place the pudding in a steamer compartment over the saucepan or stand on a trivet in the saucepan. Cover tightly with a lid and steam for about 2½ hours, topping the water level up as required, until the pudding is risen and firm to the touch – insert a skewer into the centre of the pudding to make sure the fruit is tender.

6. To serve, unwrap the pudding and invert on to a warmed serving plate with a lipped edge – the pudding will be very juicy when cut. Serve at once with custard.

✱ **Freezing:** make in a freezer-proof and heatproof pudding basin and allow to cool completely. Wrap well and freeze for up to 3 months. Defrost in the refrigerator overnight and reheat as for cooking – the pudding will take about 1½–2 hours to reheat.

Recipes: Desserts, puddings and bakes

Poached rhubarb with blackcurrant syrup

If it's been a good summer you may be able to pull the last stems of your rhubarb while picking your first blackcurrants. If not, remember to freeze some blackcurrants and try this recipe out the following spring.

Serves 4

100 g (3½ oz) prepared fresh or frozen
   blackcurrants
200 ml (7 fl oz) water
350 g (12 oz) rhubarb, trimmed
115 g (4 oz) caster sugar
Crème anglaise, to serve (see Cook's note)
Blackcurrant leaves, to decorate

1. Put the blackcurrants in a small saucepan with the water. Bring to the boil and simmer for 4–5 minutes until very soft and pulpy. Set aside.

2. Cut the rhubarb into 10 cm (4 in) lengths, and slice each piece through the middle to make thinner stems. (If you are using older rhubarb, cut it into shorter lengths, and if necessary, cut the stalks in half lengthways.)

3. Place the sugar in a medium frying pan and strain the blackcurrants through a fine nylon sieve into the pan, pressing them through to add the pulp as well. Heat gently, stirring until dissolved, then bring to the boil and simmer for 3 minutes.

4. Arrange the rhubarb in the pan, laying the pieces side by side. Bring back to the boil, cover and simmer for 3 minutes. Carefully, turn the rhubarb over, re-cover and cook for a further 3–4 minutes until just cooked. Remove from the heat and allow to cool completely.

5. Transfer to a serving dish, cover and chill for 2 hours before serving with crème anglaise (see Cook's note). Decorate with blackcurrant leaves.

🍳 Cook's note

For crème anglaise, pour 300 ml (10 fl oz) single cream into a saucepan and heat until hot but not boiling. Remove from the heat and add a split vanilla pod; leave to infuse for 30 minutes. Discard the vanilla pod. In a heatproof bowl, whisk 4 egg yolks with 3 tablespoons of caster sugar until pale, thick and creamy. Gently whisk in the vanilla cream. Put the bowl on top of a saucepan of gently simmering water and cook stirring until thick enough to coat the back of a spoon – this will take 10–15 minutes. Remove from the saucepan, cover with a layer of buttered greaseproof paper and set aside to cool, then cover and chill until ready to serve.

✱ Freezing: follow the recipe to the end of Step 3. Allow to cool then transfer to a rigid freezer container. Cover and seal, then freeze for up to 3 months. Defrost overnight in the refrigerator before serving as above. The crème anglaise will not freeze.

FOR PICTURE, SEE PAGE 117

Strawberry syllabub

A deliciously light and very simple, yet sumptuous dessert, this mixture of fruity berries and whipped cream can be served on its own or spooned on top of sponge to make a trifle.

Serves 4

50 g (2 oz) caster sugar
150 ml (5 fl oz) dry rosé wine
Few splashes of rosewater
350 g (12 oz) strawberries, washed and hulled
300 ml (10 fl oz) double cream
Strawberry leaves, to decorate

1. Place the sugar, rosé wine and a dash of rosewater to taste in a bowl. Cover and chill for 1 hour.

2. When ready to serve, place half the strawberries in a blender or food processor and blend until smooth. Slice the remaining strawberries and divide between four dessert glasses.

3. Pour the cream into a mixing bowl and begin whisking. As the cream begins to thicken, gradually pour in the wine mixture and continue whisking until just peaking.

4. Carefully fold in the strawberry purée to give a marbled effect and then pile into the glasses. Serve immediately, decorated with strawberry leaves.

🍴 Cook's note

You can prepare this dessert up to 30 minutes in advance and keep in the refrigerator. After this time, the juices begin to separate from the cream.

✱ **Freezing:** not suitable.

FOR PICTURE, SEE PAGE 118

Damson and gin jellies

I usually make a batch of damson gin each year, ready to enjoy at Christmas. Because the flavours marry so well together, I thought I'd put them together for a more instant fix.

Serves 4

450 g (1 lb) damsons, stalks removed
115 g (4 oz) granulated sugar
2 tsp juniper berries, lightly crushed
150 ml (5 fl oz) water
5 sheets fine leaf gelatine
100 ml (3½ fl oz) London gin
Clotted cream, to serve

1. Place the damsons in a saucepan with the sugar, juniper berries and water. Heat gently, stirring, until the sugar melts. Bring to the boil. Cover and cook over a low heat for about 10 minutes until the damsons are very soft. Keep covered and cool for 10 minutes, then push through a nylon sieve to make a soft purée. Set aside to cool completely.

2. Cut the gelatine into small pieces and place in a heatproof bowl. Spoon over 3 tablespoons of cold water and set aside to soak for 10 minutes. Melt the gelatine over a pan of simmering water, and set aside to cool.

3. Pour the gelatine into the damson purée, add the gin and mix well. Divide between four small tumblers, and chill for at least 3 hours to set before serving topped with a dollop of clotted cream.

🍴 Cook's note

You can also try this recipe with plums or gages, but you may prefer to replace the juniper berries and gin with a cinnamon stick and amaretto liqueur – adjust the sugar accordingly. The quantity of gelatine used in this recipe gives a softer set, more refined jelly. Use an extra sheet if you want to make the jelly in moulds for turning out.

✱ **Freezing:** not suitable.

Recipes: Desserts, puddings and bakes

Rhubarb and raspberry crump

As soon as I heard about this delightfully named West Country pudding I knew it would be one for me. My sister-in-law passed on the family recipe, and this is my version using rhubarb and raspberries, but any stewed fruit is suitable.

Serves 6

350 g (12 oz) rhubarb, trimmed and cut
   into 1 cm (½ in) thick slices
50 ml (2 fl oz) freshly squeezed orange juice
165 g (5½ oz) granulated sugar
175 g (6 oz) raspberries
115 g (4 oz) butter, very soft
150 g (5 oz) plain flour
Few drops of good-quality vanilla extract
Clotted cream, to serve

1. First prepare the fruit. Put the rhubarb in a saucepan with the orange juice and 50 g (2 oz) sugar. Bring to the boil, then simmer gently for 5–6 minutes until just tender. Stir in the raspberries and set aside to cool. Transfer to four individual 300 ml (10 fl oz) pie dishes or a large 1.2 L (2 pt) oval pie dish.

2. Preheat the oven to 180°C/350°F/gas 4. For the crump topping, put the butter in a bowl with the remaining sugar and beat together until soft and creamy. Add the flour and vanilla extract and mix together until well combined and it forms a soft, buttery dough.

3. Break up the mixture and dot all over the cold fruit filling, covering it as much as possible (it will merge slightly on cooking). Stand the pie dishes on a baking tray and bake in the oven for 30–40 minutes, depending on the size made, or until firm and lightly golden. Best served warm with clotted cream!

✳ **Freezing:** make in a freezer-proof and ovenproof dish, allow to cool completely then wrap well and freeze for up to 3 months. Defrost overnight in the refrigerator. To reheat, cover with foil and place in a preheated oven at 180°C/350°F/gas 4 for about 25 minutes until piping hot.

FOR PICTURE, SEE PAGE 119

Recipes: Desserts, puddings and bakes

Vanilla-cherry compôte and chocolate blancmange

Although this dessert may look like something from the 1970s, chocolate and cherries will never go out of fashion. This rich, chocolatey blancmange is set in a ring mould and filled with a luscious vanilla-cherry mixture.

Serves 8–10

FOR THE CHERRIES
115 g (4 oz) caster sugar
200 ml (7 fl oz) unsweetened apple juice
500 g (1 lb 2 oz) fresh cherries, stoned
1 Tbsp cornflour
1 vanilla pod, split

FOR THE BLANCMANGE
100 g (3½ oz) cornflour
650 ml (22 fl oz) whole milk
175 g (6 oz) 85% cocoa dark chocolate,
    cut into small pieces
150 ml (5 fl oz) double cream
75 g (3 oz) caster sugar
1 tsp good-quality vanilla extract

Pouring cream, to serve

1. To prepare the cherries, put the sugar in a saucepan with all but 2 tablespoons of the apple juice, and heat gently, stirring until dissolved. Bring to the boil and add the cherries. Simmer gently for 4 minutes, stirring occasionally.

2. Blend the cornflour with the remaining apple juice and stir into the cherries. Bring back to the boil and cook for a further minute to thicken or until the cherries are tender. Remove from the heat, add the vanilla pod and allow to cool completely. Discard the vanilla pod. Transfer to a serving dish, cover and chill for 2 hours before serving.

3. Meanwhile, make the blancmange. Put the cornflour in a bowl and blend with sufficient milk to make a smooth paste.

4. Put the chocolate in a saucepan, and pour over the remaining milk. Heat very gently, without boiling, stirring occasionally until the chocolate has melted into the milk. Stir in the cream and sugar.

5. Bring the chocolate milk to the boil and stir in the cornflour mixture; keep stirring as the mixture becomes very thick. Cook for a further minute, then remove from the heat, stir in the vanilla extract and quickly spoon into a wetted 1.2 L (2 pt) ring mould. Level off the surface and cover with cling film to prevent a skin forming. Allow to cool completely and set firm, then chill for 2 hours.

6. To serve, remove the cling film and dip the mould in hot water for a few seconds to loosen. Turn the blancmange on to a serving plate and spoon the cherry mixture into the centre to serve. Accompany with pouring cream.

✱ **Freezing:** not suitable.

Spicy carrot and pine nut cookies

If you can have carrot cake, why not have carrot cookies? As well as pretty orange flecks, carrot adds sweetness and a moist texture to these tasty bakes.

Makes 20

175 g (6 oz) butter, softened
250 g (9 oz) light brown sugar
2 free range eggs, beaten
150 g (5 oz) pine nuts
50 g (2 oz) grated carrot
400 g (14 oz) plain flour
1 tsp baking powder
2 tsp mixed spice

1. Put the butter in a bowl with the sugar and beat until pale and creamy. Gradually beat in the eggs – don't worry if the mixture separates at this stage.

2. Stir in the pine nuts and grated carrot, then sieve over the flour, baking powder and spice and carefully mix the ingredients together to form a soft dough. Cover and chill for 1 hour.

3. Preheat the oven to 180°C/350°F/gas 4. Line two large baking trays with baking parchment.

4. Take tablespoonfuls of the dough and form into 20 balls. Arrange, spaced about 5 cm (2 in) apart, on the trays and flatten well. Bake for 10–12 minutes until firm and lightly golden. Allow to cool on the baking trays, then transfer to an airtight container to store for up to 5 days.

✱ **Freezing:** allow the baked cookies to cool then pack in a freezer bag between layers of greaseproof paper or freezer sheets. Seal well and freeze for up to 3 months. Allow the cookies to defrost at room temperature for about 30 minutes before serving.

Recipes: Desserts, puddings and bakes

Berry cake with sugar crunch topping

This cake is bursting with flavour and colour. It's a proper cakey cake, dense and moist. It's definitely better if you leave it for 24 hours before cutting it.

Serves 12

175 g (6 oz) butter, softened
175 g (6 oz) caster sugar
175 g (6 oz) self-raising flour
3 large free range eggs, beaten
75 g (3 oz) ground almonds
150 g (5 oz) golden marzipan,
    cut into small pieces
300 g (10 oz) prepared mixed small berries and
    currants (such as blueberries, raspberries,
    alpine strawberries, blackberries, redcurrants
    and blackcurrants)
115 g (4 oz) sugar lumps, lightly crushed

1. Preheat the oven to 180°C/350°F/gas 4. Grease and line a deep 20 cm (8 in) cake tin. In a mixing bowl, beat together the butter and sugar until pale and creamy.

2. Gradually whisk in 4 tablespoons of flour with the eggs, then sieve in the remainder. Fold in the ground almonds, marzipan and berries.

3. Pile the mixture into the prepared tin and smooth the top. Sprinkle with the crushed sugar lumps and lightly push them into the top. Bake in the centre of the oven for about 1¼ hours until golden and firm in the centre. Leave to cool in the tin, standing on a wire rack.

4. Remove from the tin, wrap and store for 24 hours before cutting.

✳ **Freezing:** allow baked cake to cool then transfer to a freezer-proof plate or board. Wrap well and freeze for up to 3 months. Allow to defrost, in the wrappings, at room temperature for a few hours before serving.

FOR PICTURE, SEE PAGE 120

Recipes: Desserts, puddings and bakes

Preserves

Choosing and preparation

It is essential that you start with the best-quality produce in order to prevent rapid deterioration during storage. Fruit and vegetables should be slightly under-ripe or perfectly ripe (depending on the recipe), blemish free, and free from mould and mildew. They should be correctly prepared.

Cooking fruit

Prepared fruit is often simmered either on its own or with liquid before sugar is added. Cook the fruit slowly, without covering (unless otherwise stated), stirring occasionally until just softened. This will allow you to obtain the maximum amount of juice from the fruit. If there is a lack of juice, add a bit more water – this might occur if the fruit is firmer than usual. Take care not to overcook the fruit at this stage otherwise flavour and colour will be impaired.

Testing for setting point

There are two main ways that I use to find out if a preserve has reached the right point in order to set.

1. **Using a sugar thermometer:** For jams, marmalades, conserves and fruit cheeses, an acceptable reading range is 104–105.5°C (219–222°F). The lower temperature, used for conserves, will give a softer set than the higher one. Use the higher temperature for fruit cheeses. For jellies, use 104–105°C (219–221°F).
2. **The wrinkle test:** Take the saucepan of boiling preserve off the heat and quickly spoon a little preserve on to a cold, flat plate; allow to cool. If the preserve is ready, a slight skin will form and it will wrinkle when pushed with your finger. Bring the preserve back to the boil if it isn't ready and retest in about 2 minutes.

Sterilizing storage jars and bottles

Use sound glass containers and bottles with no chips or cracks. Wash thoroughly in very hot water with mild detergent, and rinse well. Put them open-side up in a deep saucepan, cover with boiling water and boil for 10 minutes. Carefully lift out with tongs and leave to drain upside down on a thick, clean towel. Dry with a clean cloth if necessary and place on a baking tray lined with a few layers of kitchen paper; keep warm in the oven on the lowest setting until ready to fill.

Filling the jars

A clean ladle or small heatproof jug will be useful to help you transfer the preserve to the prepared jar, or a funnel will help fill bottles. If the preserve is very fruity or contains rind and small pieces, stir well before putting in the jars. Fill to within 6 mm (¼ in) of the top of the jar. Half-filled jars of any preserve should be cooled, sealed and kept in the fridge and eaten as soon as possible.

Sealing

To prevent spoiling during storage it is essential to achieve an airtight seal on your preserves. As soon as the preserve is in the jar, place a waxed paper circle directly on the top of the contents – available in packs of jam pot covers. Either top with a screw-on lid or seal tightly with the transparent jam pot covers and an elastic band or allow the preserve to cool completely in the jars before sealing with waxed paper circles and lids. Avoid covering semi-cold preserves as too much condensation will form and this could encourage mould to grow during storage. For chutneys, pickles and other preserves with vinegar, make sure the seals used are non-corrosive.

Storage

Don't forget to label your preserve jars and bottles with its contents and the date it was made. Keep in a cool, dry, dark place in order to preserve colour and quality. If perfectly prepared and stored, most jams and jellies will keep for up to 12 months; chutneys, pickles and vinegars for around 6–8 months and fruit cheeses up to 6 months. See specific recipes for other storage instructions.

Red onion and rosemary relish

If you're not growing a pink variety of onion, this recipe works just as well with white onions. If you replace the vinegars below with cider vinegar , you'll end up with a lovely golden-coloured white onion relish.

Makes about 600 g (1 lb 5 oz)

2 Tbsp cold-pressed rapeseed oil or olive oil
700 g (1 lb 9 oz) red onions,
   peeled and thinly sliced
1 tsp salt
Freshly ground black pepper
2 Tbsp very finely chopped fresh rosemary leaves
175 g (6 oz) granulated sugar
100 ml (3½ fl oz) raspberry vinegar
100 ml (3½ fl oz) white wine vinegar

1. Heat the oil in a saucepan and gently fry the onions with the salt for about 10 minutes, stirring occasionally, until soft but not too browned.

2. Stir in the pepper, rosemary and sugar. Cook, stirring, until the sugar dissolves, then continue to cook gently for a further 15 minutes, stirring occasionally.

3. Pour over the vinegars, bring to the boil and simmer for about 15 minutes, stirring occasionally, or until the liquid has evaporated sufficiently to leave a thick syrup.

4. Spoon into small, warm sterilized jars and seal with non-corrosive lids (see Sealing on page 178). Allow to cool and store for 2 weeks before eating. It keeps for up to 6 months if stored correctly (see page 178). Once opened, keep in the fridge and use within 2 weeks.

Recipes: Preserves

Pickled cauliflower and shallots in spiced vinegar

Soaking the vegetables in salted water gives a softer pickle. If you decide to use different vegetables that are softer to start with, such as marrow or cucumber, just sprinkle with dry salt and leave as below.

Makes about 900 g (2 lb)

75 g (3 oz) salt
900 ml (1½ pt) water
400 g (14 oz) cauliflower curds, broken into
  small florets (weight stated is with thick
  stalks removed)
250 g (9 oz) small shallots, peeled and trimmed
2 dried red chillies (optional)
1 quantity cold sweet spiced vinegar
  (see Cook's note)

1. Put the salt in a large non-corrosive bowl and pour over the water. Mix well then add the cauliflower and shallots. Cover loosely and leave somewhere cool for 24 hours to soak.

2. The next day, drain and rinse the vegetables well in cold water and then shake off the excess water. Pack into a cold 1 L (1¾ pt) sterilized jar with the chillies, if using.

3. Cover with the cold spiced vinegar and seal with a non-corrosive lid (see Sealing on page 178). Allow to mature for 1 month before using. Store in a cool, dark, dry place for up to 6 months – the cauliflower may become mushy after this time.

🍞 Cook's note

For sweet spiced vinegar, mix 2 teaspoons each of mustard seeds, black peppercorns, cumin seeds and coriander seeds with 1 dried bay leaf and 2 whole dried red chillies, and then tie in a small square of clean muslin. Add to a saucepan containing 570 ml (19 fl oz) distilled malt vinegar. Bring to the boil and simmer gently for 10 minutes. Stir in 4 tablespoons of caster sugar and 1 teaspoon of ground turmeric. Allow to cool then discard the spice bag. Bottle in sterilized bottles and store until required. For a more savoury spiced vinegar, reduce or omit the sugar.

FOR PICTURE, SEE PAGE 121

Candied cherries

Although it takes a few days to make candied fruit, it is a simple process and the rewards are great. You can use the quantities and method for other firm fruits such as plums, pears and apples.

Makes about 450 g (1 lb)

500 g (1 lb 2 oz) firm, ripe, blemish-free
  dessert cherries
Approx. 1 L (1¾ pt) boiling water
675 g (1½ lb) caster sugar

1. Carefully remove the stones from the cherries using a cherry stoner. Put the fruit in a saucepan and pour over sufficient boiling water to just cover. Bring to the boil, cover and simmer for 5–10 minutes (depending on ripeness) until tender. Remove the cherries using a slotted spoon, reserving the liquid, and place in a heatproof bowl.

2. Discard all but 300 ml (10 fl oz) liquid and add 175 g (6 oz) sugar. Heat gently, stirring until dissolved, then bring to the boil. Pour the hot syrup over the fruit and leave to cool. Cover loosely and set aside in a cool place for 24 hours.

3. The next day, remove the cherries using a slotted spoon and place in another heatproof bowl. Add another 50 g (2 oz) sugar to the syrup and heat gently until dissolved. Bring to the boil, remove from the heat and pour over the cherries. Cool and leave as above. Repeat this step for a further 5 days so that the syrup becomes more and more concentrated.

4. After the 5 days, place the fruit in a non-reactive bowl. Add half of the remaining sugar to the syrup and heat, stirring, until dissolved. Add the fruit and simmer for about 3 minutes. Transfer the fruit and syrup to a non-reactive bowl, cool, cover loosely and leave in a cool place for 48 hours. Repeat the step again with the remaining sugar, but leave the fruit in the syrup for 7 days.

5. Lift the fruit from the syrup using a pair of tongs and carefully transfer each cherry to a wire rack to dry. Cover with a dome of foil, making sure it is clear of the fruit, and leave in a warm, dry place for about 48 hours, turning the fruit twice a day, until it is dry enough to pack. Store in an airtight container, between layers of greaseproof paper.

Bottled peas

This is an old-fashioned preserving method to try. You do need to use a pressure cooker in order to make sure any harmful bacteria is destroyed. Bottled vegetables can be reheated and used in the same way as canned vegetables.

Makes about 500 g (1 lb 2 oz)

300 g (10 oz) blemish-free, shelled,
   young fresh peas
½ tsp salt
1 tsp caster sugar
Approx. 1.2 L (2 pt) boiling water

1. Bring a saucepan of water to the boil and blanch the peas in a basket for 2 minutes. Lift out, drain and transfer to a large bowl of iced water to cool. Drain thoroughly and then pack into a sterilized 500 ml (17 fl oz) preserving jar (see page 177). Do not pack too tightly and leave a 2.5 cm (1 in) gap at the top of the jar.

2. Mix the salt and sugar into 250 ml (9 fl oz) boiling water and pour over the peas. Put the non-corrosive lid on the jar, and then release the lid by a quarter turn to loosen. You must now sterilize the contents of the jar immediately.

3. Put a folded clean cloth in the bottom of a pressure cooker and stand the jar inside. Wedge cloths around the jar to prevent it touching the sides of the pressure cooker.

4. Pour in sufficient of the remaining boiling water to no more than half-fill the pressure cooker. Close the lid, aligning the top and bottom handles correctly, and place on the heat. Following the manufacturer's guidelines, bring the pressure cooker to 4.5 kg (10 lb) (medium) pressure and maintain this pressure for 35 minutes.

5. Allow the cooker to cool gradually. Carefully remove the jar and tighten the lid immediately and allow to cool. Test the seal to ensure it is tight, then store in a cool, dark, dry place and use within 12 months. If the seal isn't secure, store in the fridge and use within 10 days.

🍴 Cook's note

Follow the exact same method for bottling sweetcorn kernels and shelled, small, fresh broad beans.

FOR PICTURE, SEE PAGE 122

Whisky and raspberry cordial

Traditionally this old-fashioned 'nip' was taken diluted with hot water for medicinal reasons. It certainly makes a delicious warming winter drink with or without the water.

Makes about 700 ml (1¼ pt)

350 g (12 oz) raspberries
70 cl (24 fl oz) bottle whisky
Thinly pared rind of 1 unwaxed orange
2.5 cm (1 in) piece root ginger,
   peeled and chopped
225 g (8 oz) well-flavoured honey,
   such as Scottish heather honey

1. Pat dry the raspberries with kitchen paper and place in a clean, non-corrosive bowl. Crush lightly using the end of a rolling pin covered in cling film.

2. Pour over the whisky and mix in the orange rind and ginger. Cover with cling film and leave to stand in a cool place for 24 hours.

3. Strain through a nylon sieve (don't push through) into another clean, non-corrosive bowl and gradually whisk in the honey.

4. Transfer to sterilized bottles (see page 177), seal tightly and store in a cool, dark place for up to 6 months. To serve in the traditional way, dilute one part cordial to four parts hot water.

FOR PICTURE, SEE PAGE 123

Recipes: Preserves

Loganberry 'marmalade'

These tangy berries combine excellently with citrus fruit to make an unusual preserve for your morning toast. The recipe will also work with other hybrid berries (see page 87).

Makes about 750 g (1 lb 10 oz)

6 strips pared unwaxed orange rind, finely
   shredded
150 ml (5 fl oz) boiling water
450 g (1 lb) prepared loganberries
3 Tbsp freshly squeezed orange juice
1 Tbsp lemon juice
450 g (1 lb) granulated sugar

1. Put the orange rind in a small saucepan with the water. Bring to the boil and cook for 5 minutes to soften. Drain well.

2. Put the berries in another saucepan along with the citrus juices and soaked orange rind. Bring to the boil and simmer for about 5 minutes or until just softened.

3. Stir in the sugar, and stir over a low heat until the sugar dissolves. Bring to the boil and then boil rapidly for about 10 minutes until setting point is reached (see page 177). Skim off any surface foam using a flat spoon. Stand for 10 minutes then stir to distribute the rind. Spoon into warm, sterilized jars and seal as described on page 178.

FOR PICTURE, SEE PAGE 124

Rhubarb and ginger jam

It is best to use main crop rhubarb for this recipe rather than the early forced crop.

Makes about 600 g (1 lb 5 oz)

450 g (1 lb) trimmed rhubarb
450 g (1 lb) granulated sugar
2 Tbsp lemon juice
50 g (2 oz) preserved ginger in syrup,
    drained and finely chopped

1. Cut the rhubarb into 1 cm (½ in) pieces and place in a non-corrosive bowl. Mix in the sugar and leave to stand for at least 4 hours, stirring occasionally, in order to draw out the liquid.

2. Transfer the mixture to a saucepan and stir over a low heat until the sugar dissolves completely. Add the lemon juice and ginger. Bring to the boil and then boil rapidly for about 15 minutes until setting point is reached (see page 177). Skim off any surface foam using a flat spoon. Stand for 10 minutes then stir to distribute the ginger. Spoon into warm, sterilized jars and seal as described on page 178.

Apple and pear curd

Usually, fruit curds are made with citrus fruits, but here I'm using orchard fruits. This recipe also works well with gooseberries, but you should omit the lemon juice.

Makes about 500 g (1 lb 2 oz)

350 g (12 oz) cooking apples
350 g (12 oz) ripe pears
3 Tbsp lemon juice
225 ml (8 fl oz) water
Approx. 40 g (1½ oz) unsalted butter
Approx. 175 g (6 oz) caster sugar
Approx. 3 medium free range egg yolks

1. Peel and core the apples and pears. Chop roughly and place in a saucepan with the lemon juice and water and bring to the boil. Simmer for 6–8 minutes until thick and pulpy. Push through a nylon sieve to form a smooth purée.

2. Measure the purée and place in a large heatproof bowl. Add 40 g (1½ oz) butter and 175 g (6 oz) sugar per 225 ml (8 fl oz) purée. Stand the bowl over a saucepan of barely simmering water and cook, stirring, until the butter melts and the sugar dissolves. Add 3 egg yolks per 225 ml (8 fl oz) purée and cook, stirring, until sufficiently thick to cover the back of a wooden spoon – this will take approximately 30 minutes.

3. Spoon into small, warm, sterilized jars and seal as described on page 178. Allow to cool and store in the fridge for up to 1 month. Once opened, keep in the fridge and use within 1 week.

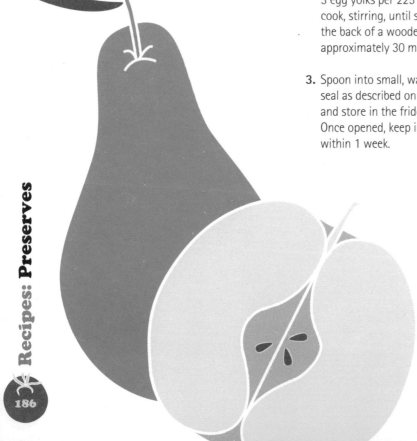

Autumnal chutney

A tasty chutney is a great way to use up orchard fruit and some of the leftover vegetables towards the end of the ripening season. This one's perfect for serving with the Christmas roast leftovers. Use plums instead of the tomatoes if preferred.

Makes about 1.5 kg (3 lb 5 oz)

225 g (8 oz) peeled onions, finely chopped
300 ml (10 fl oz) cider vinegar
450 g (1 lb) cored and peeled cooking apples,
    finely chopped
350 g (12 oz) green tomatoes, chopped
450 g (1 lb) peeled and seeded marrow,
    finely chopped
350 g (12 oz) granulated sugar
115 g (4 oz) sultanas
2 tsp cumin seeds, crushed
Salt and freshly ground black pepper

1. Place the chopped onions in a saucepan and pour over half the vinegar. Bring to the boil and simmer gently for about 10 minutes. Add the apples, tomatoes, marrow and remaining vinegar.

2. Stir in the sugar, sultanas and cumin. Stir over a low heat until the sugar dissolves, then bring to the boil and simmer gently, stirring occasionally, for about 20 minutes until soft, mushy and slightly juicy. Stir in seasoning to taste.

3. Spoon into warm sterilized jars and seal with non-corrosive lids as described on page 178. Allow to cool and store for 6–8 months. Once opened, keep in the fridge and use within 2 weeks.

FOR PICTURE, SEE PAGE 125

Recipes: Preserves

Tomato ketchup

My version of the nation's favourite condiment.

Makes about 400 ml (13½ fl oz)

900 g (2 lb) ripe tomatoes, chopped
75 g (3 oz) granulated sugar
100 ml (3½ fl oz) white wine vinegar
1 tsp salt
1 bay leaf
Few sprigs of thyme
Sprig of rosemary
Pinch of cayenne pepper
½ tsp smoked paprika

1. Put the tomatoes in a saucepan and heat gently until simmering, then cover and cook gently for about 10 minutes until very soft and pulpy. Push through a nylon sieve into a clean saucepan to remove the seeds and skin.

2. Add the remaining ingredients and heat gently until the sugar dissolves. Raise the heat and simmer for about 30 minutes until the mixture is the consistency of thick cream.

3. Transfer to warm, sterilized bottles using a funnel and secure with non-corrosive lids, but do not tighten. Stand the bottles in a deep, narrow saucepan on a trivet and wedge with cloths to prevent them touching each other and the sides of the pan – I find an asparagus steamer good for bottles and tall jars. Fill the saucepan with warm water to just cover the bottles and place the lid on top. Heat to simmering point – 88°C (190°F) – and maintain a steady simmer for 20 minutes.

4. Carefully lift the bottles on to a board, seal tightly and cool. Store in a cool, dark, dry place for up to 8 months. Once opened, store in the fridge and use within 10 days.

FOR PICTURE, SEE PAGE 126

Useful contacts

Seed merchants/Plant suppliers/Garden centres

Chiltern Seeds
www.chilternseeds.co.uk

Notcutts Garden Centres
www.notcutts.co.uk

Dobbies Garden Centres
www.dobbies.com

Suttons Seeds
www.suttons.co.uk

Samuel Dobie & Son
www.dobies.co.uk

O. A. Taylor & Sons Bulbs Ltd
www.taylors-bulbs.com

Mr. Fothergill's Seeds Ltd
www.mr-fothergills.co.uk

Edwin Tucker & Sons Ltd
www.edwintucker.co.uk

Hillier Garden Centres/Nurseries Ltd
www.hillier.co.uk

Westland Horticulture Ltd
www.gardenhealth.com

E W King and Co. Ltd
www.kingsseeds.co.uk

Wyevale Garden Centres Ltd
www.wyevale.co.uk

Associations/Organizations/Websites

Garden Organic
Organic growing charity.
www.gardenorganic.org.uk

GrowVeg
An innovative garden planning tool.
www.growveg.com

National Allotment and Leisure Garden Society (NSALG)
Charity to protect, promote and preserve allotment and leisure gardening.
www.nsalg.org.uk

The Royal Horticultural Society
Gardening charity dedicated to advancing horticulture and promoting good gardening.
www.rhs.org.uk

The Soil Association
Main charity campaigning for organic food and farming.
www.soilassociation.org

Bibliography

Berry, Mary *The Complete Book of Freezer Cooking* (Octopus, 1975)
Foley, Caroline *The Allotment Handbook* (New Holland, 2004)
Food from your Garden (Reader's Digest, 1977)
Hawkins, Kathryn *The Allotment Cookbook* (New Holland, 2007)
Hessayon, Dr. D. G. *The Vegetable & Herb Expert* (Expert Books, 2000)
Patten, Marguerite *Jams, Chutneys, Preserves, Vinegars and Oils* (Bloomsbury, 1995)
Royal Horticultural Society *Encyclopedia of Gardening* (Dorling Kindersley, reprint, 1994)

Acknowledgements

I would like to give special thanks to my brother Christopher for his expert gardening advice and for helping me put the book together; and to my mother, Margaret, for supplying me with her tried and tested gardening tips. I'd also like to thank Morgan Barr for helping me with the recipe testing and to other friends and family who have helped me out with recipes and tasting along the way.

Useful contacts

189

Index

Page numbers in *italic* refer to illustrations